D1568996

Grammar, meaning and the machine analysis of language

Yorick Alexander Wilks

Grammar, meaning and the machine analysis of language

London   Routledge & Kegan Paul

First published 1972
by Routledge and Kegan Paul Ltd
Broadway House,
68–74 Carter Lane,
London, EC4V 5EL
Printed in Great Britain by
Unwin Brothers Limited
Woking and London
© Yorick A. Wilks 1972

ISBN 0 7100 7035 7

To F.A.S.

Contents

Acknowledgments

The research described in this book has been supported by grants from HM Government Office of Scientific and Technical Information and from AFOSR (OAR), Washington, DC, USA, administered by the Trustees of the Cambridge Language Research Unit: and also by a contract from AFOSR, monitored by Mrs Rowena Swanson and administered by the Institute for Formal Studies, Los Angeles, California, USA. This research grew out of the work of the CLRU and I am most grateful to its Director, Miss Margaret Masterman, for her encouragement. The computation described was done on the time-shared on-line system at Systems Development Corporation, Santa Monica, California, and I am grateful to Dr R. F. Simmons, then Head of the Language Processing Division, for the use of his facilities. I am also indebted to Mr D. S. Linney, Professor R. B. Braithwaite, Professor D. M. Emmet, Dr K. Sparck-Jones, Dr R. M. Needham, and Dr D. G. Bobrow for their helpful suggestions, criticisms and comments.

References

References are numbered throughout the book by numerals in square brackets which refer to the bibliography at the end of the book.

1 Meaning and machines

'He then led me to the Frame, about the sides whereof all his
pupils stood in ranks. It was twenty Foot square, placed in the
Middle of the Room. The Superficies was composed of
several Bits of Wood. . . They were all linked together by
slender Wires. These Bits of Wood were covered on every
Square with Paper pasted on them; and on these Papers were
written all the Words of their Language in their several Moods,
Tenses and Declensions, but without any Order. The Professor
then desired me to observe, for he was going to set his Engine
to work.'

Swift, A Voyage to Laputa

1.1 Introduction

The main purpose of this book is not to survey research efforts,
nor is it to give a conceptual analysis of the words in the title, but
to describe a system of semantic analysis: a system for expressing
the meaning of pieces of English text. The system I describe has
actually been applied to a number of English texts with the aid of
a computer, or electronic machine, and I shall come to the concrete
detail of the analysis in due course, but there are a number of
questions that must be discussed first. These concern both the systems
of other writers and a number of very general matters that would

normally be called philosophical, since almost any enquiry that uses the word 'meaning' can be so called. But that need not mean just another rewarming of an old and well-known menu. For the familiar questions about what 'meaning' means have been changed, and in an interesting way, by the efforts of the last fifteen years to programme computers so that they can be said to understand, or at least to process, the meaning of texts in a natural language.

The advent of computers has already had an important effect on the theory of logic, and of logical description in particular: roughly, that all logical description must be part of some effective procedure that could be carried out by a possible machine. Work on the computer handling of natural language has had to impoze similar constraints on the expression of information about linguistic items. Such information must be far more precise and explicit than is usually necessary when giving the same information to human beings. For example, I can say to almost any speaker of British English, 'Would you please take these letters down to the post', and he or she will know that I want them pushed through a slot in a wall or box, and that I *don't* want them taken to an upright stake, or to any other of the many things that 'post' can mean in English.

All this is obvious to the reader, and tedious to describe, but how is one to express the relevant linguistic information in a formal manner, so that even an automaton would know which sense of 'post' is the one in question when it reads that sentence? It is clearly more than a matter of explicitness and precision, in that an automaton can do nothing that it is not instructed to do. It is also a question of what exactly is the information that has to be made precise and explicit. The immediate and natural answer is that the correct sense of 'post' is to be selected by use of context. But as it stands that description does no more than disguise our ignorance, because it suggests no real *procedure*. It gives no hint as to what information should be attached to the symbol 'post' so that the automaton, seeing the other symbol 'letters' in this sentence, would correctly judge that the 'post as a place for depositing mail' sense of 'post' was the one in question. In a more realistic example this judgment would have to be made for each *occurrence* of each word. For example, 'bar' might be used in a sentence to mean 'the metaphorical place that QCs are called to', and then in the next sentence of the same text it might be used to mean 'a part of a public house' that they repair to between sittings. In such a case one would naturally expect 'bar' to be tied to two different explanations of its sense on the two occasions of its use.

The task I have described, of tying occurrences of words in text to their correct sense explanations, is not at all a trivial one, even though human readers and speakers do it all the time, and rarely think about what they do. No one has any real idea how they do it, either, though if a computer could be programmed to do the job in a reliable fashion then that alone would suggest how humans may actually do it. But it could never be more than a suggestion, because no one has *direct access* to the way human brains process language. To argue, as some have, that because both humans and computers read text and then produce similar output, *therefore* they must have gone through the same procedures, is like saying that anyone who goes from London to Edinburgh *has* to go through Carlisle.

I shall return to this problem of sorting out the senses of words in text; indeed, it will be the main practical problem to which this book addresses itself. Why it is a paradigm of the problem of 'meaning and the machine' will become clear from a brief history of the enterprise known as Mechanical Translation (MT for short) from which the problem arose.

MT research began in the 1950s with large grants from United States Government Agencies. It was not wholly disinterested research support: the Agencies thought how nice it would be to know what was in *Pravda* every day without actually having to read it. There was also the more serious problem of reading an increasing number of scientific publications in Russian, and of getting, if not full MT, at least some crude translation that would show which documents were worth translating properly.

MT research started in great style. It was believed firmly to be no more than a short-term problem: all that was needed was energy, money and fast computers. By and large, all that early work came to nothing in terms of working systems, though the United States Air Force does still have an MT programme that digests the Russian newspapers every day. The approaches that were used varied from research centre to research centre, but none of them tried to construct what, in this book, I shall call a meaning structure. Those approaches all envisaged an initial grammatical analysis of the given, or input, language text; then a replacement of those structures by grammatical structures of the output, or target, language; and, finally, the replacement of the input words on a one-for-one basis by words of the target language. So in a Russian-English translation system, for example, each Russian word in the mechanical dictionary would be tagged to one and only one English word.

It was projects like those that produced the famous spoof translation of the English sentence 'The Spirit is willing but the Flesh is weak' into Russian, and then back again as 'The whisky is fine, but the steak's not so good'. The example is not wholly serious, but it makes the point perfectly: real words in real languages have many senses and there's no point in starting this sort of enterprise unless you take account of the fact. The trouble with the output produced by those systems, as with the example above, wasn't that they were a bit wrong, in that expensive human editing was needed to correct the output. On the contrary, the output was often so hopelessly wrong that there was nothing to edit. The basic message of the original completely failed to get across, and that situation is worse, in a sense, than having no translation at all. For, if you have only the Russian then at least you have some idea whether you understand it or not depending on your knowledge of that language. But with a hopeless translation, like the example above, you may be led to think you understand it when in fact you don't.

The first official epitaph [161] on all those research efforts has now appeared, and the gist of its verdict is that 'non-garbage' MT is in principle possible using the sort of straightforward method I described, but the cost of the human editor required afterwards is the same, or greater, than the cost of an ordinary human translator. An editor would be one who reads the machine output and sees, where it is possible, what the original 'must have meant', and corrects grammatical slips at the same time. He would not need to understand the input language.

But even before this 'black book' on MT appeared in Washington, it had been clear for some time that the era of simple-minded MT was over. That realization gave impetus to two new and growing disciplines, 'Computational Linguistics' and 'Artificial Intelligence', that took up different attitudes to the virtual collapse of MT research (I shall refer to these subjects, respectively, as CL and AI for short).

CL is a direct descendant of the North American tradition of behavioural psychology. Those parts of the field of CL that had been influenced by the thought of Noam Chomsky (whose work is discussed in detail in the next chapter) inferred from the MT *débâcle* that what had been shown was the need for a correct and proper theory of natural language. That can be called the 'think harder' response. AI is, by contrast, the 'work harder' response. The name AI covers a multitude of activities (the most comprehensive bibliography is given in Feigenbaum [86]), all of which aim at the construction of mechanisms, or computer programmes, that display features characteristic of intelligent human activity: learning, problem solving, game playing and so on. AI has until recently been a rather easy-going discipline: unlike CL it has not developed large-scale theories demanding assent. Research efforts in AI have been perhaps too unhampered by theory, and this has often made communication between workers in the two fields rather difficult. There is sometimes little to argue about or discuss in AI, and not even much to be drawn on a blackboard. All that can be done is actually to display the device that has been constructed or programmed. At the beginning, these devices were seldom linguistic in any strong sense: the early successes of AI were chess-playing programmes and problem solvers. But in the last ten years many linguistic programmes have appeared with such names as conversation continuers, question answerers, information retrieval systems, and so on.

The reaction of CL to the MT crisis was, as I said, to look for a correct theory of natural language. The most influential theory that has been developed within linguistics has undoubtedly been that of Noam Chomsky, though I do not think that its advent has in any way shifted the MT problem as I described it. AI, on the other hand, has contributed to the solution of the MT problem, though its contribution has been partly inadvertent. The reaction of AI workers to that same MT crisis was to undertake the construction of computer programmes that would acquire language in the way that humans do it, that is to say to learn it. Speaking very roughly, one could say that the most influential AI argument on this point was as follows: a machine will only be able to translate from one language to another when it can go through the process of learning to understand the two languages. The key notion here is understanding, but what must a machine do in order to be said to understand a natural language?

In a much celebrated article [280] Alan Turing once suggested that some operational test be adopted to settle the otherwise vague question of whether or not a machine could *think*. In brief, his proposed test envisaged a machine communicating with a human being by means of a mechanical typewriter or a telephone line. The human being is not told whether the thing on the other end of the typewriter wire, or phone line, is a machine or another human being. Turing suggested that if, after some agreed time, the human being decides that the thing with which he is conducting a 'conversation' is a human being (or if he cannot decide whether it is a human being or not) then we should say that the machine being used is thinking. The article had considerable influence, and set a general standard for subsequent research in the field of AI, since there is no great step from the notion of thinking to the notion of understanding.

However, a recent piece of work by Weizenbaum has passed Turing's test, and has done it by such simple-minded procedures as to devalue the notion of 'understanding by machines' as an approach to the problem of 'meaning and the machine', of which the MT problem is one aspect. Weizenbaum's mechanical conversation system, called ELIZA [293], is a very simple and elegant one, yet it operates by means of tricks of conversation familiar to anyone who has been to a boring cocktail party. Here is a small sample of ELIZA output (the human being's words are in lower-case, and ELIZA's in upper-case, type):

Men are all alike
IN WHAT WAY
They're always bugging us about something or another
CAN YOU THINK OF A SPECIFIC EXAMPLE
Well, my boyfriend made me come here
YOUR BOYFRIEND MADE YOU COME HERE
He says I'm depressed much of the time
I AM SORRY TO HEAR YOU ARE DEPRESSED
It's true. I am unhappy
DO YOU THINK COMING HERE WILL HELP YOU NOT TO BE UNHAPPY
I need some help, that much is certain
WHAT WOULD IT MEAN TO YOU IF YOU GOT SOME HELP
Perhaps I could get along with my mother
TELL ME MORE ABOUT YOUR FAMILY

ELIZA works by means of a general rule that fixes upon certain words in the line it has just read from the human party to the conversation, and asks more about them, or about words closely related to them. From the machine's point of view, as it were, it is like keeping a conversation going with someone you are not at all interested in. The example quoted above was set in psycho-analytic interview form, but it has been used in a number of different ways, and in almost all cases the human being refused to believe that he had been talking, or rather typing, to a machine.

The importance of Weizenbaum's work with ELIZA is in showing that it is much easier than anyone thought to programme a computer so that it understands or thinks, at least by the generally accepted test for what it is for a machine to understand or think. And in that sense Weizenbaum's work has, from within AI itself, produced a disappointing answer for those who hoped that 'machine understanding' would provide a solution to the MT problem.

I do not want to suggest that the contribution made by AI to the solution of that problem has been in general negative and inadvertent. On the contrary, it has made two very important positive contributions. Firstly, it kept alive the discussion of meaning, and of possible ways of encoding meaning, during CL's most ascetic period from 1957–64. The way in which most of CL dismissed the notion of meaning, and its subsequent volte-face, will become clear in the next chapter.

Secondly, AI work has produced a number of linguistic examples of feedback, reflexive, or self-modifying mechanism,[1] and some feature of that sort is, I believe, essential to any representation of meaning in a machine. What I mean by that statement is the real subject of the present chapter, and it will I hope be clear by the end of it, but nothing at all mysterious is intended by those words. The main point I want to make can be put in abstract terms as follows: all the systems of CL can be expressed as systems of *rules*, and those rules are used to try and separate off what is meaningful, or in many cases what is grammatical, from what is not. A rule could be something as simple, and totally wrong, as 'Every sentence consists of a noun followed by a verb'. Armed with that rule we would be able to decide that 'John talks', for example, is a sentence, but would have to conclude that 'John talks a lot' is not. The major point I want to make in the latter part of this chapter is that no set of rules whatever can separate off the meaningful from the meaningless by the operation of rules, however complex (I shall discuss the other case, of separating off the grammatical from the ungrammatical, in the next chapter). I shall also argue that the only useful attack on the problem of what is meaningful, and what is not, by formal

B

methods is by means of a system of rules *together with* some feature, of the sort that AI would call a reflexive or a feedback procedure, that can modify the set of rules whenever necessary. Only in that way, I believe, can one begin to cope formally with the way in which human beings can extend their language at will, can pick up quite new senses of words from context, can coin new senses of words, can 'get a meaning across' by further explanations, and so on.

All those matters will, I hope, become clearer in due course. Let me return to something more straightforward: to the problem that, as I argued earlier, was at the heart of the MT breakdown, namely, specifying the correct senses of words as they appeared in texts. At the beginning of this chapter I discussed how we might decide in a formal way that 'post' in 'Would you please take these letters down to the post' means 'place for depositing mail' and not 'upright stake driven into the ground'. Sometimes, of course, people decide this sort of question by looking at the real physical world. One might go into an art gallery and see the title 'The Monarch of the Glen' on a painting, and only realize that it meant an animal, and not a man, after one had raised one's eyes to the picture. But in this book I shall be concerned only with ambiguities of word-sense that can be settled by looking at other words.

I shall call a text, or utterance, *resolved* if one can, by any process, tag each of its words to one and only one of the possible senses for that particular world. I shall call such a process *disambiguation* or *ambiguity resolution*, but I do not mean to suggest that the words in ordinary texts are usually ambiguous, in that a reader cannot decide which of its senses each word is being used in. All I am referring to by the phrase 'ambiguity resolution' is getting a computer to do what all of us do all the time when we read or speak with understanding: to tie each word to one and only one of its possible senses. Many word-sense ambiguities cannot be resolved within the bounds of the conventional text sentence; there simply isn't enough context available. So, for example, if someone reads, in British English at least, 'I'll have to take this post after all', then he does not know, without more context, whether he is reading about an employment situation or one concerned with the purchase of gardening equipment. If that sentence were analysed by any ambiguity resolution system, as part of a larger text, we would expect as a report on the word 'post' either 'post as a job' or 'post as a stake', depending on the larger text of which this example sentence was part. I shall call an utterance *isolated* that cannot be resolved without access to more text. There is always the additional possibility that any given ambiguity is what one is tempted to call a 'genuine ambiguity' in that it represents a careless fault on the part of the writer or speaker, or perhaps, on the other hand, a deliberate cleverness of style on the part of a poet who intends some word in a poem to be understood in two senses simultaneously.

Let me describe, very simply and by way of example, an approach to word-sense ambiguity resolution that was tried at the Cambridge Language Research Unit in the very early days of MT. This early attack on the problem at the heart of MT was by Masterman [39] and made use of Roget's *Thesaurus*, the widely available classification of English words. One looks up a word in the list at the back of that document and is given a number of very general concept names, called heads, such as Darkness, Opposition, or Sequence. In the main body of the *Thesaurus* each head is given with a block of partly synonymous words grouped under it.

For a pilot thesaurus translation scheme a passage of Virgil's *Georgics* was taken, and each Latin word-stem in it was looked up in a standard Latin-English dictionary. A working coding was obtained for each Latin word-stem by taking the main English words, given against it in the dictionary and looking them up in Roget's *Thesaurus*. By this two-stage method, each Latin word-stem was attached to a list of Roget heads as its coding.

The next procedure was to compare the list of Roget heads for each Latin word with the similar lists for all the *other* words in the sentence in turn, and to keep *as the coding for the initial word* only those heads that occurred at least twice for words elsewhere in the sentence. In the case of the sentence 'Agricola incurvo in terram dimovit aratro', for example, the heads still attached to the three noun-stems after that procedure were as follows:

AGRICO: Region, Agriculture
TERR: Region, Land, Furrow
AR: Agriculture, Furrow, Convolution

As one might expect, these lists have members in common, for the procedure adopted is causing the 'coherence' of sense between the words of the sentence to show itself in a determinate way. If there were not this coherence of sense it would probably not be possible for a human being to understand the sentence, unless each word in it has one and only one sense.

The next procedure was to take the list of remaining heads for each word of the sentence in turn and to find the English words occurring under all those heads in the main body of the *Thesaurus*. So, if one takes the heads Region and Agriculture in Roget, one finds that their only common words are 'farmer' and 'ploughman'. Those two words then become the final output for the Latin word 'agricola'. By the same procedure, the output for 'terram' is 'ground' and 'soil', and for 'aratro' is 'plough', 'ploughman', and 'rustic' (in its adjectival sense). It was then assumed that grammatical considerations would remove the adjectival sense of 'rustic', and beyond that the choice of output (as between 'ground' and 'soil' for 'terram' for example) would be random.

Those experiments were done ten years ago, and were somewhat rudimentary by today's standards, yet they were surprisingly successful. One of the main difficulties was that Roget's was by no means the ideal thesaurus, and those using it were finding all the time that words had not been classified under all the heads they should have been. And, of course, there was always the more general objection, frequently raised by critics, that the *Thesaurus* was an *ad hoc* classification of words made up by P. Roget, and so could not be the basis of any serious scientific work.

But there are other, more important, troubles about the Thesaurus method. Consider the sentence, 'Our village policeman is a good sport really'. It is obvious that 'sport' in that sentence means 'sport as agreeable man' and not 'sport as recreational organization'. But if any procedure considers all word-sense possibilities in the way the thesaurus procedure does, how can we be sure the latter word-sense is eliminated? If the sentence analysed were actually 'Our village policeman is a good sport, he captains the cricket team every Saturday', then it is pretty certain that the thesaurus procedure would settle for the *wrong* sense, because of what I have called the 'coherence of sense' between the notions of sport and cricket. Important as the notion of coherence of sense is for ambiguity resolution, the last example shows that it is not a sufficient tool. There needs to be some method for refusing even to consider the sort of absurd combinations of word-senses that would result from using a simple thesaurus procedure on the last example sentence. I now want to consider, in brief outline, a somewhat stronger system for ambiguity resolution that considers only certain combinations of word-senses.

1.2 A preliminary sketch of the CSD system

Suppose for a moment that there was a set of rules that could produce representations of the possible messages, or 'gists', of what human beings can say or write. Such rules might be expected to produce a representation for 'a man is a certain sort of man', for that is the gist of the sentence about the policeman, but not for 'a man is a certain sort of recreational organization', because that is not something that one can say. If one could attach such representations to texts in some appropriate way, then an ambiguity resolution could be read off from them; just as the fact that 'sport' means 'sport as agreeable man' in the example sentence can be read off from the first, though not the second, suggested representation or gist.

That notion of gist forms the basis for the system of semantic analysis to be described in detail in Chapters 2 and 4 of this book, though some very general description of it (I shall refer to the system as the CSD system which is short for Computable Semantic Derivations) is appropriate at this point. In the experiments to be described in Chapter 4, texts were initially segmented into fragments for the purposes of the analysis, and in the final computer output each fragment is given with a list of sense explanations for all the words in it which are resolved (or which had only a single sense-entry initially, and so are trivially resolved). A list is also given of words not resolved, if any. Here, by way of example, is the final computer output for a sentence consisting of two fragments:

```
(((BRITAINS TRANSPORT SYSTEM ARE CHANGING)
 ((WORDS RESOLVED IN FRAGMENT)
 ((TRANSPORT AS PERTAINING TO MOVING THINGS ABOUT)
  (BRITAINS AS HAVING THE CHARACTERISTIC OF A PARTICULAR PART
   OF THE WORLD)
  (SYSTEM AS AN ORGANIZATION)
  (ARE AS HAVE THE PROPERTY) (CHANGING AS ALTERING)))
 ((WORDS NOT RESOLVED IN FRAGMENT) NIL))
 ((WITH IT THE TRAVELLING PUBLICS HABITS)
 ((WORDS RESOLVED IN FRAGMENT)
 ((TRAVELLING AS MOVING FROM PLACE TO PLACE)
  (IT AS INANIMATE PRONOUN)
```

(HABITS AS REPEATED ACTIVITIES)))
((WORDS NOT RESOLVED IN FRAGMENT) NIL)

RESOLUTION OUTPUT FROM THE LISP 1.5 PROGRAMME

The original English form of the sentence to which the two fragments correspond is 'Britain's transport system and with it the travelling public's habits are changing'. The way in which the sentence was broken up into the fragments, and the significance of the 'NIL' symbols in the programming language LISP 1.5, will appear later on.

The sort of decision-making made by the computer in arriving at such output assumes that it is useful, even when not completely perspicuous, to speak of 'senses of words', and that ordinary speakers of English can be got to agree that in 'I won a round of golf today' and 'One round of sandwiches, please', the word 'round' is being used in two different senses. Not all linguists would agree with this common-sense intuition, and they have a case in that it is very difficult to assign word occurrences to 'sense classes' in any manner that is both general and determinate. Even the common-sense intuition cannot be pushed very far: in the sentences 'I have a stake in this country' and 'My stake on the last race was a pound', is 'stake' being used in the same sense or not? If 'stake' can be interpreted to mean something as vague as 'stake as any kind of investment in any enterprise', then the answer is yes. So if a semantic dictionary contained only two senses for 'stake': that vague sense together with 'stake as a post', then one would expect the word 'stake' to be tagged to the vague sense for both the sentences above. But if, on the other hand, the dictionary distinguished 'stake as an investment' and 'stake as the initial payment in a game or race' then the answer would be expected to be different. So then, word disambiguation is relative to the dictionary of sense choices available, and can have no absolute quality about it.

The first requirement for any semantic system of this sort is a coding scheme that can distinguish the different senses of words in a dictionary. Let us assume, by way of example, that we want to distinguish two senses of 'salt': namely 'salt as an old sailor' and 'salt as the substance sodium chloride'. Two natural markers, or code items, to use for that purpose would be one meaning any substance, let us say STUFF, and one meaning any human being, let us say MAN. These markers represent the highest useful level of classification for each word-sense. That is to say, for example, that the class of men includes the class of sailors, and so of old sailors. So MAN will be the main marker, or *head*, in the coding for that sense of 'salt'. But it will be clear that something more complex than a single marker is needed in general to distinguish among word-senses. For, although the difference between MAN and STUFF suffices to distinguish the two senses of 'salt', single markers will not distinguish, say, 'salt as a sailor' from 'pawn as someone used helplessly by another for some purpose', since both those senses would presumably be coded with MAN as their main marker. Let us suppose, then, that the two senses of 'salt' can be expressed by *formulae* made up from such markers nested, or otherwise combined, to any degree of complexity needed to distinguish the senses. The head* of any formula will be simply its main category marker: so it will be MAN for 'salt as an old sailor', and STUFF for 'salt as the substance sodium chloride'. If then we analyse a text containing the word 'salt', and by any formal method select for that word-token the formula whose head is STUFF, we will, by that process, have selected the 'salt as the sodium chloride' sense for that occurrence of 'salt'.

The marker names used here are Anglo-Saxon monosyllables for purely mnemonic reasons. Marker names more familiar to linguists (such as 'Human', etc.) will do just as well except that they take longer to read and type.

But we also need to express more complex structures than senses of words. We need to cope with what may be loosely called the meanings of sentences (and so of texts of any length) in order to provide a representation from which an ambiguity resolution can be read off in the way described earlier. Anyone who has ever tried to understand a sentence, in a language he does not know, with the aid of only a dictionary and grammar book will have probably realized that the meaning structure of a sentence *cannot* be simply a list of word-senses, nor even a list of word-senses together with a grammatical structure. If that is so, then a natural device worth trying as a way of representing meaning structure is message-forms, or *templates*, which are no more than an attempted formalization of the notion of 'gist'. These are patterns which pick up only certain permitted structurings of word senses from coded texts. Templates are not simply lists of senses, but can be interpreted directly as the

* 'Head' will, from now on in the book, be used quite differently from its use in connexion with the thesaurus.

content of utterances. So, for example, if we were analysing a left-right sequence of formulae, each representing some sense of some word, and the heads of these formulae in left-right order were MAN BE KIND, then we could say that we had attached to that sequence of formulae the template MAN+BE+KIND, which can be interpreted directly as 'a human being is a certain kind of human being'. We would expect to detect that template in the analysis of utterances like

'My father is over-bearing',
'The Pope is Italian', and perhaps even
'The postman is happy in his work',

because in each case the message expressed could be said to be 'a human being is a certain kind of human being'. The use of templates, or message-forms, does not require any support from psychological speculations as to how human brains actually process language (even though there is some evidence that people operate not so much with single words as with the 'gists' of longer pieces of text). Templates are used here only as experimental devices in their own right.

In the written form of the template MAN+BE+KIND, the symbol '+' means only 'to the left of'. It simply formalizes the spatial relationship in which the constituent markers stand [see 230]. At the beginning of this section I wrote of 'producing' the items that I have now called templates with the aid of rules. The notion of producing, or as it is sometimes called generating, linguistic items with the aid of a rule is not a difficult one. The kind of rules I refer to most frequently in this book are called *phrase structure rules*, and in their simplest and most useful form they merely say that one symbol can be rewritten as a left-right string of other symbols. So, if 'T' were the general symbol for template, a rule that could generate the example template would be T→MAN+BE+KIND, where '→' means only 'can be rewritten as'. All this is no more complex than arithmetic equations, which could themselves be written in the form of such rules. For example, the equality $12=20-8$ could be put in the form $12→20+-+8$, provided we remember that in those rules '+' means 'to the left of' and not 'plus'.

One important disclaimer is appropriate here. In describing the template I have not intended in any way to bring in the notion sometimes called 'the sentence dictionary'. That notion enshrines the idea that word-sense ambiguity problems would be solved if only sentences could be looked up in some (impossibly long) list of sentences, in exactly the way that single words are looked up in a dictionary. It might be thought that I am proposing that sentences be looked up in some such way, and the appropriate template found. But that is not so at all, and, as will be clear later, I am proposing that the appropriate template for a piece of language should be *computed*, by means of rules, from the possible formulae for the words of the piece of language.

As is to be expected, short lengths of text, in isolation from more text, remain ambiguous with respect to templates. Consider a sentence like 'The old salt is damp'. In British English that sentence allows of two quite different interpretations that could be written 'a certain kind of human being is in a certain state' and 'a certain kind of chemical substance is in a certain state'. If we suppose now that all formulae corresponding to senses about sorts, types, and states have KIND as their head marker, then the two interpretations of the sentence 'The old salt is damp' can be, as first approximations, interpretations of the templates MAN+BE+KIND and STUFF+BE+KIND respectively. And until we know whether the sentence is part of, say, a sea story or a laboratory story, we cannot decide which template to assign to it.

The solution to that problem, naturally enough, is to specify rules that relate templates together so as to correspond to a 'proper sequence' of text-fragments. Suppose we consider now 'The old salt is damp, but the cake is still dry', where one would naturally assume that the correct sense of 'salt' is the 'salt as sodium chloride' sense. So, if the two templates discussed earlier were both possible message-forms for 'The old salt is damp'; and, let us suppose, STUFF+BE+KIND is the only one assigned to 'the cake is still dry', then for the whole sentence there would be two possible template sequences:

MAN+BE+KIND	and	STUFF+BE+KIND
STUFF+BE+KIND		STUFF+BE+KIND

In the absense of any overriding considerations, a rule of template sequence could take the second (and correct) sequence in preference to the first on the basis of the repetition of the marker STUFF. That rule would be, of course, an absurdly over-simplified expression of the sort of coherence and repetition of ideas that almost certainly has to be present in written and spoken language for it to be under-

stood. By 'proper sequence of text-fragments', I mean a sequence
that allows a single interpretation to be imposed on the whole by
rules of that sort. It is easy to construct examples of fragment
sequences for which it would be very difficult to impose a single
reasoned interpretation on the whole text, because the constituent
fragments lack this coherence: 'I stepped on a train, and won a
case yesterday', for example.

Slightly more complex rules then deal with sequences of templates
which are possible matches for longer strings of fragments in the
original text, and in that way also it is possible to, as it were, knock
out irrelevant templates and, at best, to be left with a single string
of templates as a representation of the whole text under examination.
An ambiguity resolution can then be read off from the string of
templates in the way described, and the text is resolved.

It is to be expected intuitively that a coherent text can be matched
to a single representation in some way like this, for writers who are
not poets or philosophers by profession usually go on writing until
their meaning is clear; until there can only be one generally acceptable interpretation of what they are saying.

A word of warning is necessary at this point about the odd nature
of examples in the field of ambiguity resolution. It is an important
fact about a natural language like English that there are *no* examples
of ambiguity resolution that are *beyond question*. Consider, for
example, 'The bar was shut' which is clearly ambiguous as it stands.
It is not clear whether the sentence concerns a barrier or a drinking
place, to name only two possibilities. If that sentence is now embedded in 'The bar was shut because the barman was sick', then
most speakers of English would agree that the sentence was about
a bar to drink in. But, even so, that unanimity would be a matter
of luck. It could never be put beyond question, for it would always
be possible for someone to embed that longer sentence in some odd
story text: possibly one about a man who tended a bar for a living,
but who also had some kind of apparatus which he opened and
shut across his driveway whenever he went in and out. There is no
solution to the general difficulty raised by this example, and I
mention it only to try and keep the discussion away from carping
about examples. It should, as I said earlier, be possible to assess the
output from any ambiguity resolution programme without any
knowledge of the system used, but agreement among the assessors
will always depend upon common sense and goodwill, however

vague those notions may be, for absurd stories can always be thought up to refute any suggested resolution whatever.

The CSD system of analysis, as I have sketched it, may fail to ascribe a representation to a text. There might be a number of reasons for that, and one could never infer that there was necessarily something wrong with the text. Even if the system of rules is correct in some sense, there might well be something wrong with the initial dictionary. No semantic dictionary, even if it contains all the senses specified in the Oxford English Dictionary, can be said to exhaust the possible ways of using the words in the language. It would always be possible to make up a story like the one about the bar above, which would have the effect of forcing some new sense on to a word, and yet the whole utterance would still be comprehensible to a reader. We all know of poetry that is perfectly comprehensible while containing words used in senses not specified in any dictionary, however large. As Bolinger [35] draws the moral for theory: 'A semantic theory must account for the process of metaphorical invention. . . . It is a characteristic of natural languages that no word is ever limited to its enumerable senses.'

The CSD system contains an attempt to provide such an account, albeit a sketchy and tentative one. It is called a *sense constructor*, and is a self-modifying procedure, brought into operation whenever the system cannot produce a resolution. It works, like ELIZA, in an on-line mode under the control of a human operator at a teletype. The system makes suggestions to the operator as to how the dictionary could be augmented, with an additional sense explanation for a word, in such a way that a resolution might be produced. The operator can reject the proposed extension of sense on the grounds that it is unthinkable that such-and-such a word could ever be used to mean so-and-so, but if he does not then the text analysis is tried again with that possible sense explanation added into the sense dictionary. In making the suggestions, the sense constructor assumes that there is sufficient coherence, in a broad sense, present in the text under examination to force a sense on to a word: either a new original sense, or simply one that the dictionary maker has forgotten to put in. That assumption is very like the one made by the reader of a difficult poem who assumes that, if indeed the poem is a properly written one, then there are enough clues present in it to allow him to find out what are the senses intended for the puzzling words in the poem.

The sketch of the CSD system I have now given has been a very rough and rapid one, sufficient only for the rather general points I want to make in the remainder of this chapter. Nowhere, for example, have I said what I mean by the 'meaning of a word', for I want to defer discussion of such difficult questions until the next chapter. For the moment, all I want to say is that, if the fact that most words have many senses is taken seriously, then it is just unclear to ask for *the* meaning of, say, 'post'. That word has about twenty meanings, or senses, listed in a fair-sized dictionary. In the case of highly technical words like 'psoriasis' it might seem more reasonable to ask for the meaning. If you ask someone the meaning of 'psoriasis', and they happen to know what it is, then you will hear a string of words such as 'a chronic disease of the skin'. To say that those words (though not, of course, those marks on the page) *are* the meaning of 'psoriasis' in English seems to me much the simplest way of looking at what is sometimes called The Problem of Meaning as a provisional view of it, at any rate. For experimental purposes it is certainly a more useful view than other well-canvassed philosophical views of what a meaning is: an entity in the brain or mind, or the physical object referred to by a word. For none of those entities can be represented in any straightforward way inside a computer. Words, on the other hand, can.

Again, I have written of 'meaning structures' and 'representing meaning' with the aid of such structures, and, on the other hand, I have devoted considerable space to the discussion of two simple linguistic systems designed to resolve word-sense ambiguity. And those two notions, of meaning structure and actual working systems, are not self-evidently the same. The difference can be seen by contrasting the two systems I described: CSD and the thesaurus method. Both of them were intended to resolve the senses of words in texts, but only the CSD system makes use of items, the templates, that attempt to represent meaning, namely to represent the gists of the possible messages that human beings can convey to each other. The thesaurus system contains no such structures, and that is one of its chief drawbacks, as I pointed out. So there can be no *necessary* connexion of any kind between notions of 'meaning structure' and any particular linguistic system designed to remove word-sense ambiguity.

There need be no confusion on this point, and considerable light is thrown if one sees that the question 'What is *the correct* representation of the meaning of natural language?' can be a trap, for the representation chosen always depends on the chooser's purposes. Consider the silly question 'What is the correct representation of a house?' It is quite obvious that the answer is that there is no such thing, and that the representation you choose will depend on whether you want a painting of a house to hang on your wall, a plan from which a builder can build, or any one of a number of other things.

So then, the 'meaning structure' a research worker chooses depends on his purposes, just as the choice from among the possible translations of a Shakespearean line into another language may depend on whether you want to convey some clear information about the nature of life, or to elevate in the way the original does. This book began by discussing MT, and new systems to tackle that vast problem will probably have to wait upon a number of new linguistic and computational advances. The CSD system, described in this book, tackles only the important subproblem of the resolution of word-sense ambiguity. And since meaning structure is dependent upon the purpose for which it is used, it does not follow that the structure used by the CSD system, even if that system were wholly successful, would be the correct representation of meaning for an MT system. However, it would possess a number of the necessary characteristics, the most important of which would be its ability to resolve word-sense ambiguity, which was after all the problem that halted the MT enterprise in the first place. It is for that reason that the CSD system described in this book is a step, however small, in some direction and not simply a self-justifying device in applied linguistics.

1.3 Characterizing meaningfulness

If one takes any two numbers whatever, then there is a definite procedure of division that can be gone through to decide whether or not one of the two numbers is divisible by the other. In certain particular cases, as when the divisor is three, there is an even simpler procedure that will settle the question, namely adding up the digits of the dividend. Since there are such definite procedures, the predicate 'divisible by n', where n is any number, may be said to be a *decidable* predicate.

In an outstanding piece of logical work [102] Gödel showed that 'true' is not such a predicate in mathematics, and that, in general, the truth of propositions cannot be decided by the application of formal rules of proof.

Consider now the following claim: 'A single natural language, like English, contains Gödel's theorem. That is to say it is rich enough for its statement, since it is possible to refer to a formula that is in a certain sense equivalent to itself. Because of this feature it follows that the natural language cannot *itself* be a decidable system: there can be no general procedure for deciding of a string of words in the language whether or not it is true.'

But, of course, that claim is not something that anyone who thought about the matter for a moment would deny, namely that we cannot formally and generally decide the truth of English sentences.

Even those who believe firmly in the distinction between analytic and synthetic sentences (and hence there are at least some sentences, the analytic ones, whose truth can be formally decided) would not want to make so general a claim. For if the truth of English sentences could be *generally* decided then, at the very least, there would be no need for scientific experiment. There would be no need to look at the real world, for procedures with sentences would do instead. 'Whoever thought we could, except possibly Leibniz?' someone would correctly reply. But that reply should not cause anyone to dismiss two other, more interesting, questions: one about what are usually called grammatical English sentences, and the other about meaningful English sentences. Is either of these sets of sentences decidable? Could there be procedures that would determine whether a string of English words was, or was not, either grammatical or meaningful?

Attempts have been made to construct both sorts of procedure: in the case of meaningfulness there is Carnap's theory of Logical Syntax [40, 41]: in the case of 'grammaticality' there is Chomsky's more recent work in the field of linguistics [46–56]. Carnap's work rested upon an analogy between the ungrammaticality of sentences like 'Caesar is and' and the apparent meaninglessness of sentences like 'Caesar is triangular'. Carnap thought that, if the rules of grammar were supplemented and extended by what he called rules of logical grammar, then the meaninglessness of 'Caesar is triangular' could be shown by the same procedures as dealt with the more obviously odd 'Caesar is and'.

I shall discuss the work of both those authors in some detail in the next chapter, and in the remainder of this chapter I want to look generally at the question of whether or not one could decide that a piece of language either was or was not meaningful. That is a question quite separate from the discussion and exposition in the chapters that make up the body of this book. It is, however, a question of some independent theoretical interest, and one that has not been sufficiently discussed.

It might be objected at the outset that considerations about decidability are of a purely syntactic nature (in the sense of 'syntactic' in which Gödel's theorem is said to be a purely syntactic theorem), and so they can have nothing to do with questions of meaningfulness, or 'grammaticality' in a linguistic sense. The premise is perfectly correct, but I am not trying to introduce meaning, truth or grammaticality where it cannot belong. I am simply raising the question as to how one might interpret the notion of 'theoremhood' in certain 'canonical languages' of the kind described by Post [223, 224]. Chomsky himself has observed [54, p. 9] that his own system of transformational rules can be viewed as a system of production rules for a canonical language, in Post's sense. A canonical language has a finite alphabet, a finite number of productions, or inference rules, and a finite number of axioms. The axioms are concatenated strings of items in the alphabet, and any string which can be produced from these axioms by means of a finite number of applications of the production rules can be called a theorem. The decision problem for the language is determining whether any given string is a theorem or not. The analogy between systems of linguistic rules and this formulation of proof theory depends upon considering as 'theorems' the strings produced by the operation of the linguistic rules (or 'rules of inference'). Only the last, or what Chomsky calls the terminal, string of a production is interpreted as having the property associated with theoremhood, which is called 'grammaticality' in a conventional grammar, and would be 'meaningfulness' if it turns out to be possible to have a linguistic system of rules that can ascribe that property to pieces of language.

The best-known calculus to which these metamathematical considerations apply is the Propositional Calculus in elementary logic. In that calculus it is possible to decide formally, of any well-formed formula in the calculus, whether or not it is a theorem (i.e. logically true). The decision procedure consists in certain computations on what are called truth tables. However, there is also a partial *survey* of what it is to be a theorem of the Propositional Calculus independent of the truth tables, for they are not needed to know that '$p \supset p$' is a theorem. If that were not so one could not discuss decision procedures at all. For example, when expressing Gödel's theorem in the form 'no consistent language can be adequate for the expression of mathematics, and at the same time be capable of proving all true propositions in elementary number theory', it is implied that there is some survey of what it is to be a true proposition in elementary number theory, independent of any axiomatization or decision procedure. Otherwise Gödel's theorem loses its point.

Logical truths, then, can be surveyed prior to the construction of any system for their explication. Moreover, the notion of logical truth can itself be *characterized* in terms of other concepts. These characterizations, such as Leibniz's 'true in all possible worlds' are ultimately unsatisfactory in general; but, unless such characterizations could be proposed and sustained by argument, it would probably be pointless to look for decidable systems to explicate logical truth.

So then, the first questions to be asked about the notion of meaningfulness are whether it can be characterized in terms of other concepts, and whether meaningful utterances can be surveyed. On the face of it there does not seem to be any problem about a survey. It seems easy enough to think of utterances that are clearly meaningful, and must be shown to be so by any system that might be proffered as an explication of the notion. Moreover, native speakers of a language seem to have some procedure available for settling the meaningfulness or otherwise of disputed utterances: they usually try to embed a disputed utterance in a story or explanation so as to show that it can be used sensibly.

So for example, those who were concerned to defend the meaningfulness of the celebrated 'grammatical nonsense' sentence 'Colourless green ideas sleep furiously' would try to embed it in some ingenious story, one, say, about the nature of the brain's activity during sleep, and perhaps making clear during the story that 'green' was being used in the sense of 'new', or 'untried'. If such a story seemed plausible then it would normally be concluded that the sentence was meaningful, or could be 'made meaningful'. I shall come back to this point later because I think the consequences of the success of that procedure are more disruptive than appears at first sight. But let us assume for the moment that there is no problem about surveying meaningfulness and turn to the question of characterizing it.

It is a matter of philosophical record that there have been many attempts to characterize the notion of meaningfulness. I shall discuss one of them in some detail in the next chapter, but here I shall assume that it can be done, and go on immediately to suggest a fresh characterization: one that may seem odd, and, at the same time, obvious.

I propose[2] that we call an utterance meaningful, in some primary sense, if and only if we can decide which of a number of things that it might mean it actually does mean. Or to put the suggestion another way: to be meaningful is to have one and only one of a number of possible interpretations.

If these two apparently different concepts, meaningfulness and sense resolution, can be brought together, then some light might be thrown on an old puzzle about meaningfulness: when grammarians deem a sentence meaningless, or when Carnap deemed a metaphysical sentence [41] meaningless on the grounds of its incorrect logical syntax, then it might not have been the case that such sentences *had no meaning*, but rather that each had several meanings or interpretations, though taken as single sentences in isolation from others they could not be resolved as having some particular interpretation, and so they were deemed meaningless. However, had they been put back into the context from which they came, or had other suitable context been constructed around them, they might have been susceptible of one and only one interpretation, as in the case of 'colourless green ideas sleep furiously' embedded in the simple story I suggested for it.

The most alarming consequence of accepting the proposed characterization concerns isolated utterances: those, like 'I'll have to take this post after all' in the earlier example, that cannot be resolved without more context. Again, if I say 'I found I hadn't got a jack', then that cannot be resolved, because a hearer cannot resolve 'jack' without knowing whether the sentence belongs to, say, a card-playing story or a car-breakdown story. What I am maintaining is that, in some primary sense of 'meaningful', the sentence 'I found I hadn't got a jack' is meaningless apart from some context, or context-substitute, in just the way that 'Colourless green ideas sleep furiously' is usually held to be meaningless.

Before answering charges that what I have just claimed is either

c

absurd or just straightforwardly wrong, I want to say a little more in justification of the claim that primary meaningfulness is of resolved segments of language. I think some general justification can be constructed along the lines of Quine's discussions of synonymy, where, in the course of a detailed examination and criticism of the assumptions of descriptive linguistics [232, 233, 235], he describes a situation of confrontation with a speaker we do not understand at all. Quine begins by distinguishing what he calls the activity of the grammarian from that of the lexicographer: the former seeks to catalogue significant* sequences in a language, the latter to catalogue the synonym pairs within a language, or between languages. Quine points out that their enterprises are intimately related in that one is concerned with what it is to have meaning, while the other is concerned with what it is to have the same meaning. Furthermore, those enterprises are such that either of their principal terms, 'meaning' and 'same meaning', can be stated in terms of the other, rather in the way, Quine might have added, in which Russell reduced the problem of number to that of having the same number. Quine then directs his attention to the lexicographer's problem, which he discusses in the conventional terms of substitutions of putative synonyms within larger contexts that remain synonymous as wholes. That way of discussing 'having the same meaning' is not a referential† one at all, where by 'referential' I mean all sense, designation and (Fregean) dualist theories of meaning. For on any of those theories one should determine whether or not words are synonymous by inspecting the objects or concepts (or both in a Fregean universe) to which they refer, and seeing whether or not they are the same. Quine's view is essentially a monistic, intralinguistic, view of meaning and it concerns only relations between strings of words. I see no real difference, on Quine's view of things, between saying that two utterances have the same meaning and saying that each is the (or a) meaning, interpretation, or paraphrase of the other. The problem then immediately arises of *which* of a number of possible strings of other words, and it is here that substitution comes in again, as what Quine calls 'a retreat to longer segments':

* Quine is discussing the older descriptive linguistics of Bloomfield. The term 'significant' had not then been purged by Chomsky and the 'structural linguists'.
† This use of 'referential' is somewhat broader than Quine's, who usually uses it to mean only 'designatory'.

... a retreat to longer segments tends to overcome the problem of ambiguity or homonymity. Homonymy gets in the way of the law that if *a* is synonymous with *b* and *b* with *c*, then *a* is synonymous with *c*. For, if *b* has two meanings (to revert to the ordinary parlance of meanings), *a* may be synonymous with *b* in one sense of *b* and *b* with *c* in the other sense of *b*. This difficulty is sometimes dealt with by treating an ambiguous form as two forms, but this expedient has the drawback of making the concept of form dependent on that of synonymy. . . . We may continue to characterize the lexicographer's domain squarely as synonymy, but only by recognizing synonymy as primarily a relation of sufficiently long segments of discourse. [232, p. 58.]

But what other function for a 'retreat to longer segments' can there be than an overcoming of sense ambiguity? And what is a 'sufficiently long segment' other than one that resolves such ambiguity? Quine does not say explicitly, but I think one can reasonably infer from the passage quoted that he does mean a segment sufficiently long to resolve the ambiguity of the segment, and so of the members of a synonym pair when either of them is substituted in it. The sufficiently long segment must also give mutual resolution of *all* the words in the segment, and not just of the synonym pair in question. For one could not know that the mutual substitution of a putative synonym pair 'did not change the meaning of the whole' unless one also knew what each of the other words meant as part of that particular linguistic whole.

Quine goes on: 'So we may view the lexicographer as interested, ultimately, only in cataloguing sequences of sufficient length to admit of synonymy in some primary sense'. So the difference between Quine's primary synonymy of resolved segments and the non-primary synonymy of their parts is that the former synonymy is context independent. No question arises of substituting resolved segments in anything longer, for there is no more to make clear.

Let us return to the grammarian, who was said by Quine to have the same problem as the lexicographer. If that is so, then the grammarian, too, will 'retreat to longer segments'. So corresponding to Quine's remark about 'primary synonymy' we might expect one to the effect that 'primary significance is of resolved sequences'. I do not think that Quine draws this inference in the course of his arguments, but it seems to me a correct one, and a way of stating the necessary condition involved in the characterization of meaningfulness I suggested earlier.

What is one to make of this necessary condition: the claim that a piece of language is meaningful only if it has one (and only one) interpretation; and hence that it fails to be meaningful if it has none, or two or more?[3] The claim may sound reasonable enough for utterances whose meaningfulness is in dispute, where, as with 'Colourless green ideas sleep furiously', the procedure used to show that the utterance is meaningful usually consists in constructing a narrative round the sentence so that it does have a single interpretation. I am using the term 'interpretation' loosely here, and will do something to make it more precise later on, but I think the general idea is sufficiently clear if we assume some notion of paraphrase, interpretation or synonymy between utterances. For the moment let us assume it to be Quine's 'primary synonymy' of resolved utterances.

So then, if the utterance 'He fell while getting to the ball' is embedded in a football narrative, then all proper paraphrases of it will be equivalent to 'A man fell to the ground while trying to reach the object in play in the game'. And the assertion that the second sentence is a paraphrase of the first would resolve the first utterance in just the way that inserting it into the football narrative would. In the case of either procedure, inserting or giving a paraphrase, we would then know that 'ball' was not being used in the sense of a 'formal dance'. It is also important to notice, in passing, that resolving a whole utterance by giving a paraphase or interpretation is not the same thing as resolving its constituent words. Knowing that the two sentences just given *are* possible paraphrases or interpretations of each other is *also knowing* that, for example, 'ball' is being used in its 'ball as round object' sense. But the converse is not necessarily true, since the interpretations of sentences are not simply computed[4] from the interpretations of their constituent words, as anyone knows who has tried to make himself understood in a foreign language with the aid of only a dictionary.

But how reasonable is the application of the necessary condition to a sentence such as 'He fell while getting to the ball', whose meaningfulness would not normally be in dispute? Is it not absurd to say that that sentence is meaningless just because, taken in isolation, we do not happen to know which of two likely interpretations it bears? However, if challenged to show that, or how, the sentence is meaningful, a speaker will almost certainly embed the sentence in some story or anecdote so as to give it one of its two more obvious interpretations. And that is the same procedure as the one adopted by the defenders of the meaningfulness of 'Colourless green ideas sleep furiously'. In other words, use is made of a procedure that does give the questioned utterance some particular interpretation. I am not taking refuge at this point in some highly general view such as 'meaningfulness can only be discussed with respect to an entire language', or anything like that. I am calling attention to a particular *procedure* of sense resolution, in which a particular interpretation is assigned to a questioned utterance by means of telling a surrounding story, uncovering more of a surrounding book page, or perhaps simply by producing utterances with the form of what I shall call *dictionary entries*, such as 'ball as round object'.

Yet, even if the necessary condition is plausible (and there are further considerations against accepting necessary conditions for meaningfulness that I shall discuss below), that does not shed any light on the nature of the 'primary significance' that only resolved segments have. In Quine's discussion of a 'primary synonymy' he gave a quite different explication of that notion in behavioural terms. But here I think we can push the characterization in terms of sense resolvability a little further, and get something like a sufficient condition for meaningfulness as well.

The sufficient condition for meaningfulness would be that a text was meaningful if it had one and not more than one interpretation. But in virtue of what can a text be said to have a single interpretation? Why does one want to say that 'I must take these letters to the post' has a single interpretation, though 'He fell while getting to the ball' has two? The difference cannot be simply that 'ball' has two senses while 'post' has one, for 'post' usually has more senses listed in a dictionary than 'ball'.

If an English speaker is asked to explain, in informal terms, how he knows that 'I must take these letters to the post' has only one interpretation, he will probably say that the notion of 'letters' is connected to only one sense of the notion 'post', and so if the word 'letters' is present in an utterance then it can only be the 'post as mail' sense of 'post' that is intended. But in the case of 'He fell while getting to the ball' there is no such overlap, or coherence, of notions to disqualify either of the two natural interpretations of the utterance.

The common-sense explanation can be put quite naturally in terms of any system of linguistic markers. So, to take a system even simpler than the CSD system described earlier, if there was a marker MAIL in use, then we would expect to find it attached to only one sense of 'letters' (not the 'alphabetic items' sense) and to only one sense of 'post'. We might then examine the sentence 'He took the letters to the post' armed with the rule 'if the marker MAIL is attached to senses of *more then one word* in the sentence, then select those senses'. This rule would be a very simple-minded one, though it would work in this case. However, such rules can be made as complicated as necessary and there is no more mystery about the attachment of suitable markers to word-senses than there is to the construction of the conventional entries in an English dictionary that distinguish the senses of words from each other. We can perfectly easily imagine a rule like the one involving MAIL being superimposed on the structures of the CSD system: if we have a text of fragments with a number of possible template structures for each fragment, and two fragments are such that for each there is one template containing the MAIL marker then, in the absence of any overriding consideration, one would expect those two templates to appear in the representation produced for the whole text.

Now consider a different example, which I shall call a *pseudo-text*: 'Do you like my car. I always wear a flower. The seats are leather.' An utterance like that would almost certainly be said to be meaningless, even though it is not inconceivable that an ingenious person could embed it within some intelligible story, perhaps as an entry for a literary competition. It is not easy to say why that pseudo-text seems meaningless; the simplest way of putting the matter is to say that there is nothing that it is about, in that the ideas the utterance expresses do not cohere together sufficiently for there to be an interpretation that is not identical with the utterance itself.

What is suggested here by the sufficient condition for meaningfulness, given above, is that the pseudo-text *would be* meaningful if there were sufficient coherence between its constituent concepts, of the sort expressed in linguistic terms by means of the MAIL marker, to enable rules to select a single interpretation for the whole text. What is important for the present discussion is that the meaningfulness condition expressed in terms of 'having one and only one interpretation', must refer to an overall interpretation, located by means of coherence rules of the sort I have discussed. It cannot refer simply to the sense resolvability of the individual words of the utterance under scrutiny.

The last point requires that we look at the pseudo-text again. Each of its three constituent subsentences is such that one can see, for each word in it, in which of its senses it is being used. That remains true whether the three sentences are considered separately or as parts of the pseudo-text. So there is no problem about word-sense ambiguity in the pseudo-text, and hence, *if* the meaningfulness condition were expressed in terms of word sense ambiguity resolution, rather than the provision of overall interpretations, then the pseudo-text would satisfy the condition and so be meaningful in terms of it. But the pseudo-text is, by assumption, not meaningful, so we can conclude that the meaningfulness condition must refer to an overall interpretation and not to the sense resolvability of the individual words of the text.

I have given only the crudest example of the way in which a vague notion like 'conceptual coherence' can be operationally expressed by means of procedures involving linguistic markers. Such procedures are almost always more complex in fact than the simple co-occurrence of a single marker, and it is easy to see that such a simple 'threshold' notion of coherence will usually not suffice to establish meaningfulness. On this last point, consider another pseudo-text: 'All kings wear crowns. All crowns are coins. All kings wear coins.' That pseudo-text is like the last in that each subsentence is resolved as regards word-sense ambiguity, yet the whole pseudo-text does not seem to admit of a single interpretation. Though, and unlike the last example, it is not that there seems to be *no* interpretation, but rather an oscillation between two alternative ones, depending on the sense of 'crown' selected. Yet this example would satisfy the very crudest standards of conceptual coherence, or what I called a threshold, in that each subsentence would have an overlap of markers (given any reasonable choice of markers) with either of the two other sentences comprising the pseudo-text. Hence, any rules applying to such markers would have to be more structured than the simple example rule using MAIL that I gave earlier.

I have been defending the suggested characterization of meaningfulness against charges of absurdity and wrongness, but is it nonetheless vague? After all, *what* precisely is being characterized as meaningful? Earlier on, I described a procedure often used when the meaningfulness of an utterance is challenged: a speaker defending its meaningfulness attempts to embed the utterance in a story or narrative whose overall meaning is clear. But, in terms of the characterization, the utterance so embedded is properly deemed meaningless if it does not have one clear interpretation in isolation; and, if the whole story containing it is clear and unambiguous, then it is that whole story that is shown to be meaningful by the embedding procedure, and not the embedded utterance. Furthermore, no inference can be made from the meaningfulness of the whole story to that of the embedded utterance, any more than one can infer that p is a theorem because it is a proper part of the theorem $p \supset p$.[5]

If the last point is correct, then it is not proper to speak, as I did earlier, of the procedure of embedding an utterance whose meaningfulness is questioned as one giving a survey of meaningful utterances. The possibility of such a survey is not put at risk at this point (though see below) because it is perfectly possible to look for paradigms of meaningful utterances without examining any whose meaningfulness is questionable, and without looking at any that admit of more than one interpretation.

However, another important point has surfaced here, and what it brings out is that the present formulation of the characterization of meaningfulness is incomplete: it requires to be augmented as follows, '. . . one and only one interpretation with respect to some dictionary, or dictionary substitute'. Consider again the utterance 'He fell while getting to the ball'. My claim was that it is meaningless in isolation, in that one could not decide whether its proper interpretation contained the 'ball as round object' or the 'ball as formal dance' sense of 'ball'. But that judgment assumed a conventional dictionary containing those two senses of the word 'ball', even though a considerable proportion of English speakers do not know that 'ball' can be used to mean 'formal dance', and so to them the utterance might be said to be unambiguous and so perfectly meaningful.

What I am saying here can be put as a series of assertions in which X stands for the utterance 'He fell while getting to the ball' and Y stands for what I shall call 'the dance text': a story about a dance and containing the sentence X. Then, in terms of the augmented characterization, X is meaningful with respect to Y; X is meaningful with respect to a contracted dictionary (one containing 'ball as round object' but not 'ball as formal dance', or vice versa); X is meaningful with respect to a text containing the sentence 'a ball is a round object' and X; X is meaningless with respect to a conventional dictionary (one containing both 'ball as round object' and 'ball as formal dance'); Y is meaningful with respect to the conventional dictionary.

The words 'with respect to' are being used in two different ways here: in 'with respect to a dictionary' they mean considered in regard to such-and-such possible sense explanations; but in 'with respect to a text' the words naturally mean considered as properly embedded in such a text, as proper parts of it, etc. The main point made is a simple one: the sentence X is not meaningful with respect to a conventional dictionary; the dance text Y, in virtue of its presumed internal coherence discussed earlier, is meaningful with respect to the same dictionary. The augmentation of the characterization removes the prima facie absurdity of saying that X is meaningless, since it is now proper to say that X is meaningful with respect to any text (or dictionary) that does duty for Y.

However, if nothing is specified after 'with respect to', then one has to assume that it is a conventional dictionary that is intended, and in that case the utterance X remains meaningless. In those terms the rejections of, for example, metaphysical sentences by Carnap were perfectly correct: if sentences of the sort he rejected have, as I think they can be shown to have, more than one interpretation with respect to a conventional dictionary, then they are properly rejected when considered in isolation. But, and this is the important proviso, why consider such utterances in isolation in the first place if one's aim is to understand what is being read? If the present characterization is at all correct, then there is no proper inference from such a judgment of meaninglessness to 'there is no text Y with respect to which this X is meaningful'.

1.4 Meaningfulness and decidability

If meaningful utterances can be surveyed and meaningfulness characterized, then it is possible to ask the important question, 'Is it possible to decide formally of any utterance whether it is meaningful or not: whether any given arbitrary string of words can be placed into one and only one of two classes, the meaningful and the meaningless?'

There is no general theoretical problem about deciding meaningfulness that can be expressed in the same form as truth decision problems. Discussions of Gödel's theorem often include informal paradoxes of the following sort: given a table of named statements, consider the following two items in the table:

m . . . . . . 'The sentence n is false'

n . . . . . . 'The sentence m is true'

Examples of that sort cannot be produced for the case of meaning for, if 'true' and 'false' in the example are replaced by 'meaningful' and 'meaningless' respectively, then there is no paradox. Nor is there any paradox if only one such replacement is carried out: the result is a pair of statements of the same truth value (both true or both false). The same goes for Tarski's example, the one he considered to be an informal representation of Gödel's theorem:

```
┌─────────────────────────────┐
│                             │
│      The sentence in this   │
│      square is false.       │
│                             │
│                             │
└─────────────────────────────┘
```

If 'false 'is replaced by 'meaningless' then again there is no paradox, only a false statement. It is true, on the other hand, that 'The sentence in this square is meaningless' (in the square) implies that the same sentence is meaningful, since all true sentences are meaningful. Thus its truth implies its falsity. But the converse is not true, and hence there is no paradox in any strong sense. There is not the oscillation of truth values associated with the word 'false', and the situation can, as it were, come to rest when the truth value 'false' is ascribed to the sentence 'The sentence in this square is meaningless' (in the square).

But the absence of any real 'paradoxes of meaning', and the argued possibility of characterizing the notion of meaningfulness, do not, of course, suffice to show that meaningfulness is a decidable property in the sense that divisibility by three is. The implication of the earlier discussion about characterization is, on the contrary, that meaningfulness is not a decidable property, and that meaningful utterances do not form a recursive set.

Consider again the tentative claim, made earlier, that meaningful utterances can be surveyed. A parallel was drawn with the Propositional Calculus where some survey of theorems (of $p \supset p$, for example) is possible prior to any particular axiomatization. However, in a survey of the Propositional Calculus one also knows, again prior to any axiomatization, that $p \supset \sim p$ is *not* a theorem. Is there any parallel in the case of meaningfulness, in that there are utterances known in advance to be meaningless? In terms of the characterization discussed, the answer must be no.[6] In the course of the earlier discussion, two kinds of paradigms of meaninglessness were produced: those with no interpretations (the pseudo-texts), and those with more than one, like 'He fell while getting the ball'. But, as became clear in the discussion, those utterances were deemed meaningless with respect to some particular dictionary (what one might call a conventional or standard dictionary), or surrounding context equivalent to such a dictionary. There is no way of knowing that those same utterances would not be meaningful with respect to some other, unconventional, dictionary or context, and in the case of such examples as 'He fell while getting to the ball' it was trivially easy to construct the dictionary required.

This feature of natural language is quite independent of the particular characterization of meaningfulness proposed in this chapter for, given any characterization of the notion of meaningfulness, we can never know of any given string of words that human ingenuity cannot render it meaningful with the aid of sufficient assumptions of the form 'X as Y' where X is a word in the string, and Y is some other, suitably chosen, word. Any suggested boundary[7] to meaningfulness defined by means of any set of rules only constitutes a challenge to that ingenuity.

If there can be no true paradigms of meaninglessness, then there can be no proper survey of meaningful utterances, and hence no reason to expect them to form a recursive set. However, the characterization of the meaningfulness of utterances with respect to particular dictionaries or texts, as having one and only one interpretation, can lead to some formal assessment of meaningfulness. It can, I think, though this suggestion and what follows is highly tentative, lead to some formal assessment of *degree* of meaningfulness of utterances or texts. That would be quite a different matter from any attempt to divide utterances into the meaningful and the meaningless, in the way that a decidable logic divides putative theorems into theorems and non-theorems. It would be quite possible, in principle, to order utterances by degree of meaningfulness while admitting that any utterance whatever might find a place at the far end of the scale of meaningfulness.

Now consider some possible linguistic system for deciding meaningfulness. Let us suppose it consists of a system of production rules starting with an initial symbol, just as generative grammars do. Suppose, too, the rules are of a straightforwardly decidable sort, like simple phrase structure rules [21]. That stipulation cannot, of course, make meaningfulness decidable in any sense; it is simply a property of the formal system used that for any string, it either produces the string, or shows that the system cannot produce it. Now suppose that there is an additional procedure, let us call it *Expand*, outside this system of rules, and having the following property: given an utterance A which the rules certainly cannot produce, Expand produces an additional rule which, when added to the existing system of rules, allows the augmented system to produce A. Let us suppose that Expand can be applied recursively in such a way that we can know that after some finite number of such applications the system of rules obtained by that time *will* be able to produce A.

What can one say about such a constructible series of rule systems? The metamathematical analogy has now been almost entirely jettisoned, for the procedure for adding a rule so as to produce a meaningful] but rejected, A is not at all related to the procedure Gödel discussed for adding a true, but undecidable, sentence to the axioms of a logical system. In the present case what is added is not the recalcitrant item itself but a different one, namely a fresh rule of inference. In any case, Gödel's point was that to add such a sentence to the axioms is useless because there would always be *at least one more* true but undecidable sentence. But in the present case I do not think the procedure I have described need be useless. Each particular set of rules is decidable, and if each is thought of as an explication of the characterization of meaningfulness canvassed here, namely having one and only one interpretation, then rejection by any particular set, in that the rules cannot produce that utterance, gives no assurance that Expand cannot add sufficient rules so as to yield a set of rules that does produce the utterance in question. Since any particular set of rules expresses, among other things, the dictionary with respect to which meaningfulness is being assessed, then it is quite in accordance with the suggested characterization that meaningfulness with respect to any particular set of rules should be decidable.

However, what is to be said about the whole constructible series of rule systems; that is, those constructible from some initial set of such rules plus the Expand procedure? The set of utterances that can be produced by the whole series of such systems might possibly explicate the other, non-primary and more shadowy, sense of meaningfulness that has been discussed here.* In this other sense of meaningfulness, any utterance whatever might be meaningful, in that it could conceivably be used, or be made sense of, with respect to some possible dictionary. It was part of the definition of the Expand procedure that it could add sufficient rules so as to yield a system of rules capable of producing any utterance whatever. But if there can be real boundary to meaningfulness, then that is precisely the sort of explication of the concept one would expect.† The series of constructible systems of rules could then explicate meaningfulness usefully as a matter of degree only; in that an utterance X might be said to be more meaningful than an utterance Y if it required fewer applications of the Expand procedure to yield a system of rules capable of producing it. That feature would save the important intuition that some utterances are undoubtedly more meaningful than others, even though with sufficient effort and imagination any utterance whatever might be made meaningful.

All this is very tentative indeed, yet if some procedural and linguistic flesh can be put on these rather bare bones, it would have another philosophical implication. It could be argued that all that has been said in this section of this chapter is merely an elaborate restatement of the contemporary philosophical platitude that all meaningfulness is with respect to some presupposed area of discourse, or within some *language game*. Defences of particular language games, such as theology and aesthetics, along these lines have become commonplace. However, if some concrete expression could be given to the constructible series of rules systems sketched here, then they might also give a hint as to how it is possible to pass, as it were, from one language game to another. For it is surely an ultimately unsatisfactory view that human language games, whatever they may be, are wholly separate and unconnected structures.

* And it is that sense of meaningfulness (not the primary sense) that is characterized by the ability of speakers to embed *any utterance whatever* in some story context.
† Though it makes no sense in terms of the analogy, drawn earlier, with metamathematics, where, if a system can produce any string (i.e. any well-formed formula is a theorem) then the system is by definition inconsistent.

It is not hard to see how, in principle, a system of phrase structure rules could express the characterization of primary meaningfulness argued for here: namely, having one and only one interpretation. Phrase structure rules are simply rules which allow one item to be rewritten as a string of items. It can be seen right away that a conventional dictionary entry can be put in this form (and I have several times referred to the equivalence of dictionary entries and rules of this sort). For example, two different entries for 'post' could be written in phrase structure form as post → items + that + can + be + mailed, and post → a + stake + fixed + in + the + ground. In that form the '+' sign has the same meaning as before, namely 'to the left of'.

Let us assume, in addition to the rules expressing the dictionary, a set of phrase structure rules capable of producing representations or symbolic forms of interpretations, by means of rewriting, and from them in turn producing paragraphs and sentences of written English.

Such a set of rules would be expected to produce the clearly ambiguous sentence 'The old salt is damp' via two different representations. Such a 'semantic parsing' would be in rather the same position as a grammatical parsing of a sentence like 'They are eating apples', where it is usually said that the sentence can be produced via two quite different strings of grammar codes with the aid of some phrase structure grammar.

This is where the characterization of primary meaningfulness I argued for would come in; meaningfulness with respect to a given set of such rules would be translated naturally as 'can be produced by the set of rules in one and only one way'. Thus the sentence 'The old salt is damp' would not pass this test and so would be rejected by that set of rules. But, of course, if it were produced as part of either a sea story, or, alternatively, as part of a grocery shop story, then the whole story might well have a single interpretation provided there are also rules producing only certain combinations of the structurings of markers.

It will come as no surprise to the reader to find that the CSD system, described earlier, is a system that can be described by phrase structure rules. Concatenations of markers forming templates, such as MAN + BE + KIND, are produced by such rules, and in the case of the sentence 'The old salt is damp' one would expect, as I wrote earlier, to produce it via two different representations, MAN + BE + KIND and STUFF + BE + KIND. But again, if that sentence were produced as part of a larger story text, then as with the recurrence of the MAIL marker in the example discussed earlier, there would be rules opting for either the MAN + BE + KIND or the STUFF + BE + KIND structure on the basis of the markers to be found elsewhere in what might be a grocery or sea story. To choose either of these two representations is to impose a single interpretation on the sentence, and hence to render it meaningful with respect to the story of which it happens to form a part.

If all this seems wildly optimistic it is because I have over-simplified by assuming the attachment of only a single marker to a word, such as MAN to the 'salt as a sailor' sense of 'salt'. The dictionary must in fact be more complex than that and the structurings of markers attached to the senses of words have to be as complex as is needed to distinguish each word-sense from every sense of every other word in the dictionary. But that is again a matter of linguistic detail, and the principles are not affected. It cannot be in principle difficult to select, say, the 'sailor' sense of 'salt' in a sea story because any human being, reading the story and encountering the example sentence, makes the required inference immediately. Unless this inference is made by occult means it is reasonable to assume it is done on the basis of the other words occurring in the story. If the reader also sees 'ships', then he's pretty sure that it is the 'salt as a sailor' sense that is in question.

It is equally easy to see how, in principle, the CSD sense constructor might fill the role of the Expand procedure. Suppose a given set of CSD rules fails to produce any representation for some text, and suppose, too, that it is possible to examine the attempts to produce a representation with the rules, and to find the word in the text that is holding up the process, as it were, in that, given the dictionary entries for the word, its markers do not cohere sufficiently with the other words of the text for a representation to be produced. Suppose now that, having found the recalcitrant word A, Expand can look at the dictionary entries for all the words in the text and find b, the word-sense of word B which is closest in sense, in terms of some defined procedure, to the recalcitrant word A. Expand could then add a rule to the system which is equivalent to adding that close sense b to the possible senses of the recalcitrant word A. With the new rule added we have a larger rule system and the analysis can be tried again to see if a representation can now be produced for the text. A reasonable inference, if the new augmented system does succeed in producing a representation, is that 'yes, this text can be meaningful if A can mean B in it'.

This is not a fanciful suggestion, but is, I suggest, how people may actually cope with difficult texts, especially those, like poetry and philosophical texts, that use ordinary words in new and apparently improbable ways no one would expect to find in a conventional dictionary. In a very real sense Spinoza's *Ethics* becomes comprehensible only when such a new possibility has been considered: in the case of that text one might say that the key-sense extension that a reader must consider is that 'substance' means 'the whole Universe'. The interesting question, if one were to analyse 'difficult' texts with the aid of such a linguistic system is *how many*[8] applications of a procedure like Expand would have to be made in order to resolve any particular text. The Expand procedure must eventually allow an interpretation to be produced for any text because, after a sufficiently great number of applications of the procedure, so many word-senses in the text will have been mutually identified that some trivial resolution will be produced.

The real upshot of this discussion is a distinction between two senses of 'meaningfulness': one is characterizable in terms of giving sense to an utterance by embedding it in some story whose meaning is clear. The utterances corresponding to that characterization are all possible utterances, which are therefore trivially surveyable and the set of them is trivially decidable because everything goes in. The other sense, what I called primary meaningfulness, is characterizable in terms of having one and only one interpretation, and corresponds to sets of utterances that can be surveyed and decided only with respect to particular sets of dictionary rules, and so cannot be decided in any real or interesting sense.

The importance of the Expand procedure, or sense constructor, is that it offers a possible way of bringing some determinateness to this apparently unpromising formal condition of human language; by showing how utterances, which are clearly meaningful or not, as the case may be, within some particular language game, and may be quite otherwise within some other language game (defined by some other decidable set of rules), yet may all have places on the continuum of meaningfulness which consists of all the utterances producible by all systems of rules that can be produced, in their turn, by a higher-level procedure.

2 The contemporary background

'However, many of the most Learned and Wise adhere to the
new Scheme of expressing themselves by Things; which hath only
this Inconvenience attending it; that if a Man's Business be very
great . . . he must be obliged in proportion to carry a greater
Bundle of Things upon his Back, unless he can afford one or two
strong Servants to attend him.'

Swift, A Voyage to Laputa

'But what I have most at Heart, is, that some Method should be
thought on for Ascertaining and Fixing our Language for ever,
after such alterations are made in it as shall be thought requisite.
For I am of Opinion that it is better a Language should not be
wholly perfect, than that it should be perpetually changing.'

Swift, A Proposal for Correcting the English Tongue

2.1 Philosophy

'Modern philosophy', writes Findlay [87, p. 169], 'is distinguished by
the emergence of a new question; how we give meaning to the expressions used in ordinary and philosophical discourse.' That remark is
not quite fair; certainly not to Aristotle who spent considerable
time discussing such questions as whether or not 'winged' could be
predicated of 'grammar', and so could reasonably be said to be discussing a possible boundary between meaningful and unmeaningful

D

expressions. It might then seem a small step from that discussion to one about 'how we give meaning . . .'.

However, the truth expressed by Findlay's remark is that the problem arising from researches on the foundations of mathematics and logic in the early part of this century provided a quite new starting point for efforts to separate the meaningless from the meaningful. As is well known, Russell's paradox concerning the definition of certain kinds of set led to the 'theory of types' which was intended to define classes of expression that were inadmissible or meaningless. The statement of the paradox itself was to be among the expressions so excluded. Whether or not that theory, in its various forms, was successful is not of concern here. What is important is that from it, and from Husserl's [133] contemporary resurrection of[1] the notion of a Universal Grammar, sprang a number of fresh attempts to construct logical systems powerful enough to distinguish the meaningful expressions of natural, everyday, language.

From Husserl's work, and stimulated by the apparent success of the 'theory of types', there developed two traditions of attack on this enormous problem of demarcating 'the meaningful'. They can be distinguished crudely as the Polish tradition and the German tradition. Both owed much to Husserl's *Bedeutungskategorien* as starting point, and both led from philosophico-logical system-building to theories of linguistics and so to computational experiments. In the next section I shall turn from the philosophers and logicians to their heirs the linguists: for the Polish tradition [Adjukiewicz, 1] led naturally to Categorial Grammars [Bar-Hillel, 13; Lambek, 159, 160], just as Carnap's work led naturally to the work of Chomsky (Chomsky was in fact a pupil of Carnap, just as Carnap was of Husserl).

For the moment I want to restrict my attention to what I have called the German tradition in this matter, and in particular to the work of Rudolf Carnap, which I take as a *locus classicus* for an answer to the question 'Can there be a general test for the meaningfulness of a fragment of natural language?' Carnap's answer was yes, and in particular that a text was meaningful if and only if it satisfied the 'rules of logical syntax' for the language in which it was written [Carnap, 40, 41, 44].

The logical syntax of a certain language [writes Carnap] is to be understood as the formal theory of that language. . . . We will call formal such considerations or assertions concerning linguistic expressions as are without reference to sense or meaning. [40, pp. 39–40.] [And again, 41, p. 1.] By the *logical syntax* of a language, we mean the formal theory of the linguistic forms of that language—the systematic statement of the formal rules which govern it together with the development of the consequences which follow from these rules.

Three preliminary points should be made:

(i)   When Carnap writes, as in the passages above, of 'a language' he means both artificial languages, such as his Languages I and II, for which he constructed the rules, and *also* natural languages for which he has not constructed the rules. This becomes quite clear from the discussion of natural language examples in [44]. Carnap's Languages I and II contain only statements of logic and mathematics, but in all that follows I shall take the thesis of 'logical syntax' as it refers to the case of natural languages.

(ii)   In the last passage quoted above Carnap distinguishes 'the formal rules which govern [the language]' from the 'development of the consequences which follow'. This is an adumbration of the distinction he is later to make between formation and transformation rules [41, p. 2]. All that is said here concerns only the formation rules: the 'syntactical rules in the narrower sense'.

(iii)   Carnap also distinguishes between what he calls 'pure syntax' and 'descriptive syntax':

Pure syntax is thus wholly analytic, and is nothing more than combinatorial analysis, or in other words, the geometry of finite, discrete, serial structures of a particular kind. Descriptive syntax is related to pure syntax as physical geometry to pure mathematical geometry; it is concerned with the syntactical properties and relations of empirically given expressions (for example, with the sentences of a particular book) [41, pp. 6–7].

The plausibility of that distinction is thus made dependent on that between the 'analytic' and the 'synthetic', a much questioned distinction these days [Quine, 237; Goodman, 104]. However, Carnap's use of examples presumably makes use of only descriptive syntax, so what is said here should be understood to apply only to descriptive syntax. But it will be clear that any problems that arise in the consideration of the descriptive variety throw doubt on the whole thesis of logical syntax.

Having dispensed with these preliminary considerations we can now try to come to grips with the thesis of logical syntax itself. There are in that thesis at least two different strands: the first conflates a number of forms of what is usually called the 'verification theory of meaning', and the second is our quarry, logical syntax proper. The two strands correspond to the distinction Carnap makes between two kinds of meaningless statement, or 'pseudo-statement':

> A language consists of a vocabulary and a syntax, i.e. a set of words which have meanings and rules of sentence formation. These rules indicate how sentences may be formed out of the various sorts of words. Accordingly, there are two kinds of pseudo-statements: either they contain a word which is erroneously believed to have meaning, or the constituent words are meaningful, yet are put together in a counter-syntactical way, so that they do not yield a meaningful statement. [44, p. 63.]

To illustrate the first kind of case Carnap, in [44], discusses the way metaphysicians use the word 'principle'; he claims that they evacuate the original meaning of the word, but fail to give it a new one. Thus he admits the important point that words may have a number of meanings or senses (a point *not* taken account of in any of his artificially constructed languages). When he says that a word is not meaningful, or has not been given a new meaning, he means one of the following [44, pp. 64–5]:

(i)   there are no empirical criteria for the application of the word;

(ii)   sentences containing the word are not deducible from 'protocol sentences';

(iii)   truth conditions for sentences containing the word are not fixed;

(iv)   no methods of verification for sentences containing the word are known.

Carnap says, in giving the list, that its members 'ultimately say the same thing'. That is not at all obvious since (i) would seem to be much like a 'reference theory of meaning', in that a word would be said to 'mean something' only if there were some thing to which it actually or possibly referred; whereas the formulations (ii)–(iv) would seem to be forms of what is usually called the 'verification theory of meaning'. I discuss the 'reference theory' below; and

I do not propose to deal with the pros and cons of the verifiability argument at all, since they are well known. My point here is that this whole strand, of reference and verifiability, is a quite different one from logical syntax proper, and not only different in the way that Carnap seems to think, which is that the two kinds of pseudo-statement are two kinds of case. My point is that Carnap presents two different methods of detecting pseudo-statements and that *each method is in principle applicable to any case*. It is for this reason that I feel justified in ignoring one method (verification) and concentrating on the other (logical syntax); for if the two methods did apply to different cases essentially, then it would be at least dubious to restrict oneself in this way.

The second way with pseudo-statements is illustrated by the following examples [46, p. 67]:

   (i) 'Caesar is and'

   (ii) 'Caesar is a prime number'.

Carnap's case is that (i) is counter-syntactic in that the last word place should be filled with a word from other (part-of-speech) categories; whereas (ii) is syntactically correct, although it violates the rules of *logical syntax* in that it is meaningless unless the last word places are filled by a word that can be properly predicated of persons (like 'general').

This approach is quite different from that of *verification*, which can be seen by considering that it might well be thought inappropriate to talk of verifying, or falsifying, (i) or (ii). But the distinction between this kind of 'syntactical meaninglessness' on the one hand, and that of 'meaningless words', or 'verificational meaninglessness' on the other, is not simply a distinction between cases, as Carnap claims. For Carnap admits that there are instances of use of the word 'principle', say, which are not 'meaningless uses' in his sense. Hence there must be syntactical rules in his system, if he constructed it, which specify the classes to which 'principle' belongs. There will also be rules restricting its possible use in combination with other words. Now, when Carnap's system of analysis tackles a sentence containing the word 'principle' there is always a *choice* as to which of the two methods to apply, and hence the methods are quite independent, and can be treated separately. Carnap seems almost to suggest that there is some *list* of meaningless words which can be consulted, and on the basis of which sentences can be assigned to one method of treatment or the other. But, if he admits, as he does, that even metaphysical words have 'ordinary senses' then he cannot separate the cases in that way either.

So then, one comes to logical syntax proper. Here is a succinct restatement of it:

> . . . given an appropriate rule, it can be proved that the word-series 'Pirots karulize elatically' is a sentence, provided only that 'Pirots' is known to be a substantive (in the plural), 'karulize' a verb (in the third person plural), and 'elatically' an adverb. . . . The meaning of the words is quite inessential to the purpose, and need not be known. [46, p. 2.]

Thus the content of the doctrine reduces to fairly naive grammatical analysis of the sentence, and to the last statement, which even grammarians would admit to be highly questionable.

It is not an argument against the thesis of logical syntax (LS for short) that Carnap does not *in fact* produce a system of rules, for, say, English. I take LS as saying that there is, nonetheless, *some* system of rules adequate to decide the meaningfulness of a natural language like English. Such a thesis is independent of the actual feasibility of constructing the system of rules, though it is not independent of the application of a notional system to actual examples, as we shall see in a moment.

The principal drawback of LS is that, as it is described by Carnap, it cannot effectively distinguish meaningful from unmeaningful discourse in English. The point can be put in the following way: it is a matter of fact about English, say, that most of its words have a number of senses. Carnap admits this about his chosen example word 'principle', and even distinguishes a number of its major senses. It is also a matter of fact that many of the words with this property appear in English text in such a way that it cannot be decided, within the compass of the sentence containing them, in which of their senses they are being used. Carnap admits that it is necessary, in the case of 'principle', to know which of its senses it 'has' before a sentence containing it can be deemed meaningless. Yet Carnap's theory is explicitly a theory of the *sentence*, and not of the sentence as a member of a text of sentences. Hence his system cannot both decide the meaningfulness, or otherwise, of sentences *and* be a theory of the sentence out of the context of other sentences.

It should be clear that I am not saying that *no* theory of LS could cope with the fact of the many meanings of the words of natural language. On the contrary, the system described later in this book is really a LS that goes further towards Wittgenstein's desideratum for a LS [303, 3·325]: a symbolism that does not apply signs in the same way that signify in different ways. This I do by using different symbols for different senses of a single word. Carnap was aware that such an extension of his own method was perfectly feasible: 'The mistake here is unimportant; it could, e.g. be eliminated by writing "larger1" and "larger2" (for the two senses of the word "larger").' [44, p. 75.]

But he did not use that powerful notation, and he did not seem to realize how vital it is for the determination of meaningfulness in natural language.

When Carnap comes, in [44, pp. 69–73] to apply a possible, though unconstructed, system of LS to English sentences then quite new difficulties arise. For the absence of an actual system removes the whole force of Carnap's case against the metaphysical statements he is discussing. For one has no assurance that such an attack could not be mounted against *any sentence whatever* in terms of a possible, though non-existent, system of LS. In these circumstances the dispute shifts from a discussion of the properties of a system to the swapping of intuitions about the nature of particular sentences. The last enterprise may be valuable but it is certainly not one that Carnap should consider so.

The situation would be different if direct appeals were allowed to intuitions about the meaningfulness of sentences, as with what might be called Oxford appeals to 'what can be sensibly said'. In this connexion it is instructive to compare Ryle's work [257, 259] which shares a number of presuppositions with Carnap's, whatever may be their differences of approach, and attitude towards formal systems [see 258]. In the two works noted, Ryle develops the notions of a 'sentence frame', and of categories of words defined by sentence frames in whose 'gaps' they can properly be substituted. His principal example is 'Saturday is in bed' [259, p. 70] which, says Ryle, breaks no rule of grammar, but *does* break a rule of 'logical grammar'. Like Carnap, he turns his attention to metaphysical sentences which, according to Ryle, break the rules of logical grammar and are therefore meaningless. He differs from Carnap principally in that he does not think system-building is possible in this area. Ryle's work is more a discursive adding to a stock of rules of thumb.

There are well-known objections to Ryle's arguments, and I shall not go into them here, for my point is to notice that my principal argument against Carnap tells also against Ryle: his, too, is a theory of the sentence, but in view of the need to find out in *which* of its senses a word is being used on any given occasion, a theory of the sentence cannot suffice. Sir Alan Gardiner [97] has taken a number of Ryle's 'categorical nonsense' sentences and supplied them with plausible surrounding sentences so that the wholes so formed make perfectly good sense. That, I maintain, could equally well be done with the examples Carnap takes, and it is a move open to anyone once the dispute has got down to exchanging, possibly differing, intuitions about the status of sentences. For if there is no system and no definite procedure to be followed, then anything goes.[2]

My conclusion from the last section is not that the issue of deciding meaningfulness is a closed one, but rather that it would be nice to actually construct some system and then actually apply it to texts; bearing in mind that such a system must differ radically in its assumptions from Carnap's work if it is to take account of the criticisms made above. Later, and particularly in Chapter 3, I shall define the units, and state the theses, of a quite different system for the analysis of discourse. It is proper at this point to set down eight presuppositions which my system shares with the work of Carnap and Ryle described above, and, apart from the last, I shall not have cause to discuss them again:

(i)   That a linguistic classification (an assignment of words to classes or categories) can yield information which will allow a judgment about the meaningfulness, or otherwise, of a text to be made; at least in the sense that it is not necessary to know whether the statements of the text under examination are true or false. Neither Carnap nor Ryle ever suggests that, in order to know whether or not a statement is meaningful, one first needs to know whether it is true or false.

(ii)   That some system of categories related* to the traditional categories would be adequate to the task under consideration. One can see this from Carnap's explicit use of naive grammatical categories in the examples above. Ryle, even though he criticizes the Aristotelean system of categories, never suggests that a suitable system would be utterly unrelated to it.

(iii)   That to specify the category membership of words is also in some sense to specify the permissible forms of sentences in which

* What I mean by 'related to' will appear in Chapter 3.

they occur. This assumption is quite explicit in Ryle [259, p. 76], and consistent with the views of Carnap.

(iv) That it is not improper, initially at least, to restrict one's attentions to *written* language (cf. Carnap's definition in terms of 'shape').

(v) That the construction of a system for determining meaningfulness in no way implies that human beings make use of such a system in their brains or minds when they make judgments about meaningfulness.

(vi) That it is not *in general* necessary to consider theories of behavioural meaning (such as Russell's 'pragmatic meaning' or Morris's Semiotic), when assessing the meaningfulness of any piece of language.

(vii) That *any* assessment of meaningfulness of sentences is made with respect to limitations of space and time. No one making a judgment about meaningfulness imagines that he binds the usage of all future generations.

(viii) That there are, in some sense, *linguistic rules.*

2.2 Linguistics

2.21 Transformational and other theories of grammar

The last section did not provide a very wide philosophical background, but concentrated on two approaches to the problem of determining meaningfulness. By being so selective I omitted both the traditional philosophical discussion of what 'a meaning' is, and also the modern reaction against the philosophical positions I discussed in detail. That reaction is usually associated with the later writings of Wittgenstein [305, 307], one of whose aims was to show that meaningfulness cannot be circumscribed in the simple-minded way that Carnap, and indeed Wittgenstein himself in his early writings [303], had thought.

The real purpose of examining Carnap's work was to provide a background to the enormous amount of work that has been done in recent years within formal linguistics. The best-known work is that of Noam Chomsky who, like Carnap, addressed himself to the very general question of 'what would it be like to construct a system of rules that would produce, or alternatively analyse, all the sequences of words in a language that were well-formed in some respect?'

The extent to which Chomsky's work is a proper continuation of the enterprise of LS is a disputed question among philosophers,[3] though certain formal debts are obvious. Chomsky's originality, as will become clear, consists in withdrawing the whole structure of a Carnapian logic (rules of formation and transformation) to within the area that was covered for Carnap by rules of formation alone: namely, the specification of well-formed formulae.[4]

So Chomsky's work is concerned only with well-formedness, whereas for Carnap the task of establishing correctness according to the rules of LS was no more than a preliminary to the study of deductive relations between the well-formed sentences. But it is not at all obvious why Chomsky's work is to be classified along with the traditional descriptive enterprise of linguistics, rather than with LS within logic proper. If there is a real distinction between the work of Carnap and Chomsky, and I believe there is, it can only be one of emphasis; for the task to which both addressed themselves was one set by logicians. For example:

> A logically perfect language has rules of syntax which prevent nonsense, and has single symbols which always have a definite and unique meaning. Mr. Wittgenstein is concerned with the conditions for a logically perfect language—not that any language is logically perfect, or that we believe ourselves capable, here and now, of constructing a logically perfect language, but that the whole function of language is to have meaning, and it only fulfils this function in proportion as it approaches to the ideal language which we postulate [Russell, 255, p. 8.]

I think this passage makes clear the difference in emphasis I have in mind, namely that the starting point for a logical investigation is *a notation and its illuminative power*. What areas of natural language are explored with this notation is a secondary question.

A linguistic investigation, on the other hand, is directed towards a satisfactory explanation, that is a reduction to order, either of some finite corpus of utterances or of some 'native speaker's intuition'. But this distinction is one of emphasis rather than of the use or non-use of logical tools, especially in the case of formal linguistics where notations are essentially logical; and Chomsky has acknowledged his debt to Carnap in respect both of his aims and of certain specific distinctions that Carnap made.

In using the term 'formal linguistics', I implicitly distinguish it from 'descriptive', 'structural', or, as it sometimes called, 'anthropological' linguistics. Formal lingistics of the kind under discussion began as a criticism of the American tradition of descriptive linguistics whose central figure was Bloomfield. This was a clash of empiricisms: Chomsky criticized the descriptivists [52] for the use they make of the non-empirical notion of meaning; they in turn, as we shall see, criticize his approach on the grounds of untestability, and its essentially Aristotelean assumptions about what the structures of sentences are. The difference here is about the nature of the basic observations, or data, of linguistics and not about the use of logic or machines.[5] As will become abundantly clear during the discussion of Chomsky's work, it is formal linguistics that claims 'openness to' native speakers' intuitions, and in this respect, too, it distinguishes itself from descriptive linguistics which is 'corpus oriented'. I am not claiming that there is a clear distinction between these two in virtue of the faculties to which they profess allegiance; but rather that *linguistic* conclusions, of whichever kind, are answerable to some authority like actual linguistic performance, or consilient intuitions of speakers about their performances, in a way that logic pure and simple does not seem to be.[6]

Transformational grammars

Chomsky, claiming to follow Harris, has for fifteen years expounded, developed and advocated what is now called the 'transformational theory of grammar'. In his original exposition Chomsky defined the role of a grammar of a language L: it was to be a finite set of rules that would explicate, produce or analyse the set of 'grammatically well-formed sentences' of L. Sometimes he calls this set simply the 'sentences' of L, as distinct from *sequences* which are not grammatically well-formed, and I shall use this latter convention in the following discussion. Chomsky was at pains to emphasize that none of this had anything to do with 'meaning' [48, p. 15]. He was quite prepared to admit that many sequences that are not grammatically well-formed in his sense, such as 'We be here', may yet communicate. These he calls 'acceptable' but 'deviant'.[7] He was also prepared to admit that many sentences that are grammatically well-formed in this sense may yet be meaningless, some of them because their nestings of parts are too 'deep' [310] for them to be understood by human beings subject to the memory limitation of present brains, and so on. Chomsky argued in detail [47, pp. 114–

121] the superiority of the Transformational model of Grammar over two other possible models, the Markov Process or Finite State model, and the Phrase Structure model. In the cases of both these models or putative devices, Chomsky argued that they are not sufficiently *complex* to produce all and only the sentences of a natural language. By a Markov process, or finite state grammar, Chomsky meant a device which produces the words of a sentence sequentially from left to right, and which operated on the basis of pre-assigned 'transition probabilities', invoked or consulted on each occasion that a word is written down or printed out by a machine.[8] He produced two kinds of considerations against the adequacy of this device: formal and psychological-cum-physiological. He claimed, no doubt rightly, that such a device could not produce sequences of the form ab, aabb, aaabbb, etc. [48, p. 21], where a and b are different words. Secondly, and this point has been much emphasized by his psychologist-collaborators [96] and the school of psycho-linguistics they have founded, Chomsky claimed that human beings could not learn fast enough to establish such transition probabilities in a lifetime, let alone a childhood; and that even if they could, they could not store the appropriate information in their brains.

One might reply to this as follows. Are there in fact English sentences of the form quoted? (Chomsky gives no plausible examples.) Secondly, the structure, and hence the information capacity, of the human brain is very much a matter for dispute, and arguments dependent on it are therefore dubious. Given that the 'counter-examples', such as aabb, that Chomsky offers to this theory are not very convincing, in that that it is not clear that there are English sentences of these forms, one might ask why a finite state process is not adequate for the generation of English sentences *even if* it is not, as a matter of fact, a very realistic model of the way human beings produce[9] the sentences? One asks this particularly in view of the fact that when Chomsky comes to expound transforma- tional grammar, he admits that any particular transformational grammar can be represented by an elementary finite state grammar [47, p. 123]. But this is a very important admission whose significance Chomsky does not seem to see. What Chomsky did with the forms ab, aabb, referred to above, was to produce *a* finite state grammar and then show that there were forms it could not produce. It does not follow from this that there is *no* finite state grammar which could produce them. Indeed, the admission referred to suggests the opposite in the case of an interesting class of forms, namely those which a transformational grammar produces. What Chomsky would have to do to make his case at this point would be to display forms which (i) *no* finite state grammar *could* produce, (ii) some transformational grammar could, and (iii) which plausibly represent important constructions in some natural language. These things he does not do. The admission brings out another point that I shall return to later; namely that Chomsky is concerned to prescribe in advance what the particular *content of a linguistic theory must be.* When Chomsky says that a theory of grammar is inadequate he does not mean simply that it does not 'cover the data' in that there are English sentences it does not produce.[10] What he means is that it *must* cover the data in a particular way: its theoretical terms must be those of common-sense, school text-book grammar, or what he calls the 'grammatical intuition of native speakers of English'. It is a strange thing to want to specify content in advance in this way, especially in any discipline that calls itself scientific.

In a recent essay Chomsky gives an account of what it is for a grammar to be adequate [52, p. 29]

> . . . a grammar that aims for *observational adequacy* is concerned merely to give an account of the primary data . . . a grammar that aims for *descriptive adequacy* is *concerned to give a correct account* of the linguistic intuition of the native speaker; and a linguistic theory that aims for *explanatory adequacy* . . . aims to provide a principled basis, independent of any particular language, for the selection of the descriptively adequate grammar of each language.

One notices right away that Chomsky doesn't actually say that a grammar must be observationally adequate in order to count for consideration as descriptively adequate. Nonetheless, the force of the passage as a whole is that the device he has in mind, a 'model of acquisition', would derive a number of grammars, all observationally adequate for some body of data, and then select among these to give the most adequate grammar. Now it might seem quite reasonable, if faced with a choice of this kind, to choose the one closest to that actually used by human beings when they produce sentences. The trouble with saying that is that it is not at all clear how we could know what device human beings were using, if any. A possible way would be opening heads, but whatever doing that

might tell us about the mechanism of the brain, there is no reason
to suppose it would tell us anything about the devices by which
sentences are produced. The only other way we might come to know
about sentence production would be by examining what people
actually say, and seeing what production rules fit this behaviour
best.[11] But that, of course, is exactly the formulation of the problem
that Chomsky will not allow, and is what he criticizes descriptive
(or what he calls 'taxonomic' [52, p. 11]) linguists for allowing.[12]
For Chomsky, the data must themselves be well-formed sentences,
and for this reason his above-quoted account of 'adequacy' is
misleading, especially when he suggests that there will generally be
a number of observationally adequate grammars between which a
choice can be made. For if we have chosen data so as to be consistent with a particular grammar, then we will *not* in general expect
that. In fact Chomsky does not wish to choose between grammars
because of the way human beings actually function; he wants to
choose in the light of what some of them *say* about their language
structure.[13] Chomsky always assumes that these are one and the
same thing, and that is far from self-evidently true.

   Let us turn to the distinction between descriptive and explanatory
adequacy. One suspects that Chomsky hasn't got this at all clear
when the above-quoted passage goes on as follows: '. . . the theory
of transformational grammar can approach the level of explanatory
adequacy, providing a partial explanation for the speaker's linguistic
intuition' [52, p. 35]. That, surely, is more the kind of thing that
the previous passage [52, p. 29] had led us to expect of *descriptive*
adequacy. Explanatory adequacy, it will be remembered, was only
to be achieved with the provision of 'a principled basis, independent
of any particular language, for the selection of the descriptively
adequate grammar of each language'. The context of this makes
clear that the 'principled basis' would be instantiated by a device
that would produce grammars, and so serve as a model of language
acquisition. How then can a theory of transformational grammar
even approach such adequacy, for not only was it derived for a
specific language (English), but it was constructed so as to enshrine
the native speaker's intuitions. This last means that it can only be
selected *with certainty* on a principled basis if the principle is 'look
for the grammar enshrining the native speaker's intuitions (i.e. the
descriptively adequate one), and then select it'. But if that is what is
meant by a principled basis then the whole idea of 'explanatory

adequacy' is trivial. What one would have expected of 'explanatory adequacy' would be that it selected from among 'observationally adequate grammars' on grounds such as simplicity, or in terms of the number of independent parameters required for their description. But if that is what is meant by explanatory adequacy, then *one cannot know in advance* that the grammar chosen will be 'descriptively adequate' at all. Explanatory adequacy is either trivial, or it puts the thesis of descriptive adequacy *at risk* and this latter possibility is never considered by Chomsky. The whole three-decker system would be more plausible if Chomsky had put this part of it the other way round, and said that 'descriptive adequacy' consisted in choosing in a certain way among 'explanatorily adequate' grammars.

I have discussed Chomsky's view of what a linguistic theory is at some length, and have set it within the context of his view of finite state grammars, because those grammars play a special role in his general thinking. Chomsky explicitly linked three theoretical movements, all of which he considers inadequate from the point of view of a properly complex theory. They are 'atomic models of acquisition' of language, Skinner's stimulus-response theory of behaviour and finite state grammars. Chomsky considers the last to be production models for the former behavioural and associationist theories [54, p. 11]. One can see Chomsky's whole enterprise as an attempt to construct an explanation of linguistic behaviour alternative to Skinner's stimulus-response theory.[14] The account he gives of 'explanatory adequacy' in terms of an acquisitive device makes it clear that for him this is a cybernetic rather than a linguistic task. Chomsky's principal ground for an out-of-hand rejection of Skinner is his own 'creative' view of language [52, p. 8]. This is simply that new sentences are continually being produced and recognized by human beings, on the spur of the moment, and that the phenomenon is not accounted for by rote-learning or stimulus-response explanations, but is accounted for by his own theory of transformational grammar. 'It is clear', Chomsky writes, 'that a theory that neglects this creative aspect is of only marginal interest' [52, p. 8].

The thesis of this book is that, whatever the truth of that last remark of Chomsky's, our attention should have shifted by now to creative aspects of language *not* explained by Chomsky's model, aspects in view of which Chomsky's last quoted remark might well apply to his own theory. By that I mean our undoubted ability to recognize and understand words being used in a new, or possibly metaphorical, sense as in Dylan Thomas's 'A grief ago'. People use language in this way all the time, and we both understand and imitate them. Chomsky has attempted to deal with this phenomenon elsewhere when discussing what he calls deviant [53] utterances. But that is not essentially part of his system of analysis, although there are good grounds for thinking that such a facility is essential to any computable manipulations of language for practical purposes, simply because, for any handling of general texts not considered in advance, one cannot afford to be tied to pre-assigned dictionary entries only.

Chomsky does, it is true, distinguish between 'rule-governed' and 'rule-changing' creativities [52, p. 22]. The former he associates with his own kind of creativity, and the latter he associates with 'analogic' change, that is to say with the interesting case where a word acquires a new sense. Chomsky does not explain why he thinks that 'rule-changing' activities cannot themselves be 'rule-governed', but he does make it quite clear that he is not interested in analogic change, and for the very good reason that his system was not designed to cope with it.

Let us now turn to Chomsky's objections to the thesis that phrase structure grammars are devices sufficient to generate all and only the 'grammatically well-formed sentences' of English. Chomsky's arguments on this point are of a much less radical character. Indeed, some of them seem to be no more than internal diplomacy in the field of formal linguistics. Moreover, Chomsky includes a phrase structure grammar as an essential component of his own transformational system.

Phrase structure grammars, like transformational grammars, depend upon an applicable *grammar code*. That is to say they depend, at the lowest level, on an inventory of classifiers, or markers, like 'N' (Noun) and 'V' (Verb), that can be assigned, without too much trouble, to the words of the language under examination. There are, of course, troubles about doing this for English; the chief one being that the grammar code was derived by classical grammarians for Latin, a language to which it can be applied in a semi-formal way. Attempts have been made by Dolby and Resnikoff [80] to apply such classifiers to English words in a formal way, but their results are inconclusive at present. When pressed, grammarians using this code sometimes fall back upon a determination of the scope of the classifiers by means of 'substitution frames'. Thus one might say, 'I will apply the grammar classifier "N" to any word which can stand for the blank in the frame "The . . . is made of wood"; where by "stand for" I mean "replace it so as to leave a grammatical sentence".' Yet it is not clear that grammarians concerned with explicating the set of 'grammatical' sentences of English can fall back on this method, for it assumes the very feature that is to be explicated, namely 'grammatical sentence'. This need not be fatal, for *if* there is indeed an 'intuition of grammatical structure by native speakers', independent of the application of particular grammatical rules, then it is quite reasonable to make use of the substitution frame technique.

A more practical objection to pinning down the classifiers or grammar code in that way is that there is no reason to suppose that different 'frames' will determine the same word classes; hence the selection of any particular sentence frame seems completely arbitrary. There seems to be no agreement over the adoption of particular frames, and the classifiers are in fact treated by Chomsky and others as *sui generis*. I am not objecting to this classification on the ground that it *is sui generis*. I shall (in Chapter 3 below) propose a word-sense classification that could be attacked on just such a ground. My objection to the present classification, the grammar code, is that it is both crude and inefficient. It was not derived for English, nor does it lay any claims to interlinguality. It is *inefficient* as a classification simply because the category 'N', as defined in use, probably includes 80 per cent of English words.

These classifiers, together with others of 'higher order' like 'NP' (noun phrase), 'VP' (verb phrase), and 'S' (sentence), which in general refer to more than a single word, are the names of *immediate constituents* of sentences [Wells, 294]. They can be connected with the aid of the concatenation symbol '+'[15] to form *strings*, and one can then define a phrase structure grammar as an unordered set of *rewrite rules* of the form $\phi \rightarrow \psi$.

We say that a string S_1 follows from a string S_2 if $S_1 = \ldots \psi \ldots$, $S_2 = \ldots \phi \ldots$ and $\phi \rightarrow \psi$ is a rule. Given a single symbol 'A', and a non-null string w such that $\phi = x_1 + A + x_2 =$ and $\psi_1 = x_1 + w + x_2$; then the above rule asserts that 'A' can be rewritten as 'w' in the context $x_1 \ldots x_2$ [see Chomsky, 50].

The grammar so defined is a *context-free* phrase structure grammar

E

if and only if 'ϕ' is a single symbol. In examples of phrase structure grammars I shall refer only to context-free, as distinct from context-sensitive, grammars. Chomsky always expounds transformational grammar by contrasting it with phrase structure grammar, and has made it difficult not to follow his practice in doing this, because he includes a simplified phrase structure grammar as part of his transformational grammar. By 'simplified' I mean a phrase structure grammar without either context sensitivity, or rules applicable to 'discontinuous substituents' which is to say rules of the (discontinuous) form $a \rightarrow q + \ldots + r$. However, without going into the internal politics of the field concerning the relative merits of phrase structure and transformational grammars, it should, in fairness to phrase structure grammars, be pointed out that many of the facilities available within transformational grammar,[16] are also available within extended phrase structure grammars.

In his *Syntactic Structures* [48, pp. 26–8] Chomsky gives the following example of a PSG (phrase structure grammar):

1. Sentence→NP+VP
2. NP→T+N
3. VP→Verb+NP
4. T→The
5. N→man, ball, etc.
6. Verb→hit, took, etc.

Interpreting each rule as the instruction 'rewrite the left-hand side as the right-hand side' enables one to construct *derivations*. Using this grammar one may derive the sentence 'The man hit the ball' as follows (where the figure at the right of each line denotes the rule used to derive that line of the derivation from its predecessor):

('S' or) Sentence	
NP+VP	1
T+N+VP	2
T+N+Verb+NP	3
the+N+Verb+NP	4
the+man+Verb+NP	5
the+man+hit+NP	6
the+man+hit+the+N	2
the+man+hit+the+ball	5

A line of this derivation is called a terminal string if, and only if, it contains no symbol that occurs on the left-hand side of a production rule. Derivations must begin with the symbol 'S', and each such derivation can be associated with a unique tree diagram, or P-marker. For this particular derivation Chomsky supplies the following diagram, or P-marker:

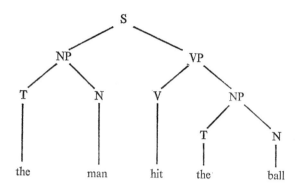

The converse association, of P-markers with derivations, is not unique since a sentence may be derivable from a given grammar in more than one way, specifically by applying the same derivation rules in different orders, so that there will be a P-marker associated with each derivation. With each such diagram a conventionally bracketed string can be associated, thus:

((the man) (hit   (the ball))), for the diagram above.
S NP   VP NP

In other cases, a given grammar may allow the derivation of a given sentence in two quite different ways, in that different rules are used in the two cases and hence different bracketings and tree diagrams are assigned to the derivations. Thus the grammar:

S→NP+VP
NP→they;NP→adj+N; NP→N
VP→are+NP; VP→Verb+NP
Verb→are+flying
Adj→flying
N→planes

enabled both the following strings to be derived [57, p. 122]:

```
( (they) (    (are flying) (    (planes))))
S NP    VP V              NP N
```

```
( (they) (are (flying (planes))))
S NP    VP  NP   N
```

This kind of ambiguous sentence is said by Chomsky to display *structural homonymity*.

Chomsky's dissatisfaction with PSGs can be put in his terminology of 'adequacy'. PSGs , he claims, are not 'descriptively adequate' in that they do not provide intuitively acceptable derived structures for sentences. At least four points should be considered in assessing this claim:

(i)   In the above case, Chomsky admits that PSG provides two derivations for the sentence, corresponding to the two more straight-forward ways we might interpret it. He claims, however, that the distinction is not 'motivated', and that a descriptively adequate transformational grammar would relate the first derivation to the sentence 'they fly planes', and the second to 'planes fly' [51, p. 935]. I am unable myself to see what such a relation would add to the distinction already marked above by the bracketing of the sentence strings.

(ii)   In other cases, such as that of the pair of sentences 'John is easy to please' and 'John is eager to please', Chomsky points out rightly that a PSG would assign the same derived structure to these two sentences. He then claims that that is intuitively unsatisfactory, in that we *know* that those two sentences should have different structures assigned to them, and specifically that 'John' has a 'passive sense' in the first and an 'active sense' in the second. This 'difference' according to Chomsky can be shown by relating these sentences to other forms by means of *transformations*. Chomsky claims that a certain transformation will produce a grammatical form when operating on 'John is eager to please', but an ungrammatical one when operating on 'John is easy to please'. He goes on: '. . . one might ask how we can establish . . . that "John's eagerness to please" is well-formed while "John's easiness to please" is not. . . . [52, p. 56]. One might indeed.

What Chomsky is feeling for here, I think, is some analogue to the traditional notion of 'logical form'.[17] He would like to be able to say that the logical form of the two sentences is different, even though that fact is not revealed by the PSG. But it may be simply that he has picked an unfortunate example in this instance, in that it in no way supports his case.

(iii) One of the cases referred to most by Chomsky when making his case against PSGs is that of active forms and their 'corresponding' passives. His case is that their structures are related and should be seen to be so, *not* that they have the same meaning. He expresses that relation as follows:

> If S1 is a grammatical sentence of the form NP1+Aux+V+ NP2 then the corresponding string of the form NP2+Aux+be +en+V+by+NP1 is also a grammatical sentence [48, p. 43].

Chomsky interprets that as a rule, and, shorn of its restrictions, it can be set out as a rewrite rule, viz.:

$$NP1+Aux+V+NP2 \rightarrow NP2+Aux+be+en+V+by+NP1.$$

That is a paradigm of what Chomsky calls a *transformational rule*, or transformation. It will be obvious that a rule of this form differs from phrase structure rules as they have been defined so far, principally in that it violates the convention that only one left-hand symbol may be rewritten on the right. That is an important restriction since upon it rests the decidability[18] of PSGs. Other transformation rules given by Chomsky in this section[19] of his exposition permute order only in certain contexts so that, in order to see whether or not one of these contexts is available at any stage of a derivation, it is necessary to examine earlier lines of the derivation. That facility is excluded by the restriction on phrase structure grammars that a rule applies to, and takes account of, only a single string.

(iv) Lastly, one should mention Chomsky's criticism that phrase structure grammars impose more structure than is intuitively acceptable, and in this way, above all, fail to reach descriptive adequacy. He takes the sentence 'the man was *old, tired, tall* . . . *but friendly*' [50, p. 15] and claims that the underlined words of it should be represented as in the left-hand figure below, but that a PSG *has to* represent it as a binary tree like the figure on the right. It does this by using recursive, or self-embedding, rules (N→A+N would be one) and in so doing it imposes *too much* structure on the sentence. He claims that it must do this because, *if the sentence were infinitely long* (i.e. if there were an infinite number of adjectives between 'tall' and 'but'), a PSG could only produce the left-hand figure by using *an infinite number of rules* (of the form $p \rightarrow q + r + s + but + t$).[20]

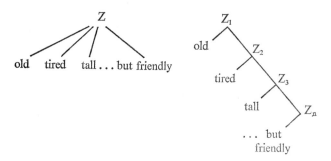

It is unfortunate that Chomsky has to fall back on the notion of an infinite sentence in order to make this point,[21] for in this particular case there is certainly only a finite class of English adjectives available to fill the gap in the sentence. And, quite apart from these quibbles, there is the continual difficulty in which Chomsky is involved each and every time he says that a sentence has *a proper grammatical structure*, over and above the structures that particular analyses assign to the sentence.

Chomsky's presentation of PSGs only as stalking horses for TGs is often unfair, in that he is led to dismiss, or ignore, those features of PSGs that make them most like TGs.[22] This approach extends even to one of his definitions of PSG, where he assumes [50] that a PSG must be the simplest possible, in that it has been selected by some 'shortness measure' applied to its list of rewrite rules. There is no talk of 'descriptive adequacy' there. One might say that the sort of formal criteria Chomsky refuses to apply to TGs, he *insists* on applying to PSGs.

After all these considerable preliminaries, I can now sketch Chomsky's original proposals for the proper production of all and only the 'grammatically well-formed sentences' of a language. Chomsky envisaged a limited PSG which would produce a number of terminal strings to be called the *kernels* of a language. All other sentences of the language would then be produced by the operation of transformations upon these kernels. A phonetic representation of each sentence would be produced by the operation of *morphophonemic rules* upon these transformationally derived sentence forms. A listing of the phrase structure and transformational rules used in the derivation of a sentence would constitute its *structural representation*. Chomsky often refers to the structure of a kernel as the 'deep structure' of *any sentence derived from it*; and the representation of the same sentence that a phrase structure grammar would give, he calls, by contrast, its 'surface structure'. Both transformations and kernels are to be thought of as finite inventories, presumably stored in the memory of some computer or other device.

I have given only the briefest account of Chomsky's original proposals, though one which suffices to make a number of general points about those proposals. Chomsky has changed his terminology somewhat in recent years, and since the publication of *Aspects of the Theory of Syntax*, at least, he no longer refers to the productions from the PSG as 'kernels'. The more generalized productions from the PSG, together with the PSG itself, are now said to form the 'base component' of the whole grammar. However, these changes are matters of linguistic detail and do not affect anything I have to say in the remainder of this chapter.

2.22 Decidability and grammaticality

The central feature of Chomsky's programme, as I have described it, was the explication of 'grammatical sentence'. It must be stressed that Chomsky does not mean by that anything like 'sentence compatible with some given grammar', for he believes that there is a class of such sentences which can be, as it were, *surveyed* prior to the construction of any particular grammar. That is implied not only by the examples of 'grammatical' sentences that he gives, but also by his use of the word 'explicate', which implies the existence of some corpus of *explicata* prior to the construction of an *explicandum*. He argues that this class of sentences does not depend on notions like 'meaning' for its characterization:

> . . . the notion 'grammatical' cannot be identified with 'meaningful' or 'significant' in any semantic sense. Sentences (1) and (2) are equally nonsensical, but any speaker of English will recognize that only the former is grammatical.
> (1) Colourless green ideas sleep furiously
> (2) Furiously sleep ideas green colourless.[23]

Chomsky later refers to this quoted passage as a demonstration of the independence of 'grammar' and 'meaning'.[24] There is no demonstration here in any strong sense: simply an appeal to observe a difference between two sentences, and moreover a difference in respect of a particular quality. I do see a difference, in that I find it much easier to be clear what the first sentence is about. I expect most speakers of the language share this perception, and even if they did not, I would expect to be able to explain it to them. This ability to 'explain the meaning of something', usually by surrounding it with more text, is part of what we mean by the ability to speak a language.[25] Not so with what Chomsky calls 'grammaticality'; I do not share his intuition, yet remain unrepentantly a native speaker of English.

Even my inability to see what sentence (2) could be about may only show lack of effort on my part. I could probably work out an interpretation for 'Furiously fought men tired weary', and might well be able to do something similar for (2). I can see no other difference between (1) and (2), unless I am provided with specific grammar rules that (1) abides by and (2) breaks.

The status of the notion of grammatical sentence, or just 'grammaticality', is important in connexion with the discussion of decidability that I began in Chapter 1. There I was discussing decidability in relation to the notion of meaningfulness, but the relation of decidability to grammaticality is rather better-mapped territory.

In Chapter 1 I described Post's notion of a logic as a set of production rules that generate strings having some property. In logic proper that property is theoremhood, or logical truth. In a grammar, cast into Post form, the property that such produced strings are said to have is grammaticality. Chomsky himself has noted [58, p. 9] that a transformational grammar can be viewed in that way. The only 'axiom' in Chomsky's system is then the string consisting of just 'S', the sentence symbol, with which all productions, or derivations, begin. It would be misleading to draw the grammar-proof analogy, as Putnam does [227, p. 41] in such a way that the grammar rules themselves stand for the axioms[26] of a proof system (and not the rules of inference), which would then operate with the usual single rule of inference 'From $A > B$ and A, infer B'. For, on Putnam's interpretation, the 'axioms' of a Chomsky system, that is to say the grammar rules, could not themselves have the property of grammaticality which is the interpretation of 'theoremhood' on this way of looking at things. For no one would say that the formal expression of the rule that produces, say, 'Mary is loved by John' from 'John loves Mary' is *itself* a grammatical English sentence. And if axioms cannot be theorems then that would be a drawback to the analogy between generative grammars and canonical languages, to say the least.

Chomsky does not claim that transformational grammars are *complete*, in that they produce all and only the grammatically correct sentences of English. Nor does he claim that they are *decidable*, in that their rules decide of an arbitrary string of English words whether or not it is grammatically correct. However, he is presumably trying to construct a system having either or both these properties for that is the programme he originally set himself, whatever his subsequent disclaimers about decision procedures [54, p. 55].

In the case of transformational grammars it is not easy to be clear about their decidability, or otherwise, because Chomsky is unwilling to give them any general form. But it does seem generally agreed that a set of transformational rules of the sort Chomsky has described characterizes a recursively enumerable set of sentences, but not necessarily a recursive set. That is to say, you can generate as many sentences as you like with the rules, but you may not be in a position to decide whether or not a given, ungenerated, sentence can be generated.

In that respect transformational systems of rules differ from phrase structure systems, which are known to be decidable in many important cases. So, in this important respect, of the decidability of the system of rules, phrase structure systems seem to start with a distinct advantage over transformational ones, for, whatever the practical advances made with heuristic transformational parsers programmed on computers [see 168 and 287] it can never be known for certain whether or not a given transformational grammar can analyse or produce a given sentence.

Chomsky has often argued against what are called finite state grammars, and by implication for transformational grammars, on the ground that there are grammatical sentences that no finite state grammar of a certain class can produce. That is to say, finite state grammars incomplete in the sense that they do not cover the known 'theorems', the real grammatical sentences.

What is important here for my purposes is to point out the assumption behind Chomsky's argument; namely that there *is* some survey of what it is to be a 'theorem to be covered' by a generative grammar, that is to be a grammatical sentence. My contention is that, on the contrary, there is not *as a matter of fact* a survey of the set of sentences Chomsky has in mind, and it is not a class of sentences about which native speakers can take reasonable decisions, in the way they can about meaningful sentences. If one asks an informant 'Is "Colourless green ideas sleep furiously" a grammatical sentence?', one tends to provoke only puzzlement; though linguists, philosophers and logicians are less unwilling to decide the question, and the diversity of their answers is an argument against Putnam's view [227, pp. 38–9] that speakers broadly agree on such questions, and hence the grammatical sentences of a language are probably a recursive set. Curry [72, p. 60] thinks such sentences are grammatical; Ziff [313] thinks they are ungrammatical but not nonsensical; Jakobson thinks that they are grammatical but false [136, p. 144]; Putnam [227] thinks they are at least ungrammatical, and certainly not false.

Chomsky's view has changed on this question: in the original formulation of his views [48, p. 15] he contrasted such sentences with ungrammatical ones. But Chomsky now [54, p. 9] considers the sentence 'Colourless green ideas sleep furiously' to be 'deviant', in that it should *not* be produced by a good grammar. Hence such sentences are now considered to be ungrammatical by Chomsky. So he might seem to be in some doubt about what is and what is not a grammatical sentence.

Yet, as I argued at some length in Chapter 1, any attempt of this sort to explicate a set of strings having some property (grammaticality in this case) requires that there is some independent survey of the set of strings before the job of explication begins. Without such a survey there is no notion of what it is to be a grammatical sentence for Chomsky's, or any other system of grammar, to produce.

Putnam has argued [227, p. 191] that the grammatical sentences of a language are surveyable, in that there is general agreement about the membership of the set, and that this justifies us in considering them a recursive set capable of being produced by a decidable generative grammar. The plausibility of his case comes from examples like 'Mary goed home', about which there would be general agreement that it is ungrammatical. But there is not this agreement, even among experts, about interesting cases of odd, or 'deviant', sentences like 'Colourless green ideas sleep furiously'. Thus Putnam's case is not made.

In Chapter 1 I also argued that, to be a candidate as a decidable property, it must be possible for the property in question to be characterized in terms of other properties, in the way that, say, 'logical truth' can be characterized. I argued that meaningfulness can also be characterized. But it is not at all easy to see how the notion of grammaticality can be characterized in any similar fashion. 'What speakers admit as grammatical' does not seem quite good enough; for, whatever the inadequacies of 'those sentences that are true in all possible worlds' as a characterization of logical truths, it is certainly better than 'those sentences that speakers (or logicians) admit as logical truths'.

Chomsky [47], and more recently Ziff [313], have suggested characterizations of grammaticality independent of the acceptance of sentences by some particular set of grammatical rules. Chomsky has suggested that an ungrammatical utterance is read with a falling tone on every word, and Ziff has suggested that an ungrammatical utterance is one that a native speaker 'balks at'. It needs no concentrated analysis to see that those suggestions will not do, and for the same reasons in each case.

On the one hand perfectly comprehensible sentences like 'Mary goed home' would almost certainly be read by a speaker with the same intonation, and as little balking, as the more conventional 'Mary went home', even though both Chomsky and Ziff would consider the first sentence ungrammatical and the second grammatical. On the other hand, even intelligent and well-disposed speakers balk at, or incorrectly intonate, sentences that are perfectly grammatical by our authors' standards, but which express some particularly striking falsehood such as 'A bear isn't really an animal you know'.

My conclusion from these arguments is not that the linguists I have mentioned are wasting their time, or engaged in some form of linguistic circle squaring, because grammaticality is not a decidable property. It is rather that if their enterprise is, as it is usually, one of testing a given string of words to see if it has a given property or not, then it would be better to call the property 'meaningfulness' than 'grammaticality', since the latter property does not admit of being attached to that procedure. Whereas, as I tried to show in Chapter 1, meaningfulness is at least a starter in that respect.

The linguistic work I have described had its roots in early twentieth-century formalism, where it was thought better to settle for whatever strings of marks a set of rules produced than to accept the disreputable advantages of notions like 'meaning'. But, naturally enough, the troubles that have beset formalistic mathematics have been visited in turn upon dependent activities like formal linguistics. And it now seems clear that something more must be said to explain 'grammatical sentence' than that the phrase refers to what some set of grammatical rules produces. Moreover, if it is intended that the set of rules shall decide of an arbitrary string whether or not it has a given property, then that property must be of a certain sort. I have argued in this section that 'grammatical' is not a property of the sort in question, and I argued earlier that 'meaningful' is more the sort of property required.

If all this is so, then the activity of many formal linguists might be more appropriately described as distinguishing between meaningful and meaningless utterances, rather than between grammatical and ungrammatical ones. And, as I pointed out, Chomsky's changing notion of 'grammatical', which once included 'Colourless green ideas sleep furiously' but now excludes it, has at present an extension very like many people's notion of 'meaningful'.

If these arguments are correct, then meaningfulness is not a poor relation of grammaticality, but rather the other way round. If grammaticality is to have a sense as well as an extension then it must, if it is to be anything, be a rather more general notion of meaningfulness. And that view is, I think, consistent with the traditional notion of grammar, though this is not the place to argue for that. Alice saw the point when she detected a very general meaning, or message, in the poem 'Jabberwocky', which has been taken to be a paradigm of 'grammatical nonsense': 'Somebody killed something, that's clear, at any rate.'

2.23 Performance and competence

Another role in which Chomsky casts transformational grammar is that of the 'scientifico-linguistic theory'. I will give a quotation to illustrate what I mean by the phrase:

> A grammar of the language L is essentially a theory of L. Any scientific theory is based on a finite number of observations,

and it seeks to relate the observed phenomena and to predict new phenomena by constructing general laws in terms of hypothetical constructs. . . . Similarly a grammar of English is based on a finite corpus of utterances (observations), and it will contain certain grammatical rules (laws) stated in terms of the particular phonemes, phrases, etc., of English (hypothetical constructs). These rules express structural relations among the sentences of the corpus and the indefinite number of sentences generated by the grammar beyond the corpus (predictions). [48, p. 49.]

The considerations I have already brought forward tell against this way of looking at transformational grammars. For, in the case of scientific theories cast in hypothetico-deductive form, there is a fairly clear notion of what it is to disconfirm a particular theory. There are difficulties about making the notion of disconfirmation (or falsification) precise: nonetheless there is general agreement about both its form and its importance. But Chomsky has formulated the theory of transformational grammar so as to rule out the possibility of disconfirmation. For when describing what it is to be an 'utterance' for the purpose of inclusion in a 'corpus', Chomsky makes it quite clear that he is not going to include what appear to be utterances, but which are sayings containing 'grammatical mistakes' [52, pp. 56–9]. And the notion of 'grammatical mistake' is defined with respect to the grammar in question, so that there can never be a rejected grammar. One is left with the scent of circularity in one's nostrils.[27]

It is important too, I think, to press the question as to what a 'theory of language L' is really a theory of. Chomsky has two quite different answers to this, which could be distinguished crudely as (i) 'a theory of language users' and (ii) 'a theory of language describers'. Sometimes Chomsky wants the latter kind of theory, as when he writes

. . . a generative grammar is not a model for a speaker or a hearer. . . . When we speak of a grammar as generating a sentence with a certain structural description, we mean simply that the grammar assigns this structural description to the sentence . . . we say nothing about how the speaker or the hearer might proceed . . . to construct such a derivation. [54, p. 9.]

Yet much of the time Chomsky seems to be after a theory of language users, viz.:

> *Obviously*, every speaker of a language has mastered and internalized a generative grammar that expresses his knowledge of his language. This is not to say that he is aware of the rules of the grammar or even that he can become aware of them, or that his statements about his intuitive knowledge of his language are necessarily accurate. [54, p. 8, my italics.]

Now in a sense there is no incompatibility between these two quoted passages, because generative grammar is indeed not a *model* of language users for Chomsky, simply because he just *knows* that there is a generative grammar inside their brains.[28]

That is the only way I can interpret his use of 'obviously' in the last quotation. But one might well not want to admit to theoretical intuitions of that sort, in which case the last quotation poses a real problem. Admittedly, it shows that Chomsky is aware that to have a theory embodying people's *views* about grammatical structure is not the same thing as to have a theory of a 'productive mechanism' inside their brains. We could properly have models for, and hypotheses about, such a mechanism though it would be inappropriate to use 'obviously' in connexion with them. But when Chomsky criticizes, for example, Yngve's phrase structure grammar on the grounds that, *whether or not it can generate sentences adequately*, it could never be a production model for speakers [54, p. 197], then it seems clear that he is again talking in the 'intuitive mechanistic' mode. If one is seeking a model for such a mechanism, then there is no reason, at the same time, to construct a model of the intuitions of speakers *about* structure. Yet, as we saw in connexion with 'descriptive adequacy' above, that was what Chomsky originally set out to do.

The distinction in terms of which Chomsky usually discusses these problems is that between what he calls 'competence' and 'performance': 'We thus make a fundamental distinction between competence (the speaker-hearer's knowledge of his language) and performance (the actual use of language in concrete situations).' [54, p. 4.] He quotes Sapir in this connexion, 'Clearly the description of intrinsic competence provided by the grammar is not to be confused with an account of actual performance, as de Saussure has emphasized with such lucidity'. [52, p. 10.] And, Chomsky adds,

'This competence can be represented, to an as yet undetermined extent, by a system of rules we call the grammar of the language'. [52, p. 9.]

In the course of this section I have distinguished three ways in which Chomsky views a transformational generative grammar: (i) as a model for sentence production; (ii) as a model for a brain mechanism; and (iii) as a model for what people say about the grammatical structure of their language. I think the above quotations make it clear that it is the last of these that Chomsky has in mind when he talks of competence, and it is what he calls a 'competence-model' that falls under the strictures of circularity set out at the beginning of this section. If indeed 'competence is not to be confused with an account of potential performance' [52, p. 10], then it is hard to see how there can be a competence model at all, let alone a non-circular one.

Chomsky thinks that performance models (models of what people actually say and write) are too difficult to construct, and also that 'grammaticality' is *not appropriate to* performance. The appropriate notion there, he says, is 'acceptability'. This, like grammaticality, is a matter of degree, but the two concepts do not coincide, or even approach each other [54, p. 11]. The notion of 'acceptability' seems almost identical with meaningfulness or significance. Competence is not at all the same as Chomsky's 'creativity', mentioned earlier: the ability to utter and understand new sentences, for that lies within the purview of 'acceptability'. Chomsky freely admits that many grammatical sentences are unacceptable; and, indeed, that they could not conceivably be used or even understood. That could be because they were too long, or too 'deeply nested' in structure in Yngve's sense [310]. And, Chomsky might well add, since 'grammaticality' has nothing to do with 'meaning', what is wrong with that? But if such sentences are too long, or too deeply nested to be understood, then I would argue that there is something peculiar about the notion of our checking up on their 'grammaticality' with the aid of those 'intuitions' about grammar that Chomsky firmly believes us all to have. Few people can be got to decide about the 'grammaticality' of a sentence as deeply nested as 'What what what he wanted cost in New York would buy in Germany was amazing'.

The structure of Chomsky's talk about 'competence' is highly reminiscent of disputes about what it is to 'have a concept', particularly in regard to the well-canvassed possibility that a man might have the concept red, say, and *never* succeed in correctly picking out red stamps from a pile of colour-assorted ones. The arguments about this situation are rather like Chomsky's defence of the notion of an intrinsic competence, or grammatical ability, if made in the case of a man who *always* split his infinitives. The parallel can be seen most clearly in Chomsky's discussion of the *acquisition* of grammar and the degree to which this requires 'specific innate abilities' and 'formal universals' [54, p. 2]. If my argument has been correct then the cash-value of the notion of 'competence' simply doesn't warrant all this investment in its philosophic defence. Belief in 'competence' cannot be refuted, in any strong sense, but the question arises 'do we need to go on about it?'

Hence I claim that there can only be performance models, and that when Chomsky talks of competence models he is necessarily talking about models for certain selections from among possible performances.

2.24 *The development of Chomsky's theories*

I have argued that Chomsky claims to be explicating a notion of 'grammaticality' that there is no reason to believe in, and on which there is no way of checking up. At any rate, there is no notion of grammaticality which enables us to explain to someone that a sentence is grammatical in the way that we can explain how it is meaningful, when either of these are in question. Chomsky continues to insist that, although grammaticality may be a matter of *degree*, it is never, at any point on a 'scale of grammaticality', to be confused with 'meaningfulness', 'intelligibility' or 'acceptability'.

There is no doubt that the proponents of the doctrine of logical syntax *were* concerned quite explicitly with the discrimination of sense and nonsense; with the demarcation of what is meaningful from what is not. I claimed earlier that Chomsky's work, too, was an attempt to make the same demarcation. There are two grounds for this claim:

(i) Despite his protestations to the contrary, Chomsky's work always has been concerned with the explication of 'meaningfulness', in so far as it has been concerned with anything at all, and, in particular, there has been a misunderstanding about whether or not 'degree of grammaticality' approaches 'intelligibility'.

(ii) Recent developments in Chomsky's work, and particularly the inclusion of a 'semantic component' *within* a grammar, have led some[29] to think that Chomsky's work is now about meaning in a way that it wasn't before. I think that this, too, rests on a misunderstanding and that, interesting as such developments are, nothing essential has changed in either Chomsky's system or his general outlook on the matter.

If I am right in these contentions it is proper to discuss Chomsky's work, at any stage of its exposition, as being one of the few systematic explorations into the jungle of determining meaningfulness.

As to (i), I rest firstly on my argument that there are not in fact intuitions about grammaticality, and that what appear to be such intuitions are in fact very general intuitions about meaningfulness. Any utterance produced as being grammatically well-formed, in the sense in which 'Jabberwocky' is usually said to be grammatical, can also be assessed as to the degree to which it expresses some very general *message* of the sort that Alice detected. Secondly, with regard to the notion of degree or scale of grammaticality, Chomsky has given two, somewhat different, accounts of what he means by that phrase [53 and 54, pp. 148 ff.]. When he insists that as utterances become more grammatical on such scales, they do not *thereby* become more intelligible, he is quite right in that the two qualities are defined with respect to two different intuitions. The trouble with putting it that way, though, is again that we do not have the intuition as to *grammaticality* pinned down in an adequate or effective way. Chomsky also associates the notion of 'degree of grammaticality' with competence, and of 'acceptability' with performance.[30] But as I have tried to show above, there is precisely the same problem about clarifying *that* distinction.

Chomsky's first suggestion for setting up a scale of grammaticality, or *non-deviance*, was by means of what he called 'formal relations to other sentences of the generated language' [52, p. 9]. Thus, to give his own example, one might impose an interpretation upon the grammatical but deviant sentence 'Colourless green ideas sleep furiously', by noting that its structure is similar to 'revolutionary new ideas appear infrequently' [52, p. 7]. The trouble with that approach is it assumes you have a non-deviant sentence to hand. If you do not then you are not given any procedure for finding one, or for knowing a sentence is non-deviant when you have found it. Chomsky's subsequent approach, which may be only the same one

F

cast in a generative rather than an analytic mode, was that one should avoid generating grammatical but deviant sentences by means of *selection rules* [54, pp. 85 and 95 ff.]. Roughly speaking, these apply a more specific grammatical classification: one intended to reduce the number of unacceptable combinations of words. Or, as Chomsky puts it, 'we suggested . . . that the distributional restrictions of lexical items be determined by contextual features listed in lexical entries' [54, p. 139]. To see more clearly what he means by 'contextual features' and 'lexical entries' it is probably best to give one of his own examples [54, pp. 85–6].

He gives the following part of a phrase structure grammar that produces the sentence 'Sincerity may frighten the boy'[31]

(23)   S→NP | Aux+VP
       VP→V+NP
       NP→Det+N
       NP→N
       Det→*the*
       Aux→M

(24)   (i)   N→(+N, ±Common)
      (ii)   (+Common)→(±Count)
      (iii)   (+Count)→(±Animate)
      (iv)   (−Common)→(±Animate)
                    etc. . . .

(25)   (*sincerity* (+N, −Count, +Abstract,
                     etc. . . .

Then, after giving other conventions restricting the introduction of the verb 'frighten', Chomsky produces the following diagram as a representation of the derivation of the given sentence:[32]

By 'lexical entries' Chomsky means the rules numbered (25), the inner parentheses of which he calls 'complex symbols'. By 'lexical features' he means the terms like 'Count' and 'Human' occurring in those lines. By 'selection rules' he means the rules numbered (24); and he contrasts them with the more familiar rules (23), which he now calls 'subcategorization rules' [54, p. 95].

The role of selectional rules is so to specify the *features* of the words constituting a putative sentence, that additional transformational rules, spanning as it were the whole sentence, will be able to eliminate deviant but grammatical forms. Thus for example, he would allow 'Sincerity frightens the boy', but not 'The boy frightens

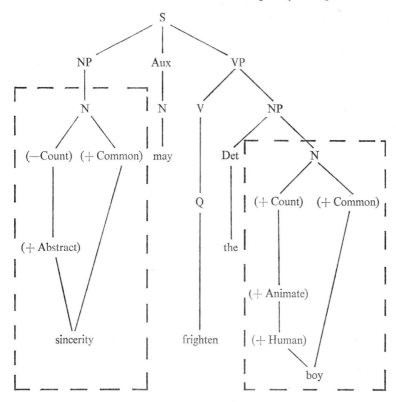

sincerity', and would hope to distinguish these two with a transformational rule that allowed a 'Count, common, abstract' noun to
precede a 'Count, animate, human, common' one in this verb
context, but not to *succeed* it. I have put this crudely, but I think
it captures Chomsky's intention. Furthermore, 'degree of deviance' is
to be assessed in terms of the number of 'selectional rules' that a
sentence breaks [54, p. 148], and selectional rules are, he claims,
formally distinct from subcategorization rules [54, p. 95].

Before going into more detail about features, I want to make a
point about this formulation of Chomsky's. Cohen [63] and Lakoff
[159] have independently produced an argument that 'degree of
grammaticality' can never be identified with 'degree of intelligibility'.
To the best of my knowledge it is not an argument that Chomsky
has produced, and it goes roughly as follows. One can produce
pairs of sentences like:

John *grasped* the ball to the left of the field,
John *thought* the ball to the left of the field,

such that the latter breaks more grammatical rules than the former, but is nonetheless more intelligible than the former.

I think that Cohen and Lakoff are mistaken in that they take the notion of 'grammatical rule' at its proponents' valuation, and then propose a measure in terms of it. They assume that one can usefully say of two sentences that one breaks *more grammatical rules than the other*. But I do not think that the underlined words are clear enough to give their argument the force they hope for. It would be quite possible to write down rules so that the more intelligible sentence broke fewer rules. One only has to conflate rules to do it, and since there is no identity criterion for grammatical rules other than the way they are written down, what is to stop one? Notice though, that no amount of rule rewriting will persuade anyone that the less meaningful sentence is really more meaningful.

Chomsky does construct a notion of 'degree of grammaticality' within his own system [53]. If he identifies that notion with the inverse of the notion of 'degree of deviance' and with the notion of 'degree of intelligibility', then he is doing what Cohen and Lakoff say cannot be done, and he is also giving up all he has stood for since 1956. He has always held that there were proper intuitions about grammaticality, though not about meaningfulness, and so not about intelligibility. But if he were to make that identification he can no longer hold that, and the question should arise for him whether, if an intuition as to meaningfulness can be explicated, need it be done via the mechanisms of syntax at all? Chomsky has already in effect abandoned his earlier form of the syntax-semantics distinction[33] by the way he now includes a 'semantic component' within a full grammar, and by his indifference as to whether selection rules are to be included in the syntactic or the semantic component of a grammar [54, p. 153]. Again, he usually calls his features 'syntactic features', but sometimes he forgets and calls them 'semantic features' [54, p. 198].

Note too that, if the 'intelligibility'-'grammaticality' distinction is abandoned, then the 'competence'-'performance' distinction that has been identified with it must be abandoned also [54, p. 11]. Chomsky's most recent attempt to preserve the former distinction is put in terms of the 'selection-subcategorization' distinction among rules, and he claims the distinction as a formal one [54, p. 148]. I argue below that it is not a formal distinction in the sense he requires. But I want to point out that *even if it is*, he has already abandoned the, to him, vital distinction between 'grammaticality' and 'intelligibility' by his use of phrases like 'grammatical but deviant'. That phrase, applied to 'Colourless green ideas sleep furiously' implies that it is grammatical: that it is such that it would be produced by what Chomsky now calls the syntactic component of a full grammar [54, p. 141] (because the semantic component is 'purely interpretive'). But the selection rules that reject deviant sentences must be put into either the syntactic or the semantic component of the grammar. If they are put in the semantic component then that component is *not* purely interpretive, it is also *eliminative*. If, on the other hand, the selection rules are put in the *syntactic* component, then there can be no 'grammatical but deviant' sentences, by definition, and what grammar measures is non-deviance or acceptability. So the onus is on Chomsky to show that, in so far as he has allowed for a degree of grammaticality, his system does not attempt to 'explicate' meaningfulness.

It is difficult to accept that there are two intuitions, one concerning meaning and the other grammar; but that one can, as it were, extend the one to meet the other, leaving a 'fuzzy area' in between. Cohen says that 'Relative intelligibility is best managed lexically, not by extending grammar beyond its normal range' [63, p. 146]. I feel it still remains to be shown that there *are* paradigm grammatical rules of Chomsky's sort available for 'over-extension'. Certainly Cohen does not show that there are any 'grammatical categories free of semantic implications' [63, p. 148], though it might, of course, turn out to be simple to do this for languages other than English.

To return for a moment to features and selection rules. Unless one takes Halliday's view that 'Grammatical categories do not apply to lexical items' [111], then the further classification embodied in Chomsky's features seems a reasonable thing to want to do. Chomsky does not provide either an inventory of features or a discovery procedure for them, but to demand these would probably be unreasonable. He claims, no doubt correctly, that there is some kind of intuitive hierarchy among such features in that 'sentences deviating from selectional rules that involve "higher level" lexical features, such as (Count), are much less acceptable . . . than those that involve such "lower level" features as (Human)' [54, p. 150].

However, as he points out, it is not in general the case that such features can be arranged 'on a tree' in respect of the inclusions of the classes of words to which they apply,[34] for there will always be what he calls 'cross-classification' of the word by the features, or what might more familiarly be called a partial ordering of the word-classes.

He indicates this on the diagram (reproduced above) for the sentence 'Sincerity may frighten the boy' by means of two partial orderings that are in fact *lattices*, which I have put in dashed boxes. Chomsky's notation does distinguish, trivially, batteries of rules that identify (different) symbols to be substituted at the bottoms of tree branches from batteries that do not. Those that do identify symbols produce lattices, and hence cannot be represented by trees, or phrase structure grammars [see 28]. *However this distinction rests on a substitution rule and not on the way the lexicon is written.* The same identification problem could have arisen with the 'old style' phrase structure grammar, without features or the introduction of the lexicon by means of 'complex symbols'. Consider the sentence 'The cut healed' as produced by a phrase structure grammar which I will write in both the 'old' and 'new' ways (in highly simplified form, and without features in both cases):

1. S→NP+VP	1′ S→NP+VP
2. NP→Det+N	2′ NP→Det+N
3. VP→V	3′ VP→V
4. Det→The	4′ Det→The
5. N→cut . . .	5′ (cut (N, V . . .))
6. V→cut, healed . . .	6′ (healed (V . . .))

Without a substitution rule which allows identification of elements in the terminal (bottom) strings, both grammars will produce the two sentence markers:

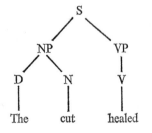 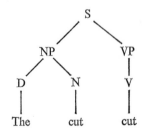

But if we allow an 'identification rule', for substitutions in the terminal string, we shall also get the sentence 'The cut', though *only with the second grammar* (rules 1'–6'). The diagram for the sentence would look like this:

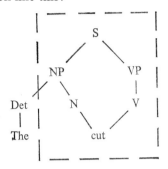

and it will contain a lattice. The point of my example is as follows: the production of figures with lattices like the one above has nothing to do with features as such at all, it simply follows from Chomsky's statement of a grammar in the style of rules 1'–6', together with a substitution rule [54, p. 84]. He calls the rule a 'lexical rule' and introduces it as follows:

A terminal string is formed from a preterminal string by insertion of a lexical formative* in accordance with the following lexical rule:
If Q is a complex symbol of a preterminal string and (D, C) is a lexical entry, where C is not distinct from Q, then Q can be replaced by D [54, p. 84].

Given the above presentation of a grammar (the right-hand one) and the lexical identification rule, we have produced such 'sentences' as 'The cut' using only the categories N, V . . . , etc. The difference made by the identification rule *is* a formal one, since lattices are not trees. But Chomsky cannot use *that* formal difference to support his claim that there is a formal difference between selection and subcategorization rules, since it is only a matter of fact that the complex symbols he gives contain features. The ones I have given in my two grammars above do not. On the other hand, I do not see that the mere *presence* of features in a rule constitutes a formal difference, since Chomsky does not give either a list of features or any other formal way of distinguishing them from category names.

* I.e. a word!

Perhaps he does attempt the latter when he defines the two kinds of rule as follows: 'Rules . . . which analyse a symbol in terms of its categorial context, I shall henceforth call strict subcategorization rules. Rules . . . which analyse a symbol . . . in terms of syntactic features of frames in which it appears, I shall call selectional rules [54, p. 95]. On the very next page he talks of subcategorization rules as imposing 'a categorization on the symbol V in terms of a certain set of frames in which V occurs', which is very like what we had been told earlier that *selection* rules did for us. So I suggest that the categories and the features are applied in exactly the same way, namely by an informed speaker on the basis of his knowledge as to how the word in question functions in his language. Since frames are never produced, talking about them only obscures that fact.

I hope that I have established that there is no formal distnction between these two kinds of rules in respect of features, which is what Chomsky claims to be the basis of the distinction. There *is* a formal distinction between the two kinds of rules that he produces; but it is in virtue of the form of the *lexical rule* and has nothing at all to do with features.

I take this as supporting even more strongly my earlier point that Chomsky cannot demarcate an untestable area of grammatical competence, and so distinguish it from considerations of meaningfulness and of deviance from it. It is true that he claims only that deviance 'correlates rather closely' [54, p. 148], with the breaking of selectional rules. Nonetheless I showed earlier that *even if one were to grant this distinction*, he has nowhere shown that the system of subclassification cannot *in principle* be extended to generate all and only the grammatical *and intelligible* sentences.[35]

Lastly, I want to say a little about how Chomsky introduces a 'semantic component' into his grammar. It is important to do so because the closely related work of Katz, Fodor and Postal (see below) is little more than a sketch for the construction of such a component, and it is through criticism of their work that I shall try to list desiderata for an adequate theory of semantics.

Chomsky's enormously extended use of the term 'grammar' began with passages like the following:

A generative grammar consists of a syntactic component, which generates strings of formatives and specifies their structural features and interrelations; a phonological component, which converts a string of formatives with a specified (surface) syntactic structure into a phonetic representation; and a semantic component which assigns a semantic interpretation to a string of formatives with a specified (deep) syntactic structure [52, p. 60].

Certain trivial criticisms can be made of this formulation, for, earlier in the same book, Chomsky wrote,

> In general, as syntactic description becomes deeper, what appear to be semantic questions fall increasingly within its scope; and it is not entirely obvious whether and where one can draw a natural bound between grammar and 'logical grammar' in the sense of Wittgenstein and the Oxford philosophers [52, p. 51].

The clear sense of the two parts of that last sentence, taken together, is that 'semantics' is 'logical grammar', and that it has to be distinguished from, and is therefore outside, 'grammar'. The deep structure 'expresses the semantic content of some well-formed sentence' [54, p. 140], and, as we saw before, this content is taken to be rather like the older notion of the 'logical form' of a sentence [54, p. 162].

The syntactic component provides the 'base', which plays a role like that of the grammar which produced the kernels in the earlier version of the system. Significant differences between the two accounts are that the base no longer contains simply a phrase structure grammar [54, p. 88], and as the above quotation about 'some well-formed sentences' illustrates, there now seems to be the possibility of an infinite number of sentences in the base, one for each of the sentences of the natural language.

This last is something of a theoretic disaster, akin to the multiplication of the number of kinds of elementary particle in quantum physics; for one of the major attractions of the earlier version of Chomsky's theory was its attempt to explain the complexity and multiplicity of the possible sentences of the language in terms of a *finite* battery of simple kernels.

My conclusion from the whole discussion is that we have to consider the possibility that, in spite of his protestations, Chomsky's work always has been an explication of meaningfulness, and that the fact has only become more explicit with the shift of his attention to 'deviant sentences', and the implied contraction of 'grammatical' so as to exclude them. As I have pointed out already, he has to contract the term in that way if the selection rules, that reject deviance, go into the syntactic component of the grammar. But if, on the other hand, they go into the semantic component, then he can no longer claim that component as to be merely interpretive.

In Section 2.32 below I shall examine the content of the semantic component, as expounded by Katz, Fodor and Postal, in order to see whether the explication of 'meaningfulness' that they give is an adequate one. I shall find that it is not, and so I shall claim that not only does Chomsky's work not give an explication of grammaticality (as he claims it does) but neither does it give a satisfactory one of 'meaningfulness' (which claim he would agree with, though he would deny that it attempted to do so). I shall then feel justified in turning the whole business on its head and seeking a direct, and in some respects simpler, explication of meaningfulness not mediated through the fiction of grammar.

2.3 Semantics

2.31 *'Non-referential semantics'*

Although Katz, Fodor and Postal have expounded, at some length, an 'integrated Theory of Linguistic Description', and, more particularly, have given an account of 'semantic competence', it can be argued that they have added little to Chomsky's notion of 'selection rules'. They do not lack articulate critics, some[36] of whom attack their specific contributions to this body of theory, while others[37] attack not only them, but, by implication, the whole of Chomsky's work on which theirs rests. They have, however, brought to wide attention certain general and obvious facts about natural language that were in danger of being forgotten, by Chomsky among others. I have in mind particularly the 'fact of polysemy', that is to say that all words are potentially ambiguous, in that they generally have many senses. Any serious analysis of natural language must come to terms with the fact, in a way that syntax analysis does not [see also Ziff, 31]. In that their work rests wholly upon Chomsky's, I shall give only a brief outline of their contribution, and hope that, in that way, I can make clearer what a semantic theory might offer.

There are two main versions of their theory of the semantic

component of a grammar:[38] Katz and Fodor are the authors of the earlier version, the later one being by Katz and Postal. Their task, as they see it, is not a generative but an analytic one: they assume that some syntactic component of a grammar will have generated a (syntactically) well-formed utterance, so that a separate semantic component can then analyse and assign a 'reading' to it. KF put the matter as follows:

> . . . grammatical markers mark the formal differences on which the distinction between well-formed and ill-formed utterances rests, whereas semantic markers have the function of giving each well-formed string the conceptual content that permits it to be represented in terms of the message they communicate to speakers in normal situations [145, p. 209].

KF make use of the performance-competence distinction in much the way that Chomsky does, but are more prone than he is to fall into the confusion between, on the one hand, describing a mechanism of process for analysing texts, and, on the other hand, describing a mechanism which has been 'internalized by all native speakers' and which accounts for their competence, but not, of course, for their mistakes. I discussed these questions above in connexion with Chomsky's work, so here I will give only an illustrative quotation of the sort of thing I mean:

> The whole process may be pictured as follows: the speaker, for reasons that are biographically relevant, but linguistically not, chooses a message he wants to convey to the hearer. . . . This message is translated into syntactic form by the selection of a syntactic structure whose semantic interpretation is this message. [KF quoted in Sgall, 265.]

I am not using the quotation to criticize the notion of 'message', for there is psychological evidence [see Wales and Marshall, 286]. that speakers and hearers do in some sense work with, process and remember the 'gist' of what they are saying, quite independently of the particular syntactic form in which it is expressed. And that is a very strong consideration against the 'fundamentalist' view of syntactic structure's role in language activity.

One of the troubles with KF is that they do not develop a *message theory*:[39] it remains for them merely an aspiration. What they do construct is a simple, and wholly syntax-based, device for resolving word-sense ambiguity up to the level of the sentence. Any clear exposition of what is meant by 'ambiguity' must be delayed until after a more detailed discussion of what is meant by 'word-sense'. But even at this point our everyday notion of word-sense can be presumed upon enough to distinguish ambiguity from 'polysemy', or multiple meaning. When we talk of polysemy we mean well-known facts of the following kind; 'bank' can mean 'rely', 'plane manoeuvre', 'boundary of a river', or 'place for money transactions', among other things. Most words have many such meanings, or senses, and it is to the credit of KF that they have reminded formal linguists of the fact, though the *need* for some such analysis can be detected within Chomsky's own work, as I shall show in a moment.

Ambiguity is different from polysemy in that it refers not to general characteristics of the performance of a word, but to specific occasions of its use. An ambiguous use is one where the surroundings, whether more text or features of the physical world, fail to provide sufficient information to decide which of the possible senses of the word is the one appropriate to that use. If features of the physical world are to provide this information, then talk of deciding between 'senses' is not always appropriate, since the ambiguity may lie in our ignorance as to which particular object, or class of objects, is being talked about, as when a speaker says 'you' and we have to look and see who he is talking to.[40]

There are difficult cases where we have only surrounding *text* to help us decide about senses, and yet the text available is inadequate. Cases like that, of real ambiguity, are hard to find in actual texts, but easier in handbooks of linguistics. A possible case, I suppose, would be a novel in which an unknown person accosted a character in the street, said 'She threw a ball', and went off never to re-enter the book. Unless some subsequent event in the novel provided more information about this meeting, the character could never decide whether the passer-by meant that some woman threw a physical object, or that she gave a large party, and nor could the readers. Nonetheless, it is a matter of simple observation that people do understand what they hear and read, in spite of the fact that most of the words used have a number of meanings and are, in that sense, potentially ambiguous. It seems reasonable to assume, therefore, that there could be some *procedure* for deciding of word occurrences, in text, in which of their senses they were being used on any particular occasion of use.

KF offer a formal procedure for tackling this difficult problem of deciding between word senses, but in so far as they limit themselves, as does Chomsky, to the '. . . semantic function of complex symbols up to the size of a sentence' [Weinreich 290, p. 127], they cannot offer a satisfactory theory. By considering only isolated sentential examples they create ambiguities they cannot resolve. One short way with the difficulty is Weinreich's, which is to say that phenomena like the irresolubility of the sense of 'jack' in 'I realized we had no jack', are '. . . in principle uncoded, and *beyond the scope of linguistics*' [290, p. 137, my italics]. But simply saying that gives one no reason to think that it is beyond the scope of linguistics, only that it is beyond the scope of the linguistics of KF and Weinreich. Another form of this difficulty is as follows; KF repeatedly say that their theory is 'non-referential',[41] which is correct. But this must lead to difficulty, if not paradox, in that by limiting themselves to isolated sentence examples in this way, they limit themselves to cases where the 'referential resolution' that the physical world allows becomes essential, as with the case just quoted.

I shall now briefly sketch the details of KF's suggestions, after showing how they arise quite naturally from the application of Chomsky's 'lexical rule'. That rule dictated that a word name was to be 'hung' from the lowest branch point of a tree when, and only when, the entry for the word in the lexicon contained all and only the classifiers at the ends of branches stemming from a single node. But, if we take any account of the classifiers that would quite naturally be attached to an English word, we can see that this rule leads to chaos unless, and this is where KF come in, one makes separate entries in the lexicon for different *senses* of the word. For example, consider the English word 'cat': in different senses it requires both the classifier 'Animate' and the classifier 'Inanimate'. Given the lexical rule as Chomsky states it, it is going to be difficult, if not impossible, ever to get this word from the lexicon into a string. Similarly with the word 'dog', somewhere in whose entry one would naturally expect the classifiers 'N' *and* 'V'. It is, however, highly unlikely that one would ever be able to apply this word in a derivation if *both* 'N' and 'V' have to be present in the terminal string for the application to be possible. Thus it seems that *some* substructure is necessary in Chomsky's lexicon, even if only to distinguish the different parts of speech[42] of the words in it, let alone the distinction between 'senses' within a single part of speech.

think the following quotation illustrates KP's notions of *multiple readings for word entries* and *selection restrictions* on their combination:

> An example of an amalgamation produced . . . is the joining of the reading *colorful*→Adjective→(Color)→[Abounding in contrast or variety of bright colors] ⟨(Physical Object) v (Social Activity)⟩ and the reading *ball*→Noun→(Physical Object)→ (Globular Shape) to produce the derived reading *colorful+ball* →(Physical Object)→(Globular Shape)→(Color)→[Abounding in contrast or variety of bright colors]. This derived reading gives the sense that *colorful ball* has in the sentence.
>
> (10) the baby is playing with a colorful ball
> An example of an amalgamation that is prevented by a selection restriction is that of the reading *colorful*→Adjective→ (Evaluative)→[Having distinctive character, vividness, or picturesqueness] ⟨(Aesthetic Object) v (Social Activity)⟩ with the reading for *ball* given immediately above. This is precluded because the selection restriction in the reading of the modifier allows it to be embedded in readings for heads only if the reading for a head contains either the semantic marker (Aesthetic Object) or the semantic marker (Social Activity) or both, and this reading of *ball* contains neither of these semantic markers.[43]

One notes right away that there is no *need* to call this kind of procedure 'semantics'; for, as Weinreich points out, the 'semantic' and 'syntactic' classifiers used by KF are often identical. K. Sparck-Jones [272] has given detailed criticism of the *structure* of their system of classifiers, or markers: principally the problems of relating their classifiers together in respect of inclusion and so on, and of relating those parts of an entry for a word which are classifiers, etc., to those parts which are simply informal exposition in ordinary language.

The two criticisms of substance that may be made are the following: (i)   What they give as the reading, or message, of a sentence is in fact a list, or heap, of word senses.[44] This trouble derives from the view they share with Chomsky, and many contemporary logicians, that the meaning of a sentence either is, or is a simple function of, its constituent words.

(ii)   Their system is completely static in that there is no account taken of the possibility of encountering a word sense which is *new*. This goes for novelty in the sense of 'not taken account of in the dictionary in use' (i.e. new to the system), and in the sense of 'correct but not taken account of by any dictionary' (i.e. genuinely new, or original, usage). KF, and especially KP, explore detailed examples of their schema in a very careful manner, and there is no space here to do justice to that care. My contention is that their idea was a simple extension of Chomsky's, and that to criticize Chomsky is in fact to criticize their theory since they base it so completely on his. I have tried to give a philosophical, rather than linguistic, criticism of Chomsky's work; but have not extended this to the work of KF and KP, not only for the reason just given, but also because their work has received a considerable amount of philosophical criticism in its own right. Chomsky has not received so much criticism of this sort, and that is because he aims less consciously at a philosophical audience than do KF and KP. However, I think that KF and KP have given too little attention to making clear what they mean by 'meaning', 'reference' and 'semantics', and I want now to examine these well-worn notions once again.

2.32 *The varieties of semantics*

In the last sections of this chapter I have not made any attempt to pin down the notion of 'semantics' with any precision, but have allowed it to function as a blank counter, taking on the values it had in the writings under discussion. That approach avoids premature formalism, but has the disadvantage of allowing the systematic ambiguity of the word to intrude into the discussion. The simple-minded, and useless, way with the word 'semantics' is to say that it means 'concerned with the meaning of words', which serves only to show that the problems about the notion of 'semantics' are the same as those about the notion of 'meaning'. Both words have two major senses; both of which have a long tradition of use in philosophy and linguistics. As I have shown in the earlier discussion, Chomsky himself has changed his usage of the word 'semantics' from meaning 'concerned with the objects that words refer to', to meaning 'concerned with the ideas that words express'. In this he is the victim of the slipperiness of the notion itself, a problem that cannot be avoided simply by deciding which of those two main uses one has in mind and then sticking to it. For there are real conceptual difficulties about opting for either alternative, as there may well be about any other proposed content for the notion. For that reason it is worth reviewing some of the difficulties concerned with the notion of 'semantics' or 'science of meaning', and even treating semantics as a subject not wholly contained by either linguistics or philosophy.

It is now a familiar observation that Frege brought the theory of meaning back from the wrong but venerable view that to mean was to name. He replaced this view with his distinction between the *Sinn* and *Bedeutung* [94, p. 29] of both words and sentences: the former, *Sinn*, was a way of meaning, and a property of words and sentences, that did not involve naming. For Frege, therefore, words* and sentences had two ways or aspects of meaning, rather as medals have an obverse and a reverse. I shall argue that this 'dualist' theory is no more satisfactory than either of its parts considered separately as a theory of meaning.

The continual oscillation and confusion between these two parts of the dualist theory can be avoided if we see that, except in those special cases when people do actually draw attention to the external world in connexion with a written or spoken statement, 'meaning' is always *other words*, and talk about 'the senses of words' is only a disguised restatement of that fact. A view of meaning along these lines is outlined by Wittgenstein in his *Bemerkungen* [308, §§43 and 45], particularly when he discusses what it is to 'apply' a piece of language, and how for this to be possible the language must, as it were, be 'in the same space' as what it applies to.

I have not so far attempted to give English equivalents for the German words *Sinn* and *Bedeutung* because the many and confused translations of the distinction they mark are themselves symptoms of the trouble in question. Those words, like 'meaning' and 'semantics' have an oscillatory ambiguity. I shall return to this point after drawing attention to the well-known drawbacks to the views: (i) that meaning is essentially designation or naming or denotation, and (ii) that it is essentially connotation or sense or intention.

The idea that all words are really names of objects, and that when we use words we draw attention to at least some of these objects, has a long history and goes back to Aristotle.[45] There is no doubt that things, including babies, are sometimes named and that 'the meaning of a word is sometimes explained by pointing to its bearer'

* Exceptions were made for proper names and 'oblique uses'.

Wittgenstein 305, §I, 43]. What is wrong is to think that language always functions in this way, or ever has done. The key arguments against the *sufficiency* of this view are Frege's, based on his example of the morning and evening stars which have the same designation but cannot be said to have the same sense; and more recent arguments, due to Wittgenstein and Quine, that pointing, naming or ostension are never clear or unambiguous simply as gestures; they presume upon the resources and surroundings of a whole natural language.

I have carefully avoided translating the word *Bedeutung* as 'reference', although this is commonly done, because the 'meaning is connotation, intension or sense' view is often put in such a form that *it, too, is a reference view* that words refer to sense-objects rather than to physical ones, and so the opposition intended between the two ways of meaning (sense and reference) is lost. Church, for example, who adopts what he considers to be a Fregean dualist view (though one in which sense is logically prior to denotation), writes, '. . . a sense (or a concept) is a postulated abstract object. . .' [60, pp. 6–7]. The difficulty about that view (and the associated view about sentences, namely that there are other abstract objects called propositions) is that it is difficult to know whether a word is to be associated with one or more of such abstract objects; and, if with more than one, how we are to decide which object the word is to be associated with *on any particular occasion of its use*. This problem of *ambiguity* arises also with a 'meaning is reference to *physical objects*' view, but there it is formally unresolvable* because of what Quine has called 'the opacity of reference'. It is difficult to discuss 'senses', let alone 'propositions', in the absence of some constructive procedure for attaching them to words and sentences respectively, and for distinguishing between them when more than one can be associated with a given word or sentence. It is just such a procedure that I shall describe in Chapter 3 of this book.

In such a procedure, decisions as to the correct sense will depend upon other (neighbouring) symbols, and so one is thus already outside the notion of reference proper, because already concerned essentially with *other symbols*. Such a procedure could express a 'sense' view of meaning that was not referential in either the designatory or the intensional sense. My quarrel with Katz and

---

* Unless, like Church, one takes the view that there could be *rules* assigning names to things.

G

Fodor at this point is that, because they limit their examination
of neighbouring symbols to the other words *of the same sentence,*
they are not in fact able to distinguish among word senses in the
way they set out to.

There is a long tradition in linguistics, too, going back to
de Saussure,[46] whose principal doctrine was different from both the
referential theories above. It was the doctrine of 'internal meaning'.
That is to say, meanings of words are essentially functions of their
use in connexion with other words.

There has been a considerable assault on this view in recent years
by British linguists like Halliday [111] and Dixon [79]. In Dixon's
case that has sometimes taken the form of attacks on Katz and
Fodor, whom he sees as paradigm exponents of bad intensional
theory. Halliday writes [111, p. 245],

The reason why 'context' is preferred to 'semantics'[47] is that
the latter is too closely tied to the conceptual method. This, in
attempting to link language form to unobservables, becomes
circular since concepts are only observable as the form they
are set up to explain. The linguistic statement of context
attempts to relate the language form to (abstractions from)
other (i.e. extra-textual) observables.

As a criticism of a pure theory of intensional meaning this seems
to me correct, though not of a theory like that of Chapter 3 below
(the CSD system), which defines its extra-textual entities in terms of
a procedure for distinguishing, or otherwise manipulating, them.
Where this work of Halliday's, and its systematic extension in the
work of Dixon, is wrong is in their notion of the *direct use of
situational context* as an aid to understanding or clarifying a statement. Situations cannot be brought up against texts directly, and
that is the point of Wittgenstein's (above-quoted) remark about a
picture having to be in the same logical space as what it pictures.
Dixon has recently, and I think seriously, suggested clipping photo-
graphs to texts for this purpose. But then the problem simply arises
in another form: what aspect of the photograph is the appropriate
one; is this a photograph of a woman, or of her head, or of a
woman standing, or what? The last line of the Halliday quotation
gives the game away with the qualification 'abstractions from'. If
this means *verbal* abstractions from a situational context then we

are back in the world of 'meaning is simply *other* words', and not in an extra-textual situation at all.

But again, Halliday and Dixon are right, in their criticism of theories like that of Katz and Fodor, if they are implicitly demanding that something else is needed, over and above a list of word senses, in order to explain or clarify the meanings of sentences; and, as Weinreich has pointed out, it must be something other than the grammar of the sentence. If we were given and could master a complete dictionary and grammar for, say, Martian we would still not understand what those creatures were saying, for we also have to know the kinds of things, in some very general sense, that speakers of a language want to say. I go on to construct a theory of message-forms, or *templates* (in Chapter 3 below), which will be such entities, but which, unlike Dixon and Halliday's 'contexts', will be in the same logical space as the text to be analysed.

I shall assume that in this section I have shown, in a rather rough and ready manner, the obvious inadequacies of pure name and pure sense theories of meaning. The same goes for the dualist theory, which is open to the intersection of the criticisms of its two constituent theories, unles it arms itself with some device for deciding which of the two aspects of a word's meaning is in play on any particular occasion of the word's use.

Wittgenstein, in his later work, and Quine from a different point of view, have put a different view of the way a language works: one that does not see either of these two ways of meaning as primary, and yet which does not take the Fregean 'dualist' stand. For Wittgenstein, reference, far from being primary, came to be a derivative function of language. For him, the act of pointing presumes upon a language understood from within, and is always ambiguous without it.[48] Furthermore, the fact that a word can be used, and properly used, in a language does not imply that there is something in the world that it *really points to* [305, I, §58]. This rejection did not lead Wittgenstein, as it did Frege, to accept the need for intensional entities, what he called the 'shadows of words and sentences'. However, Wittgenstein did continue to talk in those terms when discussing *the procedures by which we distinguish the different senses in which a word can be used.*

It is in this connexion that the 'proposition remains important' for him: he did not abandon that notion, but suggested that there are many, possibly infinitely many, such forms; and that these forms are to be assigned on the basis of the way the sentence functions 'as a member of a system of sentences' [308, §15]. In his *Bemerkungen*, Wittgenstein put the view that there cannot be rules determining the well-formedness or otherwise of the utterances of ordinary language; or at least not in the straightforward sense of rules which examine an utterance and assign it to one of two heaps, the meaningful and the meaningless. He supported this by saying that, if there were a boundary of this kind, then 'we could see on both sides of it', and so we could give meaning to the 'meaningless'. That is another form of the view that any logical grammar, as usually formulated, must exclude novelty or development in language.[49]

The notion that one can extend usage was important to Wittgenstein, and yet this point can be lost through mistranslation of his German. His word '*Anwendung*' is translated 'use' in the English edition of the *Philosophical Investigations*. With that translation of the word it is possible to read a 'static use', or logical syntax, theory into the work. However, Wittgenstein himself sometimes put '*Applikation*' in parentheses after occurrences of '*Anwendung*',[50] and this makes it clear that 'application' would be a better translation. And this is far from a trivial or verbal point; for we cannot be said to misapply a word in the sense that we can be said to misuse it. We apply what we apply, as it were. This does not mean that there *could not be* a misapplication of a word, but it does suggest an important gap between those two notions, and one that seems to have been important to Wittgenstein.

In his *Bemerkungen* Wittgenstein seems to have connected the notion of *Anwendung-Applikation* very closely with the notion of laying a linguistic measure on to the world. These are the passages I have already mentioned above: 'We cannot compare a picture with reality if we cannot lay it against reality as a measuring rod' and 'the rod must be in the same space as the object to be measured' [308, §§43–5]. This last point is near the centre of Wittgenstein's later philosophy, and contains the point made earlier that the use of words is not just a clandestine way of pointing at things. For we cannot describe the differences between things without producing differences in our uses of words.

Wittgenstein's later writing is, I am sure, the only serious philosophical groundwork for an operational semantics that is to avoid the crass pitfalls concealed in all the familiar philosophical theories of meaning. If we are to lay a measuring rod on language, and we must, then the notions we use should be defined only in terms of the operations employed in that laying on. And we should not pretend that the counters we employ in that process have some status that makes them either more or less than mere words: that makes them pointers to things, or labels for ideas, or parts of the brain.

Wittgenstein's real achievement was to convince a generation, already intoxicated with the power of formal logic, that that logic was not necessarily The Structure underlying thought and language. But although he talked much of 'deep grammatical forms', he resisted any attempt to give systematic form to any alternative structure. Chomsky's achievement has been to provide a systematic structure of forms that were not those of formal logic; to propose some real systematic alternative candidate as the Real Structure of language. The language Chomsky used was a blend of Carnap's (formation and transformation rules) and Wittgenstein's (deep and surface structures): the logical force is that of a demonstration by alternative. Here, Chomsky says in effect, is a possible alternative structure for language. The only danger is in thinking that making any such claim shows that other possible, alternative, structures must therefore be wrong.

3 Computable semantic derivations

'From Toune of Stoffe to fatten Londe'
This is a plain Designation of the Duke of Marlborough.
One Kind of Stuff used to fatten Land is called Marle and every
Body knows that Borough is a name for a Town: and this
Way of Expression is after the usual dark Manner of old
Astrological Predictions. . . . And, I think, I have not forced
the Words, by my Explication, into any other sense than what
they will naturally bear.

Swift, *Commentary on the Famous Prediction of Merlin, the British Wizard*

3.1. Word-senses, message-forms, text-fragments and semantic compatibility

In this chapter I describe the CSD system of semantic analysis. The
description is incomplete in two ways: all detail concerning the
actual application of the system to texts with the aid of a computer
is deferred until Chapter 4. Secondly, certain matters of detail, lists
of markers, and tables concerned with the construction of the
dictionary, have been omitted. Those details may all be found in the
appendices to [298].

I shall assume that it follows, in some very general way from the
discussions, of Chapter 2 above, that choice among the possible

senses of the words in a text requires some knowledge of the structure of the discourse containing them. That is a premise accepted by all the authors I have discussed, and my disagreements with them concerned the particular structures they prescribed. The present system is also a method of attaching structures to texts with the aid of codings and rules, such that, when a structure is attached to a text, particular sense codings for the words of the text can be read off from that structure. It is in that way that the attachment of such a semantic structure to a text can be said to resolve its word-sense ambiguity.

No systematic attempt is made here to survey the relations of the present system to others[1] nor is such a survey called for in a report on work still in progress. I shall therefore make such remarks only when some point of contrast is important and, for the rest, I shall assume that all theories of semantics share certain assumptions, if not goals.

However, it may be useful, if only for the purpose of communication, to compare the proposals of this section with those of Katz and Postal discussed in Chapter 2 above. My proposals differ from theirs in the following important respects:

(i)   They are designed to tackle long sequences of text and not only short example sentences.

(ii)   They are not based on a prior notion of 'grammatical sentence'; for the notion of 'meaningful sentence' is taken to be a fundamental one.

(iii)   They include a more formal procedure for semantically encoding the word-senses before the analysis starts; by that I mean the use of a budget of classifiers, or markers, rather than any unrestricted use of ordinary language one finds in existing dictionaries (cf. Katz and Postal's 'distinguishers').

(iv)   They are computable.

(v)   The interpretation of a sentence is not simply a list of appropriate word-senses, together with syntactic structure, for there are many reasons for thinking it cannot be expressed in this way. Instead, I work with a structured message-form, or *template*, which expresses the sense of a clause or elementary sentence. One such interpreted template would be 'a man is a man of a certain kind'. It is a hypothesis of this work that such structures can be used to pick up the appropriate senses of a word and reject the inappropriate ones.[2]

(vi)   They are designed to cope with new uses of words, that is to say, senses that were not fed into the programme in a coded form at the beginning of the procedure. In certain cases the procedure constructs them for itself on the basis of some considerable amount of surrounding context.

(vii)   I discuss the sense ambiguity of words only with respect to particular occasions of use in text. I think it is unhelpful to speak (as Katz and Postal do) of a word being n-ways ambiguous *simply because it has n sense-entries in its dictionary.*

The general difference between the present approach and those based on Chomsky's theory of grammar can be put as follows. Any such theory assumes as fundamental the notion of a class of *grammatical sentences*. This class pins down their notion of sentence, and the task of any particular grammar is, for Chomsky, to 'explicate' the class. A semantics is, for them, theoretically and temporally subsequent to that. My approach, on the other hand, takes *meaningful language* as the basic material for analysis and explanation. It does not assign any theoretical status to a class of 'grammatical sequences' over and above their being what some particular grammar produces, or admits, as well formed. *One aim of the present work, therefore, is to construct a theory that enables us to detect semantic forms directly, and not via a strong and conventional syntax analysis.* Thus, one can turn Chomsky's theory on its head by constructing a notion of syntax analysis as a less discriminating form of semantic analysis.Although a sequence like 'Sandwich ate a John' would, if processed by the CSD system, probably fail to have one of the semantic message forms in the inventory, it might be possible to assign to it a more general structure of the same form, though not in the inventory. Apart from that possibility one could just decline to discuss its grammaticality further, and so avoid unhelpful controversies.

My case, then, is that in analysing language it may not be necessary to consider grammatical, or syntactic, structure in any primary sense, though anyone making this claim must show how the proposed semantics 'does the job' that a conventional grammar would do (see, for example, the function of the general rule 'pack the sense-frame as tightly as possible' below). As McCarthy puts it [192, p. 69]

[this experience] has led me to the conclusion that mathematical linguists are making a serious mistake in their
concentration on syntax and, even more specially, on the

grammar of natural languages. It is even more important to develop a mathematical understanding and a formalization of the kinds of information conveyed in natural language.

The present system is intended as a tentative move along those lines. Before setting out the formal connexions that constitute the system of semantic analysis, I must convey the basic notions in terms of which it is expressed. These are of two kinds: notions applicable to texts, and notions in terms of which the text notions are formally expressed in the system. Let us call them *text notions* and *system notions* respectively.

I shall first set out four text notions: word-sense, message-form, text-fragment and semantic compatibility. The relation between these is roughly as follows: *message-forms* are to be sought within single *fragments* of text. One can decide which *sense* of the words of a fragment is appropriate by considering either the message-form appropriate to the fragment or the relation of *semantic compatibility* between the appropriate message-forms for the fragments (and so, derivatively, the compatibility between the fragments themselves).

Let us start with the difficult, but important, notion of a sense of a word. Ordinary people, linguists and philosophers talk about, and distinguish, the senses of their words all the time, though there is less reflection on 'what is *a* meaning, or a sense, of a word?' than on 'what is *the* meaning, or sense, of a word?' One could put the problem so: a given word, say 'bar', occurs in innumerable positions in actual texts; it always looks the same, yet we know that these occurrences can be classified appropriately for at least lawyers, publicans, racialists and metalworkers (and many more, for 'bar' has at least eight senses). *Yet it is not at all self-evident on what basis, or information, this classification is to be done.* It is not even universally agreed that it can or should be done. Wittgenstein, as was mentioned earlier, wrote in his *Tractatus* [303, §3·323] that what one would normally call occurrences of a word symbol in different senses of that word are actually different symbols.

More recently the linguist Antal [7] has restated the case that all occurrences of a word token mean the same. This involves him in adopting a simple designatory theory of meaning, whose drawbacks I have examined, while leaving the word 'mean' as a blank counter, by definition the same for all occurrences of a word token. One might just as easily go on to say that 'all occurrences of all words mean the same'; it would make no real difference to the view. Neither Wittgenstein's nor Antal's views shift the problem, it is simply renamed. For even if all ambiguity is 'really' homonymity, we are left with the problem of deciding which of a number of homonyms is appropriate on any given number of uses of any given word token. We are where we started, with the important difficulty of distinguishing between word-senses.

The classification of word occurrences into classes representing 'senses' may seem an intractable problem of classification if one retains a deep attraction to the primitive view that, if things are placed together in a class or subclass, *then they possess a common property*. Wittgenstein has thrown considerable light on what it is actually to classify with his hints at a theory of 'family resemblances'. This has been given extended statement by Bambrough [12].[3]

An important part of this view, as I understand it, is that there are no *privileged* classifiers in any field, but that the 'classifier words', on the basis of whose assignments we assign other words, are themselves in the same position as the 'higher-level' words. Our purposes demand that we stop somewhere, but we do not have to hunt for *the* right set of classifiers. The notion of 'family resemblance classification' can certainly be extended to linguistic classification given the presupposition that meaning is always other words. For we *in fact* classify words by other words in all cases, whether the apparent activity is classifying butterflies, human tribes or word-uses.[4]

K. Sparck-Jones [270, 273] has applied a measure of 'family resemblance' to the problem of semantic classification. She used other natural language words as her classifiers in a straightforward way: classifying each word examined by those other words that can replace the given word in a 'replacement frame' *so as to leave the meaning of the whole frame unchanged*. Her aim was to classify and distinguish the senses *so obtained*. She did not actually use this procedure to obtain the finished 'dictionary classification' of word occurrences into senses, but described how her procedures could in principle be applied at a 'lower level' so as to do this. Or, to put the matter another way, she actually started with the classification provided by a conventional dictionary having given a plausible explanation of what it would be like to produce it by the same general procedures of automatic classification.

I shall not adopt this method of synonym replacement, because as has been said above, it *begins* with the difficult notion of 'preserving the meaning of a larger whole'. The method also restricts itself to replacement frames in the form of short sentences,[5] and I wish to be able to consider wider connectivities in text, as I wrote above in connexion with KF. The importance of this work of Sparck-Jones is that it shows, in an operationally defined way, how one might go from the occurrences of words in actual contexts to that grouping of those contexts we instinctively call word-senses. And, in that sense, the work gives an operational definition of the elusive notion of word-sense.[6]

I turn now to the notion of a message-form, which rests on the following sort of example. If we are given the language segment 'Mr Smith is angry' and asked what it is really about, then it seems reasonable to reply 'a human being under discussion is in a certain emotional state'. Similarly, if one were reading a report of a committee meeting and came across the segment, 'The chair is displeased', one would want to say again that what it meant was that 'a human being under discussion is in a certain emotional state'. One interprets the last segment in that way quite naturally, and in spite of the fact that the word 'chair' usually means 'a piece of furniture for sitting on'. Everyone knows that the intended sense of chair is 'a person in control of a meeting' simply because articles of furniture do not get into emotional states. I shall call the segment 'a human being. . .' etc. the *message-form* of the two example segments.

It should now be clear that if the following three conditions were satisfied, then message-forms could be used to resolve the ambiguity of segments of text:

(i)   At any given time there are a finite number of message-forms.

(ii) There is some formal representation of message-forms.

(iii) There is some formal method of attaching message-forms to appropriate segments of text.

The satisfaction of these requirements is demonstrated in the subsections that follow, but it can already be seen how the proposed method would work. For, in an inventory of possible message-forms, one would expect 'a human being under discussion is in a certain emotional state', but *not* 'a certain object under discussion is in a certain emotional state'. So, given representations of the various senses of the words in the segment 'The chair is displeased', one would not expect to be able to attach any message-forms appropriate to the 'physical object' sense of 'chair' to the sentence. Or, to speak quite naturally in the language of substitutions, one would not expect there to be any message-forms in which the physical object sense of 'chair' was a possible substitution value.

Message-forms can thus be seen as theoretic devices by means of which the word-sense ambiguity of segments of text can be resolved; for a word-sense is assigned to a word use if and only if it is a substitution value in some message-form *which is itself finally assigned to the segment.* I say 'finally assigned' because the possibility arises that the assumption (iii) above will lead to the attachment of *more than one* message-form to any given segment. As will become clear below, this possibility is dealt with by sequence rules of 'semantic compatibility'. A message-form is finally assigned to a segment of a text only if that message-form satisfies rules of 'semantic compatibility' applied to the whole text. That a system of message-forms, functioning in this way, can resolve the word-sense ambiguity of texts is an empirical hypothesis to be confirmed or refuted by actual semantic experiments.

The view that there are permissible forms of statement is, of course, an old one going back to Aristotle, as is the notion that the typologies of ideas and statement form are interrelated. It is possible to derive further general support for this notion of a message-form, not reducible to its constituent word forms, from Wittgenstein's notion of propositional form. The essential 'category' distinction for Wittgenstein in his *Tractatus* was between facts and their elements ('The sentence-token is a fact', §3.143). This led to the development of one strand in his thought which, though it agreed with Frege and Russell that the sentence is a function of the expressions contained in it, differed fundamentally from them about the interpretation. Stenius[7] has argued that for Wittgenstein 'Socrates is mortal' would have a logical form, while 'Mortality is Socrates' would not. That would not be because a type theory excluded the latter combination of words, but because the symbols for the words of the latter could not be substituted in the propositional fact, because of the way *its* symbols are laid out from left to right. I said 'one strand' in the *Tractatus* because that view is inconsistent with Wittgenstein's other (and wrong) view that to translate the words of a sentence is *ipso facto* to translate the sentence [303, §4.025]. For, if the fact is distinguished from its elements, it is clearly possible to find equivalents for the latter without doing so for the former. It is interesting that this strand in his thought led Wittgenstein, as we saw earlier, to deny that there was 'sentence for sentence translation' [303, §4.025] even though the *Tractatus*, as we have it in English, is a very good example of exactly that.

The inadequacies of this formulation of Wittgenstein's early but important view are well-known: from the point of view of the present work there are three:

(i) His apparent view in the *Tractatus* was that there was a *single* propositional form, rather than a number of them. His renunciation of the 'single form view', and of the logic within which that form was defined, did not lead him to say that there are *no* forms underlying the 'surface grammar' of a sentence, and which relate the sentence to other sentences.

(ii) Wittgenstein did not see, at the time of his *Tractatus*, that a sentence could have a multiplicity of forms, which would be appropriate on different occasions of its use. It is essential to the notion of message-form that more than one of them might match with a language segment considered in isolation. That is, the longer segment *is itself in principle ambiguous*, and in a way not reducible to the ambiguity of its constituent words. A longer segment, then, can be ambiguous in respect of message-form. Later Wittgenstein changed this early view: 'If we take the sentence as a prescription to picture models, then their pictorial character becomes even clearer. For in order to guide my hand, *it must have the multiplicity* of the desired activity.' [308, §10, my italics.]

(iii) Whereas, in the last quotation, we are made to feel that pictures are being discussed as an *example* of how the world can be represented, in the *Tractatus* there is more than a suggestion that picturing is the form of all such representation. That is misleading if it is interpreted to mean that the relation between a propositional form and anything else is *iconic*; where by 'iconic' I mean that some relation between picture parts is identical with some relation between the parts of what is pictured, or represented. That view would, of course, limit propositions in English to the representation of things in relations of right-leftness, or possibly in relations of size or colour. I am not saying that Wittgenstein believed that propositions were iconic in this sense, but many of the right-left examples with which philosophers have subsequently discussed this work, suggest that they thought that he did hold such a view.

R. M. Needham [200] and K. Sparck-Jones [274] have both put forward criticisms of semantic analyses that employ a finite battery of message-forms: Sparck-Jones specifically criticizes the present work among others.

Needham writes as follows, after discussing the syntactic and semantic criteria to be applied in a *Gedanken* experiment he conducts in translating a passage from Camus:

> . . . we have rejected alternatives because they do not satisfy some stated criterion. What right have we to expect that one or more of the possibilities will satisfy some previously stated criterion? The answer I believe is necessarily none. To require that everything in a text must satisfy some previously stated set of semantic criteria is to require that the criteria cater for everything that can be said. . . . This is patent nonsense, and one of the great differences between syntactics and semantics: it is commonly supposed that a good grammar describes and delimits the whole corpus of grammatical sentences of language.

I would reply to this as follows:

(i)   The criticism rests on the firm distinction between syntax and semantics, which I have argued against in the course of the earlier discussion. Furthermore, whatever the generality of the impression that a good grammar does what Dr. Needham says it does, I have argued at length in Chapter 2 above that there are not, and perhaps cannot be, good grammars in his sense.

(ii)   I think his criticism is directed against a theory of semantic message forms in which the forms are *interpreted as expressing the meaning of what is being analysed with them*. I have not interpreted them in this way in the present work, but have discussed them only as heuristic devices for resolving ambiguity.

(iii)   If, however, a theory of message-forms were to be *interpreted* in this way, it would be at least as secure as a syntactic theory.[8]

It is no more *a priori* foolish to classify semantic forms than to classify logical or syntactic ones. In fact they are related enterprises. In syntactic classification one examines the behaviour of a word within a coarse framework of structures, and assigns it to large substitution classes. In semantic classification the framework mesh is finer and the substitution classes correspondingly smaller. I think it could be shown that there are syntactic analogues to basic semantic message forms: consider the message-form 'a human being in our discussion is a certain sort of human being'. This pins down a *more specific situation* than a 'Subject-Complement-Copula' form in syntax, which one may interpret as locating a *more general situation* such as 'a certain entity in the discussion is a certain kind of entity'. Semantic forms simply locate a *more specific* form of fact.[9]

(iv) Quite apart from questions of interpretation, there is an important difference between viewing an inventory of message-forms, in the way I described it (as containing variables), and viewing the same inventory with all possible semantic substitution values substituted for the variables. It is only the latter 'inventory' which could be criticized as attempting to cater for everything that could be said.

The former inventory (of message-forms containing unsatisfied variables) attempts to cater for everything that could be said *only* in the way that an inventory of syntactic forms does; for grammatical categories like 'noun' etc., are essentially variables ranging over functions of other synctactic variables and lexical items. The general reply to Needham's criticism, as to K. Sparck-Jones's queries about how the inventory of message-forms is to be set up, is to point out that the inventory should not be thought of as finite and inextensible in principle.

In keeping with the spirit of Needham's paper, which is not to show that semantic analysis of this kind *cannot be done*, but that it must have ways of accommodating what it cannot account for, I shall show below how the present CSD system also contains the possibility of extending itself in the face of what it cannot account for.

An important question which arises immediately is, what text-segments is it proposed to attach the message-forms to? I shall call such units of natural language text simply *fragments*, and all I want to stress at this point is that they are not to be equated with what are ordinarily called sentences.[10] The notion of 'sentence' *in a natural language* is a very confused one, largely because of the oscillation between structural notions on the one hand, and what is actually found between capital letters and full stops, on the other. I have already shown that Chomsky's explication of 'sentence' gives no operational assistance, nor in a different way does formal logic, in that it requires simple forms of sentence like 'aRb'. In any case, no actual logic is intended to be an exhaustive classification of natural language forms.

There is some evidence in contemporary linguistic literature [see

92 and 172] that a piece of natural language like those that are normally called clauses, or phrases, is a more appropriate structural unit on which is based an analysis of natural language. This view is not inconsistent with common sense intuitions about message-bearing units of text, since it is plausible to find the same message in the description 'the red house', and in the assertoric 'The house is red'; apart, that is, from considerations about the tense of the verb occurring in the latter form.

The precise details of the criteria and procedures for segmenting a continuous text into fragments I leave until Chapter 4, where they are set out in the context of the programmes for actually doing the job.

It is with reference to the fragment unit that two kinds of ambiguity resolution are distinguished; internal and external. For example, if one were presented with the fragment 'Jones is a rat' one could be pretty sure without looking outside the fragment that the required sense of 'rat' was not the 'animal sense'. This I call an internal resolution, and *ipso facto* the fragment is not isolated in the sense defined earlier. But in the case of 'He hasn't got a jack', one needs access to surrounding text to resolve the word 'jack', and this would be an external resolution, and so one could call that fragment isolated as it appears here.

Thus the resolution of the word 'chair' in the fragment 'The chair is displeased', would be an internal resolution. Conversely, one might expect to attach more than one message-form to 'He hasn't got a jack', and to decide between them would necessarily be an external resolution, since there is no information available from within the fragment to decide the question.

How are external resolutions to be performed? Suppose one puts the fragment 'He hasn't got a jack' into a number of contexts, as follows:

John can't repair his car.
He hasn't got a jack.   (1)
Do you have one.

John is going to lose this trick.
He hasn't got a jack.   (2)
But he had a very good hand last time.

This spot is a distant galaxy.
He hasn't got a jack.   (3)
Down the stream floated a hockey stick.

Let us suppose that what I shall call relations of 'semantic compatibility' could be set up between message-forms such that in text
(1) one could assign the 'correct message-form' to its second fragment
because only that message-form would satisfy the 'semantic compatibility relation' with the possible message-form(s) for the first
fragment. By the *correct message-form* for the second fragment of the
first text I mean the one in which the substitutions value for whatever
represents 'jack' is its 'tool' sense and not its 'high-value playing
card' sense. Put at its crudest, this would require some conceptual
overlap between the representations in the message-forms for 'jack'
and 'car', namely that they both had to do with motor vehicles.

Similarly in text (2) one would hope that such relations of compatibility would be satisfied only by the message-form for the second
fragment that represented the 'playing card' sense of 'jack', and
not by the one containing a representation of the 'tool' sense. This
satisfaction would be in virtue of a conceptual overlap between
'jack' and 'trick', in that both, in some sense, contain or convey the
notion of 'playing cards'. Thus one could expect analysis of texts
(1) and (2) to lead to the assignment of different message-forms to
the fragment 'He hasn't got a jack'. Or, in other words, the two
contexts resolve the ambiguity of that whole fragment in different
ways.

If one looks, finally, at text (3) one sees that it gives no help at all
in resolving the second fragment. Reading the whole text leaves one
no wiser. The reason for that, put crudely and oversimply, is that
its three constituent fragments do not cohere together conceptually
at all.

3.2. Semantic element, formula, template and sequence rule

I turn now to an exposition of the basic notions of the present
system of semantic analysis. Three of them are the formal representations of the text notions just discussed: the semantic *formulae*
represent word-senses; *templates* represent message-forms; and
sequence rules between templates represent rules of semantic-com-
patibility between message-forms. These three formal system notions

H

are all expressed in terms of an inventory of semantic elements, classifiers, or markers, and I shall start with them.[11]

I shall work with a set of semantic elements, classifiers or markers, and, like Katz and Fodor, I shall not try to justify the actual membership of the set. That does not mean that they are chosen at random; on the contrary, they are chosen to be consistent with the observations of linguists[12] about concepts to be found in all languages. However, I am not in using them making any claims about the human *mind* concerning linguistic universals in the way that Quine and Chomsky do.[13]

It must, however, be emphasized that the use of a particular set of classifiers, however universal, does not imply belief in a best, or right, set. They are to be thought of as Popperian terms, if I may use that expression, to be used in order to get a result, and to be assessed only in the light of that result. Garvin has said that the only useful generalizations about language are inductive ones. This is correct and important, of course, but it is no help to one who has to *start* rather than to *assess*.[14]

The semantic formulae

The purpose of the formulae is to encode and so distinguish the different senses of natural language words: one would expect to assign a different formula to each major sense of a word that a good dictionary distinguishes. Formulae consist of left and right parentheses and *elements*.

Def. 1: an *element* is one of the following fifty-three primitive semantic classifiers:

BE	FORCE	MAN
BEAST	FROM	MAY
CAN	GRAIN	MORE
CAUSE	HAVE	MUCH
CHANGE	HOW	MUST
COUNT	IN	ONE
DO	KIND	PAIR
DONE	LET	PART
FEEL	LIFE	PLANT
FOLK	LIKE	PLEASE
FOR	LINE	POINT

SAME	THINK	WHEN
SELF	THIS	WHERE
SENSE	TO	WHOLE
SIGN	TRUE	WILL
SPREAD	UP	WORLD
STUFF	USE	WRAP[15]
THING	WANT	

As I wrote earlier there cannot be a *right* set of elements, or semantic markers, but only better and worse sets, and there must be freedom to change the inventory to see whether an amendment leads to better overall results. The elements themselves are only words and so they can be expected to be as potentially ambiguous as the word-senses they are used to classify. However, there need be no circularity here, for the sense of a single word is encoded by a formula, and it is up to the dictionary maker to see that the formula *as a whole* is not ambiguous. It might be possible, ultimately, to replace the stage of formula making if there were a trustworthy thesaurus, so a formula for a word could then be constructed by rules from the formulae for those subsections of the thesaurus in which the word occurred.

When I speak of classifying a word-sense by a semantic element in order to set up a semantic formula, I mean something very simple-minded, because I am using a quite naive notion of 'conceptual containment'. For example, suppose one is considering the word 'compass', in its sense of 'an instrument pointing north', and one wants to make up a formula out of the above elements, and any of them preceded by NOT.[16] Since a compass, in this sense, is a thing one would certainly expect to use the element THING. Again, since the notion of a compass involves that of pointing, one would certainly expect to use the element POINT, and so on.

Before going on to describe exactly how a semantic dictionary is set up, I want to make clear what the *form* of that dictionary would be. I assume that one starts with access to the sense distinctions given by an ordinary dictionary, and that one can then encode those in the metalanguage of formulae made up from the semantic elements. However, it would have been *in principle possible,* as in the Sparck-Jones work discussed earlier, for these same elements to have been applied to individual word occurrences, and for these then to have been grouped into (conventional dictionary) senses on the basis of some family resemblance algorithm operating on the elements.

I shall discuss the setting up of a semantic dictionary having the following form.

Def. 2: the semantic *dictionary* is comprised of a set of ordered sense-pairs.

Def. 3: a *word* is either a natural language word or a sequence of them entered, for convenience, as a single character in the dictionary. An example of the latter is 'as far as'. (A full list of such contractions is given in Appendix iv to [298]).

Def. 4: a *sense-pair* is an ordered pair corresponding to some major sense of a word, as distinguished by a conventional dictionary. The first member of a pair is a (well-formed) *semantic formula*; the second member is a sense description of that sense of the word, which must begin with the name of the word in question. Thus a sense description for one sense of 'compass' would be 'compass as instrument pointing north'.

Either or both members of a sense-pair may be null. In Chapter 4 below I give examples of such cases: they are words like 'although' which are considered here to have no *semantic* content.

The *order* of the pairs that, as a list, constitute the *dictionary entry* for a word is the same as that of the corresponding senses when found in a standard dictionary: main sense first, at least in cases where it is proper to speak of a 'main sense'. It should be pointed out that no attempt has been made to give a *complete* dictionary entry, such as would result from coding the whole mass of information that a good dictionary gives about a word, archaic senses and all. Completeness of that kind is out of the question at the moment. Thus to take the entries from the semantic dictionary for two consecutive words at random we have:

(COMPASS((((((THIS POINT)TO)SIGN)THING)(COMPASS AS INSTRUMENT
                                        POINTING NORTH))
((COUNT DO)(COMPASS AS TO MEASURE NUMERICALLY))))
(COMPLAINTS((((MAN FOR)((NOTPLEASE BE)SIGN))(COMPLAINTS AS
                                        EXPRESSIONS OF DISPLEASURE))))

From the preceding definitions it should be clear that
(((((THIS POINT)TO)SIGN)THING) is the formula in the first sense-pair for 'compass';

(COUNT DO) is the formula in the second sense-pair for 'compass';
(COMPASS AS INSTRUMENT POINTING NORTH) is the sense description in
the first sense pair for 'compass'; and so on.

I still have not explained how a formula is put together from the
elements and the right and left brackets that it evidently contains.
That is best explained by the definitions and rules of construction,
but an informally explained example may help.

Thus to take the formula from a sense-pair at random, say;
(COLOURLESS((((((WHERE SPREAD)(SENSE SIGN))NOT HAVE)KIND)
(COLOURLESS AS NOT HAVING THE PROPERTY OF COLOUR))))).
The formula in that sense-pair can be explained as follows: 'colourless' is a sort; a sort indicating that something does not possess some
property; the property is an abstract sensory property of a certain
sort; that certain sort has to do with spatial extension. Thus the
meaning of the whole word-sense is 'a sort that lacks an abstract,
sensory, spatial property', and it is not difficult to see that that is
what (in right-left order) the formula conveys.

Formulae are defined recursively as follows:

Def. 5: a *formula* is a binarily bracketed string of formulae and
atoms.

Def. 6: an *atom* is an element, or an element immediately preceded
by NOT.

It is a purely mnemonic matter that the element names are chosen
to be Anglo-Saxon monosyllables, for their function is much like
that of the semantic markers in other systems with more sophisticated
names.

It follows from this that an element is not a formula. Not all
formulae can be assigned to sense-pairs, but only well-formed
formulae:

Def. 7: the *head* of a formula is its last atom. Thus KIND is the head
of the formula for 'colourless' given above.

Def. 8: a *well-formed formula* (wff) is (a) a formula, and (b) such that
its head is one of the following elements:

HOW KIND FOLK GRAIN MAN PART SIGN STUFF THING WHOLE WORLD
BE CAUSE CHANGE DO FEEL HAVE PLEASE PAIR SENSE WANT USE THIS

and (c) such that it satisfies the rules of interpretation R1–
R3, below.

It follows from the definition of formula and head (defs. 5 and 7) that any formula F can be put in the form;

$$(f_1;;;(f_{n-1}(f_n(cf)))\dots)$$

where f is the head (last element) and c is the left-hand (dependent) element or formula which forms a bracket pair with f. $f_{1---}f_n$ are then the successive dependents which complete the whole formula, f_n being the rightmost.

Def. 9: the *core* of a formula is the element or sub formula that is the dependent (left-hand member of the bracket pair) whose right-hand immediate constituent is the head of the whole formula. (i.e., the core of F is c in the formalization above.)

Thus

(((WHERE SPREAD)(SENSE SIGN))NOTHAVE)

is the core of the formula for 'colourless' given above. When constructing formulae the dictionary maker works with six types of bracketed group, as follows:

I. *Adverbial Group*

((TRUE MUCH) HOW) equivalent for 'enough' used as an adverb. Same function as 'rather nicely' in English. Can end with element HOW.

II. *Prepositional Group*

(MAN FROM) same function as 'to the end' in English. Cannot end with any of the elements of (b) above, and hence a II-type cannot be a well-formed formula.

III. *Adjunctive Group*

((TRUE MUCH)KIND) equivalent for 'enough' used as an adjective. Same function as 'almost black' in English. The inner bracket is of type I. Can end with KIND.

IV. *Nominal Group*

(((SIGN STUFF) FOR) SIGN) an equivalent for 'bill' used as a noun in English. Same function as 'blue book' in English. Inner brackets are of type IV and II. Can end with FOLK, GRAIN, MAN, PART, SIGN, STUFF, THING, WHOLE or WORLD.

V. *Operative or Verbal Group*

(CAN DO) an equivalent for 'can' used as a verb. Same function as '[I] have come' in English. Can end with CAUSE, CHANGE, DO, FEEL, HAVE, PLEASE, PAIR, SENSE, USE or WANT.

VI. *Sentential Group*

(THING USE) as equivalent for 'apply'. Same functions as '[They] like it' in English. Can end with CAUSE, CHANGE, DO, FEEL, SENSE, USE, WANT, PAIR or PLEASE.

The dictionary maker constructs well-formed formulae by nesting brackets of these six types in such a way that the last atom of the whole formula is always one of those listed in (b) of Def. 8 above. Thus it follows that there cannot be a well-formed formula of type II; for formulae of this type can only occur as nested subparts of well-formed formulae. A table specifying which elements can occur as immediate constituents of which of the six bracket types, and also which bracket types can be nested within which others, is given in Appendix vi of [298].

That table serves to restrict the senses in which the elements can be used, and those restrictions are made explicit in a table of 'scope notes' (see Appendix vii of [298]) which indicates how the elements are to be interpreted in each bracket type in which they can occur.*

The participation table for elements in formulae specifies whether an element can occur as second or first member, or both, in each bracket type of which it can be an immediate constituent. This is because each bracket is interpreted as having a rightwards dependency relation between its two immediate constituents. In type I it is the dependency of the qualifier of an adverb on the adverb it qualifies; in II of the object of a preposition on the preposition, and so on. This interpretation continues through the formula until in the end everything is dependent on the right-hand member of the main bracket pair. That may or may not be the head, or last atom, which in the case of a well-formed formula is one of the elements listed

---

* The scope notes give the dictionary maker some indication of the intended scope of the markers. The table contains entries like:
GRAIN: (II, IV, VI) any kind of structure or pattern
      (III)   structural or pattern-like.
The Roman numerals here refer to the six *bracket types* listed above.

in Def. 8 (b) above. The heads of well-formed formulae correspond to the basic kinds of thing, substance, action and type that form the universe of entities distinguished by the formulae. The contents of the participation table *for bracket types* can be seen by looking back at the formula for 'colourless'. Inside that formula ((WHERE SPREAD) (SENSE SIGN))is itself of type IV (Nominal group), as are both of its subparts. So a type IV bracket can be made up of two type IV brackets; just as a noun phrase in English, such as 'corn stalk' or 'power tool', can be made up of two nouns.

The table of notes therefore contains not only restrictions on which markers can participate in which bracket types, but also restrictions on which bracket types can participate in which other bracket types. From what has been said so far it follows, for example, that type IV can occur inside itself. Type II, however, cannot occur inside itself. It will also be clear, from the example of the table format given above for the marker GRAIN, that the markers cannot be exclusively assigned as either items or properties of items. GRAIN can occur in type III as a property, equivalent to 'structural', but also in type IV to stand for the item 'structure'. In all bracket types the rightmost marker is its head. However, only certain markers can be the heads of *well-formed formulae*, that is, formulae that can be the left member of sense-pairs encoding the senses of words. The possible heads of well-formed formulae are those markers underlined on the original list of markers given above. They indicate the major categories of word-sense classification, though this list, too, can only be justified intuitively. Since HOW is not underlined, and since type II can have only HOW as its head, it follows that a type II bracket can never express a word sense.

So one could say that the set of elements is composed of two subsets; the formula heads (the more general elements) and the others. Although this is the only structuring given *to the whole set*, the structuring implied by the dependencies of elements within any individual formula is of considerable value in semantic analysis, since it enables one to decide which of the elements classifying a particular word-sense are the more important ones. The advantages of using such 'structured markers' over semantic analyses employing only unstructured marker lists have been argued at length by Sparck-Jones [272].

The only exception to the dependence rule is in the use of the element PAIR, meaning 'correspond', where the relation between its two dependents (the things which correspond) is not one of dependence to the right.

Thus we may summarize the rules of interpretation:

R1: A well-formed formula is such that each bracket pair can be interpreted as being of one of the six types I–VI.

R2: The relation between an element and the bracket pair of which it is an immediate constituent is subject to a participation table as is the nesting of the bracket types within themselves and each other.

R3: A well-formed formula is such that each bracket pair comprising it can be interpreted so that the left-hand member depends on the right-hand member; except when the right-hand member at the next higher level is PAIR.

R4: A plural word can only be associated with formulae whose first element is MUCH.

R5: A verb sense of a word can only be associated with formulae whose first bracket pair is of the form (X FOR), where X denotes the principal kind of agent of such a verb: unless the formulae have BE, DO or HAVE as their heads.

R6: The left-right order of dependence of the adjuncts of verbs is fixed as follows: Agent indicator; Object (or complement); adverb; auxiliary; main verb.

Why complex formulae?

It is worth making clear at this point just why words are tagged by *complex* classifiers in the present system, rather than by a string of simple classifiers, as is usually done. By 'complex classifier' here I mean the formulae, not elements expressing complex ideas. Most other such systems, right back to Carnap's logical syntax, tag a word with a set of simple 'single-concept' classifiers, or, if they take account of polysemy of words, by a set of such sets of classifiers, one for each sense of a word. In the systems of Structural Linguistics the classifiers are usually called 'features', and are drawn from a pre-assigned inventory. In other systems such as Sparck-Jones [270] the classifiers are other natural language words that can be substituted, under certain conditions, for the word they classify. This last device is a great advance over other more simplistic methods of linguistic classification, because it is clear that the method of classification-by-substitution can be applied to any word and not simply to 'name-of-object' words, that is to say nouns. However, the classification of Sparck-Jones is directed to a goal quite different from that of the present work and of the structural linguists, namely the classification of natural language words into thesaurus classes.

The so-called feature method[17] has been applied to all 'parts-of-speech', but it is not easy to get it to deal with what one might call the 'structure of the meaning' of many words. Consider, for example, the word 'depend'. The formula assigned to its first sense in the dictionary is

(((SIGN FOR)((WHOLE(THINK SIGN))PAIR)(DEPEND AS DEPEND

LOGICALLY)).

Now, of the six elements in the formula, some could be, as it were, taken out and placed in a set of simpler classifiers; for example:

(SIGN FOR): a sign is the subject of this sense

PAIR: this is a verb signifying a form of correspondence.

However, it is not easy to continue this process for what is expressed by the remaining elements, namely that the correspondence in question is between an idea and some larger whole.

I shall now turn to discussion of the notions of template[18] and rule of semantic compatibility. What I shall call a 'bare template' consists of no more than a triple of the semantic elements described above. The triple is essentially in the order in which it is written from left to right[19] and it is to be interpreted as a message-form in a quite natural way by reading the concatenated elements. Thus,

MAN+BE+KIND

is to be interpreted as 'a man is a man of a certain sort'. In the formal exposition that follows it will be clear how a particular inventory of templates is produced with rules, and how a bare template can have each of its elements qualified by a semantic formula so as to produce a *full template*.

The rules that produce the templates have the form of phrase-structure rules of the sort described in connexion with grammars in Chapter 2 above. The sequence rules, which express the relation of semantic compatibility between message forms, are also in the form of phrase-structure rules. These rules operate in a productive form, so as to produce a pair of full templates from a single one, such that the pair produced are in the desired relation of semantic compatibility. Thus in the expression of these rules the same concatenation symbol '+' links full templates which are also semantically compatible. These rules operate on the elements of full and bare templates so as to define classes of templates semantically compatible with them.

In order to do this they make use of information in the form of 'negation classes'. This is perhaps an unfelicitous phrase,[20] but it refers to a fairly simple and well-understood notion. The negation class of a semantic element is the class of its contrary elements, that is to say concepts which can all fail to apply to some entity, but cannot all apply.

For example, the object of a word-sense could be either a 'THING' or a 'STUFF', but it couldn't be both. The negation class notion is meant to locate a well-known tendency of speakers to follow an utterance with another which is in a minimal sense both opposed to it *and* a repetition of it. Notions in this relation are like the colour words: although they can all *fail* to apply to something (i.e. it's colourless), nevertheless, if one of them applies, then none of the others can. They both exclude each other in this way, and yet also constitute a category of near synonyms. That is to say, 'red' is much more like 'green' in meaning than it is like 'table'; yet we can say of something that it is both red and a table, whereas we cannot say of it that it is both red and green.

In the first chapter I indicated how a repetition of elements occurring in different templates could serve to cast out, or reject, certain templates matching with text-fragments in favour of others. That can be seen in operation by again considering the example of that chapter, involving the fragment ambiguity of 'The old salt is damp', which can in isolation match with both bare templates STUFF+BE+ KIND (given the 'chemical' sense of 'salt') and MAN+BE+KIND (given the 'sailor' sense of 'salt'). One would expect the 'sailor' resolution of 'salt' in the sentence 'The old salt is damp but the biscuits are still dry'. Yet here, biscuits are not a substance, or stuff, like cake; they are things, or individuals. So one would expect the formula for the appropriate sense of 'biscuit' to reflect that fact by having, say, the element THING as its head. In that case the correct sequence of templates for the whole sentence would be

> STUFF+BE+KIND
> THING+BE+KIND

which could not be selected by mere repetition of heads alone, since the heads that are repeated, BE and KIND, are not those relevant to the resolution of 'salt'. At this point the sequence rules operate with the notion of the negation classes of the semantic elements.

That notion relates each element to a class of other elements that are 'semantically close' to it in some way. So STUFF and THING would be more alike (each would occur in the negation class of the other) than would be MAN AND THING. So, working with this form of preference the correct sequence above would be selected.

Very little of interest could be done with the heads of formulae alone, as the examples so far have been. The analysis actually works almost entirely with the whole formula picked up by the template pattern. By matching the *bare template* MAN+BE+KIND, say, on to a text fragment, what is actually picked up from the text in the process is: a formula whose head is MAN, followed by a formula whose head is BE, followed by a formula whose head is KIND.

Now consider 'The old salt is damp though the bed was properly prepared'. The most plausible interpretation contains the 'salt as an old sailor' sense, which requires, let us suppose, the template sequence

$$\left[\begin{array}{l} \text{MAN}+\text{BE}+\text{KIND} \\ \text{THING}+\text{BE}+\text{KIND} \end{array}\right.$$

But from what has been said about negation classes one would not expect rules using them to select this pair of templates in preference to the other pair corresponding to the 'salt as sodium chloride' sense (which would contain the head STUFF in place of MAN); since MAN is not as 'semantically close' to THING as STUFF is. Hence the whole of the semantic formulae for the senses of 'salt' and 'bed' would have to be examined at this point; in particular we would expect some indication in the formula for 'bed as an object for sleeping on' that it is *for human beings*, and so there would be some repetition of the element MAN, in the 'bed' formula and as the head of the formula for 'salt'. So a sequence rule picking up this overlap would be expected to override the one using the weaker negation classes.

I said earlier that the above interpretation might seem to be the *more likely* one for the sentence, because anyone could conceive of another interpretation, based perhaps on the presence in the dictionary of a formula for 'bed as part of a garden'. There might then be a weak (negation class) overlap between the template matching on to this sense and one matching on to the salt 'as sodium chloride' sense earlier in the sentence. Unless we had a rule to prefer the template pair with the overlap of MAN elements, we would then have two alternative template pairs for the sentence and it would remain ambiguous in isolation from more text (with one interpretation corresponding to sailors at rest and one to gardening activity). The latter pair would eventually be selected if the sentence were embedded in a longer narrative about the soil, and we had a technique for reapplying the sequence rules connecting templates together in a recursive manner, so as to end up with only a single string of templates matching a whole text. In the present system this is done using the Cocke Algorithm: the rules relating templates are applied first to pairs of contiguous templates (those matching fragments adjacent in the original text) and then to non-contiguous pairs. Rules are provided for constructing a single composite item for any pair of templates related in this way, and that item can then participate in rewritten strings. This is all precisely analogous to the rewriting of NP+VP as S in a conventional phrase structure grammar.

3.3. The CSD system of semantic analysis

Production of single bare templates

Before presenting the formal structure of a system it is important to present an outline of what it is all for. This system operates on texts, in the sense of 'text' as an ordered set of fragments. It replaces each fragment of the text by a number of strings of formulae (*frames*) constructed from one formula for each word in the fragment, so one frame is constructed for each combination of such formulae. It then searches each frame and replaces it by a number of templates, or semantic structures.

Thus, schematically one has:

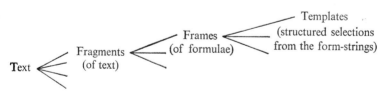

In the course of the initial procedures, therefore, each fragment of text is tagged to a number of templates, and each of those templates is tagged by that procedure to *some particular selection* of the word-senses for the words of a fragment. The purpose of the subsequent procedures is to reduce this 'fragment ambiguity'[21] by specifying a set of strings of these templates, one template corresponding to each fragment, and thus to specify a particular set of word-senses for the words of the whole text. The intuitive goal is that there should be just one string of templates in the set, and hence a unique ambiguity resolution of the text. However, the possibility of a number of independent resolutions cannot be excluded *a priori*.

The outcome of applying these procedures to a text is thus either nothing or a string of sense explanations for the words of the text. In the case where the outcome is nothing, further procedures are defined whereby the system returns, as it were, to the beginning, adjusts one or more dictionary entries in a determinate way, and then tries again to resolve the text. Thus the positive outcome described may be achieved after any one of a finite number of tries. As will be seen, there is a limit to the number of possible tries, and after all the possibilities have been exhausted the system has to conclude that the text cannot be resolved by these methods.

In this section, the formal relations between the items of the system are described. Actual algorithms, either for attaching formal items to text items, or for transforming one kind of formal item into another are not given; these are to be found in the appropriate section of Chapter 4. However, the fact that the system can be expressed formally as a set of phrase structure rules does ensure that it is possible to write the corresponding algorithms, since systems of phrase structure rules of this type are known to be computable.

The presentation to follow will give the phrase structure rules in their generative rather than their analytical format simply because convention has made it easier to discuss them that way round: that is to say in the form,

$$x+D+y \rightarrow x+A+B+C+y$$

rather than,

$$x+A+B+C+y \rightarrow x+D+y$$

However, since the presentation ought to be in the same order as its implementation (described in the subsequent sections of this chapter), I shall give the 'lowest-level' rules first, because they are the ones applied at the first stage of *analysis*. The presentation will thus end up, rather than start, with highest level rules $P \rightarrow \ldots$ where 'P' is a 'paragraph symbol', analogous to the sentence marker 'S' in conventional grammar.

Following what has been said above, one can define:

Def. 10:a *frame*, for a fragment is a string of formulae such that each word of the fragment that has a (non-null) dictionary entry is represented by one and only one formula, and that formula has the same linear order in the frame as the corresponding word in the fragment. Thus the set of all frames consistent with this definition (and with the dictionary entries for the words of the fragment) constitute an initial representation of that fragment in the system.

We can now define the fundamental notion of *template*.

Def. 11 : A *bare template* is any concatenated triple of elements that can be produced by Rules 1–6.

$R1.$ T $\rightarrow$N1+V+N2

$R2.$ V $\rightarrow$BE

$R3.$ N2$\rightarrow$KIND, THIS, GRAIN, THING, SIGN.

$R4.$ N1$\rightarrow$GRAIN, THIS, THING, PART, SIGN, MAN, FOLK, STUFF, WHOLE, WORLD.

$R5(i)$[22] (N1$\rightarrow$THIS)   + . . . + N2$\rightarrow$PART, MAN, FOLK, STUFF, WHOLE, WORLD

  (ii) (N1$\rightarrow$THING) + . . . + N2$\rightarrow$PART, STUFF, WHOLE, WORLD

  (iii) (N1$\rightarrow$PART) + . . . + N2$\rightarrow$PART, STUFF, WHOLE, WORLD

  (iv) (N1$\rightarrow$SIGN) + . . . + N2$\rightarrow$PART, STUFF

  (v) (N1$\rightarrow$MAN) + . . . + N2$\rightarrow$PART, FOLK, STUFF, MAN

  (vi) (N1$\rightarrow$FOLK) + . . . + N2$\rightarrow$PART, MAN, FOLK, STUFF

  (vii) (N1$\rightarrow$STUFF) + . . . + N2$\rightarrow$PART, STUFF, WHOLE, WORLD

 (viii) (N1$\rightarrow$WHOLE) + . . . + N2$\rightarrow$PART, STUFF, WHOLE, WORLD

  (ix) (N1$\rightarrow$WORLD) + . . . + N2$\rightarrow$PART, STUFF, WHOLE, WORLD

  (x) (N1$\rightarrow$GRAIN) + . . . + N2$\rightarrow$PART

$R6(i)$ (N1$\rightarrow$GRAIN)   + . . . + V $\rightarrow$PAIR, DO, CAUSE, CHANGE, HAVE

  (ii) (N1$\rightarrow$THIS)   + . . . + V $\rightarrow$PAIR, DO, CAUSE, CHANGE, HAVE

  (iii) (N1$\rightarrow$THING) + . . . + v $\rightarrow$PAIR, DO, CAUSE, CHANGE, HAVE

  (iv) (N1$\rightarrow$PART) + . . . + V $\rightarrow$PAIR, CAUSE, CHANGE

  (v) (N1$\rightarrow$SIGN) + . . . + V $\rightarrow$PAIR, DO, CAUSE, CHANGE

  (vi) (N1$\rightarrow$MAN) + . . . + V $\rightarrow$HAVE, USE, FEEL, SENSE, CAUSE, CHANGE, PAIR, DO

  (vi) (N1$\rightarrow$FOLK) + . . . + V $\rightarrow$HAVE, USE, FEEL, SENSE, CAUSE, CHANGE, PAIR, DO

    (viii) (N1→STUFF)   + ... + V   →PAIR, DO, CAUSE, CHANGE
    (ix) (N1→WHOLE) + ... + V   →PAIR, CAUSE, CHANGE, DO
    (x) (N1→WORLD) + ... + V   →PAIR, CAUSE, CHANGE

Since none of the rules is recursive, these six main rules allow only only a finite number of bare templates to be produced, all of the form:

Noun (or Substantive) type element
    + Verb type element
        + Noun (or Substantive) or Qualifier type element,
in that left-right order.

    Thus MAN+HAVE+PART can be produced in this way, but MAN+ BE+WORLD cannot.[23] This order is called the *standard order*, and templates are always considered and compared in this order even if located in fragments in other (non-standard) orders, or in 'debilitated forms.'

Defs. 12 and 13: If N1+V+N2 represents the *standard order*, then
                V+N1+V2 and N1+N2+V are non-standard orders,
        and

$$N1+N2$$
$$N1+V$$
$$N1$$
$$V$$

        are *debilitated forms.*

Def. 14: A fragment *matches* with templates if a frame for it contains concatenations of heads (in left-right order) corresponding to any template produced by rules 1–11.

Where:
†R7. THIS→*
R8. B2→*
R9. KIND→*
R10. V→*
[24]R11.(i) N1 + ... + (KIND→*)→KIND + ... + N1
    (ii) (V→*) + ... + KIND→KIND + ... + V
    (iii) N1 + ... + (V→*)→V + ... + N1
    (iv) (V→*) + ... + N2→N2 + ... V

†Where (*) indicates a blank item.

Rules 1–6 produce standard forms of bare template and rules 7–11 produce (by means of deletions and re-orderings) the permitted debilitated and non-standard forms. The latter rules produce actual text items, in the sense of heads (of formulae) to be located in the frames that represent fragments of text directly.

In order to produce templates that can plausibly be interpreted as *meaning structures* for fragments—in that they correspond to the heads and frames for the *correct* word-senses of the fragments—it is necessary that classes of templates be produced in a given order. There are four such ranks of classes, as shown by the following table:

RANK	'TEXT-ITEMS'	STANDARD FORM
I	N1+V	N1+V+THIS
	V+N1	THIS+V+N1
	N1+V+N2	N1+V+N2
	V+N1+N2	N1+V+N2
	N1+N2+V	N1+V+N2
	KIND+N1	N1+BE+KIND
	N1+V+KIND	N1+V+KIND
II	N1+KIND+V	N1+V+KIND
	V+N1+KIND	N1+V+KIND
	N1+KIND	N1+BE+KIND
	N1+N2	N1+BE+KIND
III	V+KIND	THIS+V+KIND
IV	V	THIS+V+THIS
	N1	THIS+BE+N1
	KIND	THIS+V+KIND

Since the rules 1–11 are non-recursive there is no problem about ordering the productions in this way. Apart from the forms given in the table, there are only vacuous cases such as *+*+*.

The above table is intended to make clear the relation between the various standard forms (in the rightmost column) and the corresponding 'item in frames' produced or recognized (middle column). Thus, in the production mode in which we are speaking, the text-

I

items are produced from the standard forms by transposition and deletion. In the analysis mode, whose implementation will be described in the sections below, the text-items are recognized in the rank order shown, and then transposed and augmented with dummy BE and THIS elements so they will be in standard form for further computation.

The actual function of the rank choice is best explained by example, particularly as regards the composition of rank I, since the ranks lower than I clearly consist of 'debilitated forms' and it is intuitively plausible to produce fuller forms first. This ordering is an example of the general rule that enables template matching to do at least the work of a conventional grammar; namely, 'pack the form-string as tightly as possible', or, in other words, produce the fullest possible template.

The presence in rank I of the 'debilitated' form KIND+N1 can be understood by considering, for example, the fragment:

(THE OLD TRANSPORT SYSTEM)

To simplify matters I shall consider only (i) the frame consisting of representations of the appropriate senses of the words in that fragment, and (ii) the frame identical with that one *except that it contains representations of 'old' in its substantive sense ('the old people') and the active (verb) form of 'transport'*. Thus, by the coding system described above, those two frames will contain the following heads, and in the order shown for the words 'the' 'old' 'transport' 'system':

    (i)   [. . . *) . . . KIND) . . . KIND) . . . GRAIN)]
    (ii) [. . . *) . . . FOLK) . . . . . DO) . . . GRAIN)]

Now the rules above generate both

FOLK+DO+GRAIN and KIND+GRAIN in rank I, the latter by transposition and deletion from N1+BE+KIND and KIND+N1. So, if the form KIND+N1 were *not* in the first rank, along with the forms like N1+V+N2, which yields FOLK+DO+GRAIN, then a phrase like this one would never get the correct interpretation, which must contain both the sense of 'transport' whose formula head is KIND ('transport' being an adjective in this fragment), and the sense of 'old' whose formula head is KIND ('old' also being an adjective in this fragment). If KIND+N1 were *not* in rank I then the matching routine would match FOLK+DO+GRAIN on to the fragment via the second frame and never look any further for debilitated forms;

and in doing so it would have got the wrong senses of 'transport' and 'old'.

Consider another fragment that is not in an assertion form, but is again a noun phrase, say, 'the black wizard'. The heads of the appropriate formulae for 'black' and 'wizard' would be KIND and MAN respectively. As there is no verb, a debilitated template of the KIND+ N1 form would match on to these two heads, and that would then be converted into MAN+BE+KIND, which is the intuitively correct interpretation. The dummy verb is added in the way described; and in cases where the first head is the predicate KIND, the order of the two heads is reversed, so as to give the MAN+BE+KIND form. In the 'old transport system' case discussed earlier, the debilitated form KIND+GRAIN will match on to both 'old+system' *and* 'transport+system'. It will be converted twice with the dummy verb to the standard form GRAIN+BE+KIND. That template can be interpreted as 'a structure is of a certain sort', and is a very general representation of both 'a system is old' and 'a system is for transport'. So far then, the fragment 'the old transport system' has been matched with two different bare template types, GRAIN+BE+KIND and FOLK+DO+GRAIN, since they were both in rank I and there is no reason to prefer one to the other at this stage. But it is important to see that the fragment has matched with three bare template-*tokens*, on the other hand. This can be represented schematically as follows, with the matched fragment words under the appropriate formula heads that make up the three template-tokens:

FOLK+DO+GRAIN
old transport system
GRAIN+BE+KIND
system (is) transport
GRAIN+ BE +KIND
system (is) old

It will be clear that the first template-token is a wrong interpretation, for the fragment is not about old people. Yet either of the other two interpretations might be correct, and I shall describe in the section on full templates, below, how a choice is to be made between the two, and why. What is important to see is that at the present stage, of matching on *bare* templates, there is no way of choosing between the above three interpretations, given the way the rank table is set up.

Again, the 'debilitated form' THIS+V+N1 occurs in rank I so as to cope with fragments like (TO TAKE SOME WEIGHT). The frame for the 'appropriate' senses of these words contains the heads [*) . . . DO) . . . KIND) . . . SIGN)]. The appropriate template here is THIS+ DO+SIGN which is a production from THIS+V+N1; THIS, the dummy substantive, being written out as a blank *. But, unless this latter form occurs in rank I of the preference table, only productions like N1+BE+KIND will produce it, via transpositions to SIGN+BE+KIND and KIND+*+SIGN. In that latter case one would have a perfectly acceptable interpretation for a fragment (WEIGHT IS SOME), but an inadequate one for the present fragment since the force of 'take' would be lost. Thus, the production THIS+V+N1 is in rank I along with N1+BE+KIND.

Production of single full templates

Further production rules limit the templates actually produced, and these require the notion of a *full template*.

Def. 15: A *full template* is two triples of formulae such that the heads of the first triple constitute a bare template (in the sense of Def. 11 above) and the second triple can be produced from the first by rules 12–16 below.

Def. 16: The six formulae constituting a full template will be called *text-values*.

The six formulae so defined give content to the corresponding bare template expressed by the heads of three of them. The rules below specify the *other* three in such a way that each of them 'qualifies' one of the three formulae containing bare template heads.

R12. (h→BE, THIS, KIND, HOW, FOLK, GRAIN, MAN, PART, SIGN, STUFF, THING, WHOLE, WORLD, CAUSE, CHANGE, DO, FEEL, HAVE, PAIR, SENSE, PLEASE, WANT, USE) $h \rightarrow F(f_1 ch)$.

That rule simply means that any of the elements constituting a bare template, can, in the bare template, be rewritten as a formula F whose core is c, whose first pair (if any) is f_1, and whose head is the element in question (see Def. 8 above).

R13.   (i) (h→THIS, FOLK, GRAIN, MAN, PART, SIGN, STUFF, THING, WHOLE, WORLD)
$$F(f_1 ch) \rightarrow_1 F^1(f_1 c^1 KIND) + F(f_1 ch).$$

(ii) (h→BE, DO, CAUSE, CHANGE, FEEL, HAVE, PAIR, SENSE, PLEASE, WANT, USE)

$$F(f_1 ch) \rightarrow_1 F^1(f_1 c^1 HOW) + F(f_1 ch)$$

(iii) (h→BE, DO, CAUSE, CHANGE, FEEL, HAVE, PAIR, SENSE, PLEASE, WANT, USE)

$$F(f_1 ch) \rightarrow_1 F^1(f_1 c^1 h) + F(f_1 ch)$$

(iv) (h→BE, DO, CAUSE, CHANGE, FEEL, HAVE, PAIR, SENSE, PLEASE, WANT, USE)

$$F((x \text{ FOR})ch) \rightarrow_1 F^1(f_1 c^1 x) + F((x \text{ FOR})ch)$$

(v) (h→BE, DO, CAUSE, CHANGE, FEEL, HAVE, PAIR, SENSE, PLEASE, WANT, USE)

$$(h \rightarrow KIND)F(f_1 ch) \rightarrow_1 F^1(f_1 c^1 HOW) + F(f_1 ch)$$

(vi) (h→BE, DO, CAUSE, CHANGE, FEEL, HAVE, PAIR, SENSE, PLEASE, WANT, USE)

$$F(f_1 ch) \rightarrow_2 F((\text{THIS KIND}) \text{ THIS THIS}) + F(f_1 ch)$$

R14. $\quad F^1((\text{THIS THIS}) \text{ THIS THIS}) \rightarrow$

Rules R13 i–iv are the rules producing, from a single formula, a pair of formulae such that the first is formally appropriate to the second. Thus, R13 i produces an 'adjective-type' formula before a 'noun-type', R13 ii produces an 'adverb-type' before a 'verb-type' and so on. R13 iv produces a 'noun-type' before a 'verb-type' such that the 'noun-type' is an 'appropriate agent' for that kind of verb.

As will be seen from the subscripts on the rule arrows, the rules fall into two classes (R13 i–v and R13 vi) and the productions from the first class are to be preferred to those from the second. Rule 13 vi merely means that a 'dummy formula' may be produced.

The ultimate production of frames *requires* that R12 and R13 be applied since single elements of the kind that compose bare templates cannot be formulae (see above). R14 expresses the fact that a dummy formula (produced by R13 vi) can be deleted in the production of the frame from the full template.

These rules concern the production of pairs of formulae from the single elements which, in triples, constitute bare templates. When producing a full template from a bare one by the application of Rules R12–R13–R14 the following meta-rule is applied.

R15. Produce preferentially those full templates in which as many elements as possible are developed by the first class of Rules 13, i.e. i–v.

This means 'produce if possible those in which each of the three constituent elements of the bare template is "formally appropriate" to its preceding formula, and the first (noun) formula can be an agent for the second (verb) formula.'

All this exposition has been rather abstract, but it all boils down to the expression of very simple relations that ensure that the template structures produced have as much internal coherence as possible. So, in the analytic mode of operation on actual texts, the rules will prefer those template interpretations that have the greatest such coherence, and reject all others.

The way in which the preference works can be seen, in terms of form-closeness, by following the 'old transport system' example through one more stage. Earlier the bare template procedure had produced three possible bare templates that could be said to match on to the fragment 'The old transport system'. By means of R12 the heads of those bare templates can now be expanded to a formula in each case, and by means of the Rules 13 each of these formulae can be expanded so as to produce another (formally appropriate) formula to the left of itself. Now we look at the (wrong) bare template FOLK+DO+GRAIN for that fragment, and imagine the rules trying to expand it to produce formulae actually present in some frame for the fragment. Apart from the vacuous 'the' there are no more words left in the fragment to provide heads and formulae for such an expansion. Hence that bare template cannot be expanded by those rules into any frame of formulae for the fragment in question.

Now suppose we look at the first bare template-token GRAIN+ BE+KIND, the one that matched on to the heads for the formulae of 'system+(is)+transport'. Again, this cannot be expanded because, although the formula for 'old' precedes the formula for 'transport' in the frames available, it is the adjective (i.e. KIND) formula for 'old' in question in both cases, and Rules 13 do not allow the production of an adjective formula before another adjective formula, which is only to say that an adjective does not qualify an adjective in English.

Now we turn to a fresh token of GRAIN+BE+KIND, the last of the three. This time it matches on to the heads of the formulae for 'system +(is)+old'. In this case it can be expanded because the adjective sense of 'transport' is a proper predecessor, or qualifier in the sense of Rules 13, for the noun (i.e. GRAIN) sense of 'system' in question. So, by expansion we get a representation of more of the fragment, namely 'transport system is old'. Only the last template-token can be expanded, so by Rule 15, it is preferred to the other two bare template-tokens.

In that way, by expanding templates and then choosing the most expanded, the one that can fill the frame as tightly as possible, the CSD system is able to do most of the work of a conventional grammar.

In the final stage of the production of full templates one wants not only those templates whose parts are 'formally appropriate' to each other but also those templates whose parts are most mutually appropriate in regard to content; that is to say, full templates such that the triple of preceding text-values are 'semantically close' to the text-values each respectively precedes. There is no attempt to recreate a syntax-semantic distinction here, between formal- and content-closeness. Those closenesses are merely expressed in terms of a different subset of the elements.

Def. 17:   Two formulae are said to be 'semantically close' if either:

(i) they share a common pair of elements;

(ii) they have one or more of the following elements in common: ONE, COUNT, WORLD, WHOLE, LIFE, LINE, MUST, SELF, SPREAD, TRUE, WRAP, WHEN, WHERE, THINK;

(iii) their cores are such that they are identical, or either is a member of the other in the sense of a list-member, or the left- or right-hand member of either core is a member of the other.

To the above R15 one can now add:

R16. Produce preferentially those full templates such that at least one of the productions from Rule 13 is a pair of semantically close formulae.

It will be seen from the definition of 'semantically close' above that we have now effectively established a partition of the class of semantic elements into three sub-classes. (1) The most general elements, that function as the heads of formulae BE, KIND, THIS, GRAIN, HOW, FOLK, MAN, PART, SIGN, STUFF, THING, WHOLE, WORLD, CAUSE, CHANGE, DO, FEEL, HAVE, PAIR, SENSE, WANT, PLEASE, USE. (2) The most specific elements (not members of (1)) given in Def. 19 above, which are such that two formulae containing one in common may be considered 'semantically close' in some minimal sense. (3)

The remainder of the elements BEAST, CAN, DONE, FOR, FORCE, FROM, IN, LET, LIKE, MAY, MORE, MUCH, PLANT, POINT, SAME, THIS, TO, UP, WILL.

When these Rules 12–16 are employed in an analytic mode, their effect will be to prefer those templates that[25] have 'head formulae' preceded by formulae that are related to them by some degree of semantic closeness. The notion of semantic closeness used here ranges widely from 'being a qualifier' to 'having constituent concepts that are related as contraries'. The last relation is the one expressed above in terms of the negation class of a semantic element.

Rules producing more than one template

The rules given concern the production of single templates. One can now consider the production of a concatenation of such templates.

Def. 18:   A *paragraph-string* is any string of templates, produced from the paragraph symbol P by the rules R17–18 below.

[26]R17: $P \rightarrow T_r + T_s$

R18: $(T_s \rightarrow F_{S1}^1 + F_{S1} + F_{S2}^1 + F_{S2} + F_{S3}^1 + F_{S3})T_S$
$\rightarrow (F_{T1}^1 + F_{T1} + F_{T2}^1 + F_{T2} + F_{T3}^1) + \ldots$
$+ (Fu_1^1 + Fu_1 + F^1u_2 + Fu_2 + F_{U3}^1 + F_{U3})$

Again, we have

Def. 19:   Two full templates $T_F + T_S$ are *semantically close* if (i) (with the above notation for full templates) at *least two* of the following pairs of formulae are such that the head of the second is identical with, or in the negation class of, the first:

$(F_{r1}F_{s1})$, $(F_{r1}F_{s3})$, $(F_{r2}F_{s2})$, $(F_{r3}F_{s1})$, $(F_{r3}F_{s3})$, and
(ii)   either they, or their qualifier formulae, are semantically close. These ten possible directions of connexion between two full templates can be shown schematically as follows:

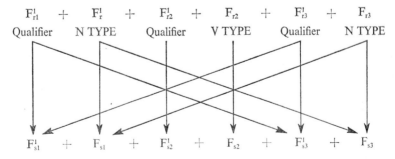

F_{r1}^1	+	F_r^1	+	F_{r2}^1	+	F_{r2}	+	F_{r3}^1	+	F_{r3}
Qualifier		N TYPE		Qualifier		V TYPE		Qualifier		N TYPE

Rule 18 above does not, as might at first appear, involve a self-contradiction. The short-hand form of rule writing is now being extended to mean that, T_s having been rewritten as $F_{s1}^1 + \text{——} + F_{s3}$, then that latter form may be rewritten as . . . , etc.

This rule I shall call the expansion-concatenation rule, since it specifies (1) the two forms with which a single full template can be replaced or rewritten; namely, those produced by R18, the first containing two of the three main formulae that make up the rewritten template, and the second produced template containing the third main formula (this is the expansion of one into two); (2) there lation of 'semantic closeness' between the two, possibly non-contiguous, templates produced.

The expansion-concatenation rule can be applied recursively to the initial productions from P (Rule 17), and thus at any stage in this process a *paragraph-string* of templates is produced, in the sense of Def. 18 above.

At any point the string can be considered terminal and with the aid of the dictionary of words and sense-pairs the paragraph-string of templates can be converted to a string of frames and so to a text (Def. 9 above). This procedure is analogous to the introduction of the word lexicon in any standard phrase structure grammar.

The following supplementary rule is applied at the terminal string level:

R19: Prefer those paragraph-strings in which the final applications of the 'expansion-concatenation' rule (Rule 18) are productions of contiguous templates.

The set of production rules thus defined will produce paragraph-sequents or strings of full templates which can finally (terminally) have frames 'hung' upon them and so produce texts of words whose respective senses are specified by the production itself. However, the *paragraph representations* are the nested structures of full templates that can be associated with each such derived sequent. None of these sequents is unstructured: as in the case of the productions used in Chapter 2 above to illustrate generative grammars, it will be possible to associate each such derived sequent with either a tree or parenthesis (bracket) structure which expresses the order of derivation of that sequent from the initial symbol P. In the case of derivations using the rules of discontinuous substituents it is necessary to use a subscript notation so as to make unambiguous the relation of the derivation order to the final internal order of the sequent.

As specified above, the rules leave completely free the *order* in which the members of a string are to be developed, whether right- or left-handedly, and whether continuously or discontinuously (apart from the terminal level, restricted by Rule 19). I can now give a definition of *resolution*: a text is *resolved* by the given set of rules if there is one and only one derivation producing a sequent of words identical to the text.

Although I have set out this system of semantic analysis in what one may call the production mode, it must in fact be used in the analytic mode. That is to say, texts will be provided and the system will be run, as it were, backwards to see if the paragraph symbol can be reached. This is analogous to the operation of systems of syntax analysis described in Chapter 2 above. There is no theoretical problem about doing that since systems of this sort are decidable and so the problem of running this system in the analytic mode is analogous to that of seeing whether or not a formula in the propositional calculus is a logical truth by means of truth tables. More precisely, the analytical method is that of constructing trees by means of the 'inference rules' given above in the way usually associated with Gentzen's formulation of the predicate calculus. What is actually done (see Chapter 4 for detailed discussion) is to replace a string of text words by all possible sequents of formulae which satisfy Rules 13 and 14, and then constructing trees of sequents 'above' each of them by recursive applications of rules of types 1–12 in an attempt to reach P, the top of the tree. If any sequent of formulae can be 'parsed' in this way then it is by definition a resolution of the text.

3.4. Sense construction

It is always possible that, for a given text and set of rules, no sequence of formulae can be parsed so as to reach the point P, i.e. there is no resolution. This can happen for a number of reasons of course, for example, the system of resolution rules may not be up to the job. However, if one assumes that this is not the trouble a number of possibilities remain. Here are two:

1 The dictionary maker has left some important sense of a text word (or words) out of the semantic dictionary.
2 The text is such that some word (or words) in it are being used in

an unusual or idiosyncratic sense, and one which a dictionary maker might well not have known about.

In case (1) it is highly unlikely that a system like the present one could offer any help. To see this difficulty in the case of *major* senses of words, one has only to remember how difficult it is to understand a sentence in a foreign language when it contains a word in a major sense of which one is ignorant. A tourist asking the way in Italy and being asked in return if he has a *'pianta'* will be very puzzled if he knows that it means 'plant' but doesn't know it means 'map' as well!

So the question remains whether anything can be done in cases of unusual or idiosyncratic word use. One is encouraged to think that something can be done by the well-evidenced ability of human beings to *make sense* of what they are reading in such situations. What they actually do in successful situations would be described in ordinary language as *'constructing a sense* from the context or surrounding text'. One can put the essential point as follows: 'constructing a sense' will be the intuitively correct thing to do provided that one is dealing with a situation of 'extraordinary use'. By 'extraordinary use' I mean language used creatively, in a novel way, so as to extend the range of uses of one or more of its constituent words. Extraordinary use is, however, natural in the sense that writers and speakers of a language use it in this way all the time. Any theory of semantics should therefore have some explanation of this phenomenon built into it. I think this is done in the present one, by the notion of the metarule that adds a rule 'at the lower level' so as to construct a new sense for some word or words in the semantic dictionary. This I called the *Expand* procedure in Chapter 1.

There is another, perhaps more important, reason for introducing some such facility into a semantic theory as early as possible, or at least into any semantic theory that seeks to choose among pre-assigned dictionary senses of words. For, only if there is some possible move open to us when these routines fail is one justified in presenting a model for disambiguation at all. That is, to be convincing, a model for disambiguation should be a self-extending one. This is because everyone knows that *a word can be applied in a particular text in such a way as to produce not nonsense but rather a totally new sense of the word.* That is what I called 'extraordinary use' of language. It is quite different from what Chomsky means when he talks about our ability to recognize sentences we have never seen before. I have in all probability never before produced or encountered 'Five thousand and nine plus eleven makes five thousand and twenty'. Yet as Chomsky rightly says, I can produce it and would recognize it and understand it if someone presented it to me for the first time. That is not the kind of novelty I mean, but rather our ability to understand 'A grief ago' within the context of Dylan Thomas' poem (Putnam's example). I think this difference can be understood in terms of Wittgenstein's distinction between the 'use' and 'application' of words, for it is in connexion with the latter notion that he speaks of 'introducing a piece into the language it wasn't yet using' [308].

There is another reason why a system possessing such a feature, and, to the best of my knowledge no other system has it, is a good candidate for explaining the use of words in natural language. It concerns the fact that speakers and writers have a very strong belief that if *any* set of rules for the use of language were presented to them they, or someone, could come up with something that broke the rules but was indubitably language. It is as if (this is a figure of Wittgenstein's) *given actual boundaries* one can always step over them, or conceive of them being stepped over, hence talk of boundaries in the ordinary sense is not appropriate. Bennett puts what seems to be the same point when he writes [26, p. 17] '. . . the senses of words cannot be laid down in a foolproof fashion in a rule, because the rule itself is a vital item whose own use is vulnerable to falsification, in just the same way if not to the same degree as the word uses it regulates.' I argued in Chapter 2 above that 'falsification' is not the most appropriate way to talk about the meanings of words, but I would agree with this passage of Bennett's that 'rule' is not wholly appropriate either. The point about Expand is that it is not a rule on the same level as the other rules of the system; it is a metarule, and might be part of a hierarchy of such rules. I think that the operation of this metarule is consistent with the way human beings behave when confronted with a text containing a word used in a sense that they have never encountered before. They try to see what, if anything, the text means, and only then, not being able to interpret it, do they go on to remarks about what it 'might mean'.

In so far then as such extension of word-sense is not a sport, or freak misuse, one might explain it in terms of the resolution rules of the present system by allowing them in certain cases to *construct* a sense for a word, and in a non-arbitrary manner, until a sense was constructed which permitted a chain of templates to represent the whole paragraph containing the words. So what is done is to construct, or find, a formula such that the rules *will work*, and in this way to cope with the well-known, but little-understood, phenomenon of new senses of words. Such a procedure provides something else that can be done if the resolution routines fail, and so it follows that all the resolution procedures are, to that degree, provisional ones.

All this requires one further assumption: that the upper limit to the length of text required to resolve an ambiguity is of the same order as the length of text required to establish a new word-sense. In both cases a paragraph (in the ordinary type-setter's sense) is assumed to be sufficient. I want to distinguish any attempt to get the present system to expand its word-dictionary from another, somewhat related, enterprise. I have in mind the work that has been done recently on constructing rules that express the way in which words in a dictionary acquire a new sense-entry. These rules would operate on words and their dictionary entries only, that is to say, they would have no access to text of any sort. Givòn gives an example of a sense-extension of this kind for the word 'grain' which he puts informally as follows [101, p. 8]:

'a single grain→"grains in the mass"'. Examples[27] of the second case would be:

(1) 'grain is grains in the mass',
(2) 'the robber stole two hundred pounds of grain'.

This second use of 'grain' is dated later than the first in the Oxford English Dictionary and can be presumed to have been novel to a reader at some time. A 'test' of rules of this sort would be if they suggested extensions like the above such that one was able to construct sentences like (1) and (2) from other sentences. One might then say that rules that produced (1) established both (1) and (2) as meaningful.

I have gone into this example in detail in order to show by contrast that this is not the paradigm of sense-extension that I have in mind in the present section. Consider, for example, the tenth paragraph analysed in the experiments of Chapter 4 below. As I shall show the word 'substance' (or rather the German word '*Substanz*') is used there by Wittgenstein in two quite different senses. In the first sense it means roughly, 'all the objects that there are' and, in the second, 'all the facts, or structurings of objects, that there are'. This second sense is the one borne by the word 'world' throughout Wittgenstein's *Tractatus*. This is a quite different kind of sense-extension from the 'grain' example mentioned earlier.

The difference lies in the fact that the extended sense given to, in this case, 'substance', is identical with a sense of some other word in the passage, in this case 'world', and that extended sense could not, in any plausible way have been derived from an existing dictionary entry for 'substance' alone (the method of Givòn). To say this is not to point to any formal difference, of course, over and above a difference in method. But, and I think this does point tentatively to a formal difference, the sentences *established as meaningful* by this latter method will not be of the same kind as (1) and (2). For example, the (3) established analogously to (1) would be (3) '*substance is (the) world*'. Now, (1) and (2) are unambiguous as they stand, in isolation, but this (3) (as with any corresponding sentence (4) from the paragraph which contains the word 'substance') would be ambiguous, since it relies upon the context of the paragraph for the resolution of 'world'. So, one might say, in this case (3) *is established as meaningful only with respect to some paragraph, or explicatory context*.

I have jumped ahead a little in the last paragraph and have presumed upon a notion of what it is to 'establish something as meaningful'. However, I think that the example is clear as it stands, and in any case the notion will be discussed at considerable length in Chapter 4 below.

The question that now arises is, what could a system of the kind described here do in those cases where no resolution is produced because the 'semantic parsing' does not reach the paragraph point P? Answering the question requires one further observation; namely that the semantic dictionary entries themselves can also be considered as phrase structure rules. For example, if F_n is a formula and α_p is some text-word for which F_n is a formula then $F_n \rightarrow \alpha_p$ is one rule of the productive system. These would be the rules to be operated last in the productive mode. They would be operated in procedures that I referred to figuratively earlier when I spoke of 'hanging frames of sense pairs on to the produced sequents'. Final rules like $F_n \rightarrow \alpha_p$ would then produce *text-words*. That particular rule would mean that there was in the dictionary a sense-pair composed of the formula F_n and some sense description of the word α_p.

Now, let us assume that we have an Expand *algorithm* having the following property: it locates the parsing which, although unsuccessful, was the one which *came nearest* to reaching the top of the tree P; it also produces a *new* rule of the above type (dictionary rules) $F_n \to \alpha_p$, where α_p is a word in the text and there is already a rule $F_n \to \alpha_q$ in the system such that α_q is also a word of the particular text. The natural way of expressing this latter facility is that Expand finds word α_p in the text and suggests adding to its dictionary entry one of the senses of the word α_q. That is, it suggests that, in this text, word α_p has one of the senses of word α_q. One can then add this *new rule* $F_n \to \alpha_p$ to the system, producing a new system, and, as it were, try again with the parsing which was the 'best effort' to see if P can be reached. The 'best effort' and the new rule are related in that it was from the best parsing that the Expand algorithm derived the new rule. One can further assume that if there is no resolution this time then the Expand algorithm can be recursively reapplied.

I shall refer to this Expand algorithm again below, since it is of some importance that this system can enlarge itself in situations of initial failure. I shall now offer an amended definition of word-sense *resolution* as follows: a text is *resolved* by a given set of rules if there is one and only one derivation producing a sequent of words identical to the text, or if such a result is produced by *any* set of rules recursively defined by the initial set of rules and the Expand algorithm.

There is no intended suggestion that the CSD system I have described is *the* linguistic system for analysing natural language. Contemporary philosophy, and the older linguistics, should have by now inhibited the search for any such Grail. It is simply a system designed to do a limited job, and based upon a number of obvious notions that have to some extent been lost to the sight of much contemporary linguistics. Nor is it to be taken as any kind of attack on the notion of 'syntax' as currently understood. I have called it 'semantics' in a fairly carefully defined sense, but it does not matter at all if someone chooses to say that it is all syntax really. For, as I pointed out in Chapter 2, there is already available within formal logic a perfectly well-defined sense of 'syntax', namely 'any formal manipulation upon a finite set of symbols', in which sense any adequately defined system is, by definition, syntax.

4 Practical semantic experiments

'The Pupils at his Command took each of them hold of an
Iron Handle, whereof there were Forty fixed round the Edges
of the Frame; and giving them a sudden Turn, the whole
Disposition of the Words was entirely changed. . . . Six Hours
a Day the young Students were employed in this Labour; and
the Professor shewed me several Volumes in Folio already
collected, of broken Sentences, which he intended to piece
together; and out of those rich Materials to give the World a
compleat Body of all the Arts and Sciences.'

Swift, *A Voyage to Laputa*

This chapter presents and applies algorithms intended to investigate
fundamental semantic structure in text, and more particularly to
resolve its word-sense ambiguity. I shall assume for this purpose
that, given a text and the kind of listing of senses that a dictionary
gives, it is *in general* possible to decide of each word occurrence in
which of those dictionary senses it is being used. If that is so, then
the results printed out by a resolution programme in a computer
can be assessed by someone quite unfamiliar with both the linguistic
system employed and the detailed manner of its programming.

The bulk of this section describes the implementation (in the
language LISP 1.5) of a method of semantic analysis, designed to
resolve the word-sense ambiguity of paragraph length texts. Ten

texts are analysed; the first five I shall call data texts, in that information gained from their analysis is used in the analysis of the other five, experimental, texts. The first five texts are from newspaper editorials. The sscond five are well-known passages of metaphysical argument.

I shall assume that the choice of experimental texts requires no particular defence, and that their structure is of as much inherent interest as that of any other text. They were, of course, the target of the philosophers of logical syntax discussed in Chapter 2 above. In a sense one could say that the whole purpose behind the construction of logical syntax was to show that texts like these experimental ones were meaningless.

I should say something about the list processing language LISP 1.5. John McCarthy developed the language as a version of Church's lambda-calculus. The main feature of the language [see 193] is that it is not, as all earlier programming languages are, a sequence of instructions. A 'programme' in LISP consists of a set of definitions of functions, and then the provision of some function(s) with appropriate arguments. The computation then consists in determining the corresponding *values* of the functions. It is an extremely powerful and subtle logical system, and most of the shorter functions one defines in use are strongly recursive, in the sense of being self-naming (their definitions contain their own names).[1]

Programme files are not programmes in the usual sense, then, but definitions of functions. The corresponding 'programme' is then only a line or so long and provides some 'top-level' function of a complex hierarchy with an argument, or arguments. I sometimes refer to an EVALQUOTE MODE. This is a feature of an *on-line* LISP system like the one in use at Systems Development Corporation and is the mode of the programme system in which functions can be evaluated (definitions, too, have the form of functions: DEFINE is just another function in the system). EVALQUOTE MODE is to be distinguished from other modes in which the 'programmes' are treated, not as functions, but as strings of characters so that they can be edited. A LISP programme cannot be edited in the way a conventional programme can, simply on the basis of numbered commands, since there are no commands to number, but only a deeply nested structure.

K

4.1 The texts

Ten paragraph-length texts were chosen for analysis: the first five were from editorials in randomly chosen copies of *The Times*; the other five were paragraphs from the works of five philosophers: Descartes, Leibniz, Hume, Spinoza, and Wittgenstein. The texts are stored on a LISP file TEXTS; each paragraph being written as a list of sentences (each sentence being itself a list) and set as the value of a symbol PARA $\#$ where $\#$ is a number from 1 to 10. The paragraphs are stored as they appeared in their original setting, except that colons and semi-colons are omitted (there being no character for them in LISP), and so are numbered references occurring in two of the texts (Spinoza and Wittgenstein). Also, some ten words have been omitted from the Spinoza text: they constituted a periphrasis in the middle of the passage which added nothing at all to its sense.

Why were these two kinds of texts chosen? The editorial texts were chosen because the editorials of that particular newspaper are often considered to be models of coherent contemporary style. It seemed reasonable, therefore, to use them as *data texts*: in that they could be assumed to resolve their word-sense ambiguity within the space of a paragraph. Relations between the basic classifiers, or markers, of the present system, set up from these data texts, are then used in the first attempt to resolve the other five, *experimental*, texts.

The newspaper texts were as follows:

PARA 1   *The Times, Monday 14 November 1966*
Britain's transport system and with it the travelling public's
habits are changing. It is the old permanent way which is once
more emerging as the pacemaker. Airlines have lately been
losing internal traffic to the modernized railways. Railways are
at last beginning to take some cars off the congested systems
to take the weight off both. If the new ideas are pressed forward,
the pattern of commuter movement and dormitory-area
congestion could be changed.

PARA 2   *The Times, Tuesday 15 November 1966*
The main reasons for the uncertainty are clear enough. The
separation of powers means that President and Congress are
elected separately. The federal structure of the huge country

means that between presidential elections the local party organizations more or less go their own way. Both parties are in fact coalitions of interests and regions and the only effective leader of either is an elected President. Losing presidential candidates find themselves without any office at all.

PARA 3   *The Times, Monday 28 November 1966*
Yesterday's complaints from members of the National Union of Students about conditions in teacher training colleges are characteristic of a growing mood of unconsidered carping. Colleges of education are needed to train teachers in greater numbers in order to reduce the size of classes, and so to improve the standards of the state education system.
Education has taken a growing share of national resources during the past five years, and the number of university places and places in training colleges has steadily risen. This represents progress, of a sort.

PARA 4   *The Times, Saturday 26 November 1966*
On one thing all shades of opinion can unite: the need for sustained pathological research, so that the fishery authorities may know more about what it is they have to cope with. The threat seems to dictate activity on their part. Yet, when the aetiology of the disease is so obscure, their activity may be misdirected. Amid so much uncertainty fishermen are haunted by the history of the terrible plague that settled on the salmon rivers of Scotland in the last decades of the nineteenth century.

PARA 5   *The Times, Tuesday 29 November 1966*
This is as far as exemption can go if a policy of restraint for the general body of citizens is to remain credible. It is, moreover, particularly important that the lower paid wage earners should not have grounds to suspect that better-off salary earners are escaping.

In setting up a semantic dictionary for the words of the ten texts, the first step was to obtain an alphabetical concordance for the texts with existing IBM 360 programmes. The whole dictionary, in alphabetical order, was then written on, and spread over, four LISP files, DIC1 to DIC4. Each file consists of a single DEFLIST function which puts the dictionary entry for each word on the property list for that word. In every case the dictionary entry is stored on the property list for 'its' word under the marker 'IDIC'.

Here, by the way of example, are the dictionary entries for two contiguous words, 'compass' and 'complaints':

(COMPASS

((((((THIS POINT)TO)SIGN)THING)(COMPASS AS INSTRUMENT POINTING
NORTH))

((COUNT DO)(COMPASS AS TO MEASURE NUMERICALLY))))
(COMPLAINTS

((((MAN FOR)((NOTPLEASE BE)SIGN))(COMPLAINTS AS EXPRESSIONS OF
DISPLEASURE))))

From the definitions of Chapter 3 above it follows that the information stored on the property list of a dictionary entry word is a list of pairs, each member of which consists of a left-hand member (a semantic formula such as ((((THIS POINT)TO)SIGN)THING)), and a right-hand member (a sense description of the meaning of the corresponding formula, such as (COMPASS AS INSTRUMENT POINTING NORTH)). Each such pair corresponds to one *sense* of the dictionary entry word. The sense description (right-hand member of pair) serves to explain to the operator, in ordinary language print-out, which particular sense of the word is being operated on, or has been chosen by the system, at any given stage of the procedure. Thus I assume, what was argued for in Chapter 3 above, that the occurrences (or tokens) of a word in a written language can be classified by some procedure into *sense classes*: classes of occurrences such that each class corresponds to one sense of that word.

Sample of the semantic dictionary in LISP (*in its initial form, before any Sense Construction*).

(EXTENDED (((((WHERE STUFF) IN) KIND)
    (EXTENDED AS BEING IN SPACE))
  ((((MORE LINE) (BE CAUSE)) KIND) (EXTENDED AS LENGTHENED))))
(EXTENSION (((((WHERE STUFF) IN) SIGN)
  (EXTENSION AS THE BEING IN SPACE))))
(FACULTY ((((THINK DO) (GRAIN SIGN)) (FAULTY AS DISPOSITION))))
(FASHION ((((DO HOW) GRAIN) (FASHION AS MANNER IN WHICH))))
(FEDERAL ((((WORLD PART) (PAIR KIND))
  (FEDERAL AS OF A GEOGRAPHICAL ENTITY MADE UP OF PARTS))))

(FIGURE ((((WHERE SPREAD) (LINE GRAIN))
  (FIGURE AS THE FORM OF SOMETHING IN SPACE))
  (((MAN FOR) ((THINK THING) USE)) (FIGURE AS THINK))
  (((COUNT SIGN) (LINE SIGN)) (FIGURE AS NUMERICAL CHARACTER))))
(FIND ((((MAN FOR) (((MAN FROM) THING) SENSE))
  (FIND AS DETECT))))
(FIRST (((((COUNT SIGN) KIND) (FIRST AS INITIAL))
  ((UP KIND) (FIRST AS IMPORTANT))))
(FISHERMEN ((((BEAST USE) FOLK)
  (FISHERMEN AS THOSE WHO CATCH FISH))))
(FISHERY ((((BEAST USE) KIND) (FISHERY AS TO DO WITH FISH))))
(FIVE (((COUNT KIND) (FIVE AS HAVING IN NUMBER))
  ((COUNT SIGN) (FIVE AS NUMBER))))
(FIXED ((((NOTCHANGE KIND) (FIXED AS NOT ALTERING))
  (((MAN FOR) ((((WHERE POINT) NOTCHANGE) THING) (BE CAUSE)))
  (FIXED AS PLACED IN A GIVEN POSITION))))
(FLEXIBLE ((((((WHERE SPREAD) CHANGE) CAN) KIND)
  (FLEXIBLE AS ABLE TO HAVE ITS SHAPE CHANGED))))
(FORMED (((((BE CAUSE) LET) KIND)
  (FORMED AS MADE THE WAY IT IS))))
(FORM (((BE CAUSE)
    (FORM AS CAUSING SOMETHING TO BE THE WAY IT IS))
    ((((THINK STUFF) WANT) FOLK) (FORM AS A CLASS OF SCHOLARS))
    (((((THIS HOW) BE) CAUSE) SIGN)
    (FORM AS WHAT CAUSES SOMETHING TO BE THE WAY IT IS))
    ((LINE GRAIN) (FORM AS OUTLINE))))
(FOR (((FOR BE) (FOR AS TO BE ASSIGNED TO))))
(FORWARD ((((((THIS WHERE) FROM) (WHERE CHANGE)) HOW)
    (FORWARD AS IN A MANNER AWAY FROM SPEAKER))
    (((((THIS WHERE) FROM) (WHERE CHANGE)) KIND)
    (FORWARD AS IN A DIRECTION AWAY FROM THE SPEAKER))))
(FREQUENTLY ((((MUCH WHEN) HOW) (FREQUENTLY AS OFTEN))))
(FROM (((FROM DO) (FROM AS AWAY))))
(FURTHERMORE ((NIL NIL)))
(GENERAL (((WHOLE KIND) (GENERAL AS NOT SPECIFIC))
  (((MUCH UP) MAN) (GENERAL AS HIGH RANKING OFFICER))))
(GOD ((((MUCH UP) MAN) (GOD AS A SUPERHUMAN PERSON))
  ((WHOLE WORLD) (GOD AS EVERYTHING THAT THERE IS))))
(GO (((WHERE CHANGE) (GO AS TO MOVE IN SPACE))))
(GREATER (((MORE KIND) (GREATER AS LARGER))))

(GROUNDS (((MUCH ((THINK CAUSE) SIGN)) (GROUNDS AS REASONS))
   ((MUCH (WORLD PART)) (GROUNDS AS GARDENS))))
(GROWING ((((MORE BE) KIND) (GROWING AS GETTING BIGGER))))
(HABITS (((MUCH (((MAN FOR) (MUCH DO)) GRAIN))
   (HABITS AS REPEATED ACTIVITIES))))
(HAD (((DONE HAVE) (HAD AS POSSESSED))))
(HAS (((HAVE HAVE) (HAS AS POSSESSES))
   ((THIS BE) (HAS AS IS OR HAS THE PROPERTY))))
(HAUNTED (((((MAN FOR) (NOTPLEASE FEEL)) KIND)
   (HAUNTED AS CAUSING PEOPLE TO FEEL UNEASY))))

That seems a generally acceptable assumption, and I shall not attempt to specify such a procedure, but will simply indicate the existence of standard dictionaries which do in fact classify the occurrences of words into sense classes in just such a way.

Some words, let us call them markers, are not assigned semantic codings in the present dictionary at all. Important as such words are logically and grammatically, it is difficult to assign any *semantic* content to them. They are entered in the dictionary as null entries, thus: (ALTHOUGH((())))). (A list of them is given as Appendix iii of [298].) Prepositions, too, are a difficult matter for a coding of this sort. Here they have been coded so as to facilitate the way in which later stages of the present analysis attach templates, or meaning structures, to fragments of text which are single prepositional phrases. Prepositions are each given a single coding in the dictionary;[2] that is, they are considered to be unambiguous words. That is, of course, an enormous over-simplification and a glance at any dictionary shows that it is not wholly realistic. However, in this pilot study I shall be concerned with the ambiguities of more 'contentful' words. Other research suggests that the ambiguity of prepositions can be dealt with by particular methods quite different from the general ones proposed here [Robison, 248].

The CSD system makes use of a number of 'secretarial functions', operating directly on the dictionary:

REPORT takes a word name as its argument and returns a list of the sense explanations present in the dictionary entry for the word at the time of application. It enables an operator to check up on how much of a word's meaning is covered by the dictionary at any given moment.

CHEQSUP takes no arguments and is called whenever a paragraph is read. It searches the paragraph and returns any word characters in it that are not in the dictionary. Its replies (at a teletypewriter in this case) are of the form ((xxxx NOT IN DICTIONARY)(OTHERWISE SET)). This function is important when, for example, a designated phrase like 'as far as' has been typed in as more than one character, or vice versa. It also reports any encounter with free NOT elements, which should only occur in combination with other elements, and with any dictionary formula which is not a well-formed formula (usually because its head is not one of the 'proper' elements).

MAKEDIC is a function that takes the name of a *paragraph* as its argument (such as PARA6). It returns NIL (the LISP symbol for the empty list) as its value, but also constructs a dictionary for the named paragraph from the main dictionaries, and puts this new dictionary on the list of files under the file name MADEDIC. It is important to be able to make dictionaries for individual paragraphs in this way, because of the storage problem in real machines. If the whole main dictionary, plus texts and, say, one longish file o operating functions, are read into the store and compiled, then there would be very little storage left for subsequent computation in most contemporary computers.

Thus it is often necessary to operate on only a single paragraph and its associated dictionary. The important point about MAKEDIC is not that it constructs such a dictionary, but that the dictionary produced is not simply compiled code that must be further operated on at once, or printed out. The new dictionary is *transferred to the list of current files* and so can be stored on tape and run in alone without the main dictionaries.

ADDIC takes as its arguments a natural language word and a sense-pair. It adds the sense-pair to the end of existing dictionary entry for the natural language word: DELDIC is the corresponding function that takes as its arguments a natural language word and a sense description. It deletes, from the entry for the word, the sense-pair that contains that sense description.

Functions operating directly on the texts

A set of preliminary functions break each input sentence up into substrings of words, and, in certain circumstances, reform discontinuous substrings into whole strings. The output from this whole process is a sentence in the form of a list of strings each of which (if it is not a single word) is either an elementary sentence, a complex noun phrase, or a clause introduced by a marker (such as a preposition). Thus, for example, the first of the chosen texts is returned as follows from a function PARA which applies the set of functions to all the sentences of a paragraph in turn, and returns the paragraph as a single list of such substrings, thus obliterating the original sentence boundaries.

((BRITAINS TRANSPORT SYSTEMS ARE CHANGING)
(AND)
(WITH IT THE TRAVELLING PUBLICS HABITS)
(IT IS THE OLD PERMANENT WAY)
(WHICH IS ONCEMORE EMERGING)
(AS THE PACEMAKER)
(AIRLINES HAVE LATELY BEEN LOSING TRAFFIC)
(TO MODERNIZED RAILWAYS)
(RAILWAYS ARE AT LAST BEGINNING TO TAKE SOME CARS)
(OFF THE CONGESTED SYSTEMS TO TAKE THE WEIGHT)
(OFF BOTH)
(IF THE NEW IDEAS ARE PRESSED FORWARD)
(COMMA THE PATTERN OF COMMUTER MOVEMENT AND DORMITORY AREA
CONGESTION COULD BE CHANGED)   )

This is a perfectly general procedure, designed to transform paragraphs containing realistically complex sentences into a string of entities each as much like an intuitive notion of 'elementary proposition' as possible.

It can be seen from the example paragraph above that the functions described do not simply segment the sentence strings in a linear manner. They also 'take out' certain kinds of clause from within a sentence and append them as separate substrings. Thus the sentence 'the dog that bit the man has been shot' would be output by PARA as ((the dog has been shot)(that bit the man)), (cf. first sentence of output paragraph above). However, and by way of contrast to that, a clause like 'President and Congress are elected separately' is *not* segmented as ((President are elected separately)(and Congress)), but is left as it is. The reason for this output must be explained with reference to the purpose for which this fragmentation of the paragraphs is undertaken. The aim of later procedures is to match the meaning structures, or templates, with each fragment in turn. Now among the templates matching with the string 'President and Congress are elected separately' will be one matching with the semantic formulae for President+are+elected, and another one matching the codings for Congress+are+elected; and it will be clear that it would not have been possible to match both of these templates with the formulae if the whole string had been cut up in the above manner as ((President are elected separately)(and Congress)).[3] Whereas, in the case of the dog and the man, it seems reasonable to match templates to the formulae for dog+been+shot and for that+bit+man, and the fragmentation proposed puts these wordstrings into different fragments.

As it will be clear from the output, the fragmentation functions operate with (lists of) marker words[4] which, in general, begin new fragments. The four lists used are given in Appendix iii of [298]. The same functions also contain subfunctions which have access to the dictionary of formulae for the words of the texts. These subfunctions inspect the heads of the formulae for any given word, and, as will be clear from the account of formulae given in Chapter 3 above, so obtain information roughly analogous to 'part of speech' information. However, apart from the four word lists and the dictionary of formulae, there is no other, specifically grammatical information supplied to the functions.

What I have said so far about the contents of the fragmentation functions can be summarized as follows: the top-level functions, with the aid of a list of markers as fragment-openers, define a recursive notion of fragment. However, as well as the list of opener-markers, the functions also have access to the formulae for the words of the text (i.e. the dictionary), and these are sufficient to define conditions for ending fragments.[5]

The fragmented paragraphs are not passed directly to the template matching functions, but are first processed by a set of functions whose 'top-level' member is REORDER.

REORDER inspects the fragmented output for a paragraph and seeks for entities like qualifying phrases beginning with 'of' or 'for'. It takes such phrases and places them before the noun they qualify and then returns the fragments. The REORDER function also moves adverbs to a position before the verb they qualify, and infinitive forms of verbs to a position before the verb on which they depend. Only after this rearrangement is a fragment handed on to the template matching functions. The reason for this permutation is that when a template match has been made with a fragment, the subsequent routines seek for the qualifiers of a noun or verb *only to the left of it*. Thus a phrase like 'A book of rules' goes to the matching routine as 'A (of rules) book,[6] just as the phrase 'A red book' would.

After all these processes a text is ready to be passed on to the real analysis procedures. The first text is in the following list form at this stage:

((BRITAINS TRANSPORT SYSTEM ARE CHANGING)
  (WITH IT THE TRAVELLING PUBLICS HABITS)
  (IT IS THE OLD PERMANENT WAY)
  (WHICH ONCEMORE IS EMERGING)
  (AS THE PACEMAKER)
  (AIRLINES LATELY HAVE BEEN LOSING TRAFFIC)
  (TO MODERNIZED RAILWAYS)
  (RAILWAYS AT LAST ARE BEGINNING)
  (TO TAKE SOME CARS)
  (OFF THE CONGESTED SYSTEMS TO TAKE THE WEIGHT)
  (IF THE NEW IDEAS ARE FORWARD PRESSED)
  (COMMA THE OF COMMUTER MOVEMENT AND DORMITORYAREA
    CONGESTION FO PATTERN COULD BE CHANGED))

Two more definitions are appropriate at this point:

Def. 20: a *fragment* is any substring of a sentence produced by the algorithms just described.

Def. 21: a *text* is any string of fragments, regardless of whether or not such a string corresponds to a whole number of sentences.

Two final points should be made: firstly that the fragmentation procedure is in no way *essential* to the system of semantic analysis, it is a convenience merely. It would be possible, for example, simply to reassign the fragment boundaries if the results of the analysis were unsatisfactory to the degree of absurdity. It would even be possible in theory to dispense with fragment boundaries altogether and to match the templates sequentially on to the whole, coded, but unfragmented, text. Secondly, there have been other attempts, quite independent of the present one, to segment text into units of this length for similar purposes, using textual information of a quite different sort, for example [Alt and Rhodes, 2].

4.2 The first template matching cycle

Matching bare templates on to fragments

This subsection describes the matching of the fragments of the ten paragraphs with the bare templates produced by Rules 1–6 (see Chapter 3 above). As I explained earlier, output from applying those rules is only preliminary to the output from the full template, or PICKUP cycles, where the PICKUP output is that obtained from applying all the rules given above. This intermediate output, then, is printed out for the first five texts (the experimental texts), only in order that relations between the bare templates which are the 'proper' ones for their fragments can be made to yield 'negation classes' inductively. The classes so obtained are then used as data in the course of subsequent computation. How this is done will be explained at the appropriate point below.

TEMPO is the main matching function: it examines in turn all the frames of sense-pairs for a fragment, and so on for all the fragments of a paragraph. It takes as its argument a frame, or string of semantic formulae, one for each of the words in a fragment under examination. The function FRAMELIS passes to TEMPO each such combination of semantic formulae in turn. TEMPO then scans each such combination in turn, starting with the string comprising all the first (main) senses of the words in the fragment. If N denotes a substantive-(noun)type semantic element, and V denotes a verb-type semantic element, then TEMPO can be thought of as searching for triplets of such elements in the order of preference given above (in that if it finds any of type I, it doesn't look for any of types II, III, IV, V or VI and so on). Each type of template given in the table above, is 'collected' by a different free variable SEARCH $\#$ (where $\#$ ranges from 1 to 6) within the function SEARCHER which examines successive CDRs[7] of every frame. If TEMPO finds nothing till it reaches the 'debilitated' N+N form, it replaces the N+N it finds by N+BE+N (BE being the 'dummy verb'). Similarly V+N and N+V are replaced by THIS+V+N and N+V+THIS respectively (THIS being the 'dummy substantive'). The function of these 'dummy features' is to supply a general form of template for subsequent processing, even when it is not wholly 'present' in the text. Suppose, once again, a fragment consisted not of an assertion form, but of a noun phrase like 'the black wizard'; where the heads of the *appropriate* codings for 'black' and 'wizard' would be KIND and MAN respectively. As there is no verb, a 'debilitated' template of the KIND+N form would match on to these two heads, and that would then be converted into MAN+BE+KIND, which is the intuitively correct interpretation (WIZARD IS BLACK). The dummy verb is added in the way described; and in cases like this where the first N head is the predicate KIND the order of the two N heads is reversed, so as to give the MAN+BE+KIND form. This transposition is defined by Rule 11i in Chapter 3 above.

TEMPO actually works by seeking the N+N pairs which are stored as a list which is itself the value of the character TEMPAR. It then seeks for any verb-like head which is to be found on the property list (under marker TEMP) of the first member of the appropriate N+N pair. For each fragment TEMPO outputs a list comprising (1) the name of the fragment itself, (2) a triplet of template heads and (3) a triplet of the sense-pairs (formulae plus sense explanations) for those senses of the words on to which the heads were matched by TEMPO.

Here is LISP output for a rather rebarbative fragment:

```
((COMMA AND THE UNIVERSITY PLACES AND PLACES IN TEACHER
        TRAINING COLLEGES FO NUMBER)
  ((THIS BE FOLK)
(((THIS) (DUMMY))
  ((BE) (DUMMY))
  ((THIS FOLK) (NUMBER AS A NUMBER OR COMMUNITY OF PEOPLE))))
  ((THIS BE SIGN)
(((THIS) (DUMMY))
  ((BE) (DUMMY)) ((COUNT SIGN) (NUMBER AS NUMERICAL ENTITY)))))
```

What we have here is a fragment tied to two bare template interpretations, together with the formulae whose heads define those bare templates.

This output serves also to illustrate the function SKIPPER, and the use that is made of the 'FO' characters that were inserted by the earlier fragmentation functions. A phrase ending in 'FO' (and beginning with 'AND' in this case) is considered to be a qualifying phrase and the SEARCHER function does not seek for bare template heads *within such phrases*.

Although a frame consists of sense-pairs, the function SEARCHER always has access to the name of the word from which any given sense-pair came, since the name of a word is always the first character in its sense explanation, and hence is the first character in the second member of every sense-pair.

There is also a function, JUMPER, analogous to SKIPPER, that prevents a SEARCHER function from connecting, within a single template, formulae attaching to two substantives linked by 'and' or 'or'. Thus in the fragment:

(THE BALL IS ROUND OR SQUARE),

one would expect templates to attach to the heads for the words:

BALL+IS+ROUND
BALL+IS+SQUARE

but not to the heads for the words ROUND+SQUARE when separated by 'and' or 'or', as they are here.

It should be noted that the output from TEMPO contains *only* 'bare template forms': for these template forms have not yet been used to pick up any content information from the fragments to which they attach. But even this intermediate stage does give a minimal resolution of ambiguity since there are not templates corresponding to *all possible* orders of heads of formulae, and so that fact already implies a selection among the coded word senses to which the heads correspond.

The procedure for obtaining negation classes

It is now possible to use the output from TEMPO for the first five (data) texts in order to set up relations between the heads of 'semantically compatible' fragments. To do this requires two quite separate analyses: first, one must be able to look at the TEMPO output for a single fragment and to decide which bare template contains the correct word-senses for that fragment as it occurs in that particular paragraph.

Secondly, one must be able, in the cases of at least some paragraphs, to decide (on reasonable grounds) which fragments are semantically compatible with which others. By a 'reasonable grounds' I mean no more than 'in such a way that most other people can see and understand what one is doing'.

There need be no argument about the first analysis: on the next page I give the bare template matching outputs for the first and second fragments of the first paragraph, and mark thus '*' what seem clearly to be the correct interpretations. The second analysis, in terms of what I have called 'semantic compatibility' is more difficult to pin down. It rests on the basic idea, outlined in Chapter 3 above, that there are proper and improper sequences of fragments and that one can distinguish them. I argued that the difference rests on semantic compatibility between fragments in proper sequence.

That means more than 'fragments conveying related concepts'; it also means 'fragments having forms related by contraries'. (I mentioned contraries in Chapter 3 above in connexion with negation classes.)

Output from first matching cycle for paragraph 1 (*crude readings*)[8]

```
((BRITAINS TRANSPORT SYSTEM ARE CHANGING)
  ((SIGN BE KIND)
   ((((MAN FOR) ((WHERE CHANGE) SIGN))
    (TRANSPORT AS MOVING PEOPLE ABOUT))
   ((BE BE) (ARE AS HAVE THE PROPERTY))
   ((CHANGE KIND) (CHANGING AS ALTERING))))
*((GRAIN BE KIND)
  (((WHOLE GRAIN) (SYSTEM AS AN ORGANIZATION))
   ((BE BE) (ARE AS HAVE THE PROPERTY))
   ((CHANGE KIND) (CHANGING AS ALTERING))))
  ((SIGN BE THIS)
   ((((MAN FOR) ((WHERE CHANGE) SIGN))
    (TRANSPORT AS MOVING PEOPLE ABOUT))
   ((BE BE) (ARE AS HAVE THE PROPERTY)) ((THIS THIS) (DUMMY))))
  ((THIS CHANGE GRAIN)
   (((THIS THIS) (DUMMY))
    (((THING FOR) (WHERE CHANGE)) (TRANSPORT AS MOVE ABOUT))
    ((WHOLE GRAIN) (SYSTEM AS AN ORGANIZATION))))
  ((GRAIN BE THIS)
   (((WHOLE GRAIN) (SYSTEM AS AN ORGANIZATION))
    ((BE BE) (ARE AS HAVE THE PROPERTY)) ((THIS THIS) (DUMMY)))))
((WITH IT THE TRAVELLING PUBLIC HABITS)
  ((GRAIN BE KIND)
   (((MUCH (((MAN FOR) (MUCH DO)) GRAIN))
    (HABITS AS REPEATED ACTIVITIES))
   ((BE BE) (DUMMY))
   (((WHERE CHANGE) KIND) (TRAVELLING AS MOVING))))
*((GRAIN BE KIND)
  (((MUCH (((MAN FOR) (MUCH DO)) GRAIN))
```

(HABITS AS REPEATED ACTIVITIES))
((BE BE) (DUMMY))
(((WHOLE FOLK) KIND)
(PUBLICS AS CONNECTED WITH THE WHOLE PEOPLE)))))

Let us consider the (fragmented) first paragraph in this light:
I shall number is fragments 1–12 as follows:

[1 ((BRITAINS TRANSPORT SYSTEM ARE CHANGING)
[2 (WITH IT THE TRAVELLING PUBLICS HABITS)
3 (IT IS THE OLD PERMANENT WAY)
[4 (WHICH ONCEMORE IS EMERGING)
[5 (AS THE PACEMAKER)
6 (AIRLINES LATELY HAVE BEEN LOSING TRAFFIC)
[7 (TO MODERNIZED RAILWAYS)
[8 (RAILWAYS ATLAST ARE BEGINNING)
[9 (TO TAKE SOME CARS)
[10 (OFF THE CONGESTED SYSTEMS TO TAKE THE WEIGHT)
[11 (IF THE NEW IDEAS ARE FORWARD PRESSED)
[12 (COMMA THE OF COMMUTER MOVEMENT AND DORMITORYAREA
CONGESTION FO PATTERN COULD BE CHANGED))

One could then argue that fragments:

1 and 2 are structurally parallel (both essentially assert that a
structure is of a certain sort:
1)—a system is changing
2)—a structure is the public's)
4 and 5 are structurally parallel (both essentially assert that something is moving)
7 and 8 are structurally parallel (both essentially assert that the
railways are near to us in time in some
way)
9 and 10 are structurally parallel (both essentially assert that something is taking something)
11 and 12 are structurally parallel (both essentially assert that some
structure is changing or about to change).

Notice that parallelisms of this sort between fragments are
sufficient to resolve at least one ambiguity in the fragments: for
example the correct sense of 'habits' for fragment 2 is 'structure of
behaviour', rather than 'articles of dress'. *Thus pointing out this
parallelism is also selecting the appropriate sense of 'habits'.*

Another point should be noted in passing; semantic parallelisms of this sort seem to have nothing to do with the mutual dependency structure of the clauses that the fragments constitute. If one marks the structure of the main clauses and their dependents on the above paragraph, then this marking seems totally unrelated to the one I have imposed. It might, one feels, have been otherwise, and such that the dependency structure offered surface clues to the structure of semantic compatibility. This, however, seems not to be the case.

I have marked these semantic connexions on the list of fragments above, and it will be noted that they are all between contiguous fragments. Other equally plausible connexions, or parallelisms, could have been located between discontinuous fragments in the paragraph, but my only concern here is to set up one such parallelism, and it seems reasonable to treat parallelisms between contiguous fragments first. Of course, it is much easier to see these parallelisms of form when considering the fragments together with the bare template that represents each, but that would lead to circularity since it is vital for the present purpose that one can set up a notion of 'semantic compatibility' *without reference to the template* structure.

In the set of connexions I have set up, fragments (3) and (6) remain unrelated to any other. Now, as the system was discussed above (as allowing of recursive application of rules which produce single representations of two compatible fragments), it seems reasonable to expect that one will be able to set up some such parallelism between, say, fragment (3), and some composite representation of other fragments. However, illustration of that requires that we assume the system to be in existence, and that would be going beyond the limits imposed on the present procedure.

I shall now assume that (*a*) the correct template for each fragment has been selected from the TEMPO output, (*b*) a set of possible semantic parallelisms have been set up between the fragments of the paragraph. So I can now list as follows the results of both these analyses for the twelve fragments of the first paragraph:

[(1)	GRAIN+BE+KIND	On the left are indicated the 'structural
[(2)	GRAIN+BE+KIND	parallelisms' between the fragments so
(3)	THING+BE+SIGN	numbered. On the right are the bare
[(4)	THIS+BE+KIND	templates which are the 'proper repre-

[(5)   THIS+BE+THING   sentations' for the same twelve frag-
(6)   SIGN+HAVE+SIGN   ments.
[(7)   THIS+DO+THING
[(8)   THING+BE+KIND
[(9)   THIS+DO+THING
[(10) GRAIN+DO+SIGN
[(11) THING+BE+KIND
[(12) SIGN+BE+KIND

One can illustrate the possible connectivities between the heads of compatible templates as follows:

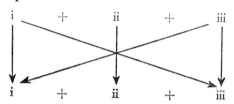

where each '→' signifies the relation 'is the same element, or the same element fused with "NOT", or the negation class of the upper element contains the lower element (element pointed at)'. The criterion for semantic compatibility suggested in Chapter 3 above is that compatible templates should have at least two such con-nexions. Clearly, the connectivity between fragment (1) and frag-ment (2) has at least three connexions on the basis of identities alone, and similarly that between fragment (4) and fragment (5). But fragment (7) and fragment (8) requires (THING ∈ [THIS]) or (BE ∈ [DO]), where that notation simply means ' "THING" is a member of the negation class of "THIS" ', or ' "BE" is a member of the nega-tion class of "DO" '.

It will be clear that, proceeding in this way through the five data texts, one can set up a table of disjunctions for each 'semantic compatibility' connectivity *not satisfied by element identities.*

Thus:

template connectivity	disjunctions
x—y	(A ∈ [B]) v(C ∈ [D]) . . .
z—a	(L . . . .
.
.
.

L

A simple algorithm then suggests itself for producing the overall smallest class of negation classes sufficient to make each of these lines 'true': one takes whichever form (P ε [φ]) occurs most often (in all the lines considered together); then assigns P to the negation class of φ and *deletes* all the lines which (P ε [φ]) occurred. (Those lines now being 'true'.) One then repeats the process for the remaining lines. This procedure must give the class of negation classes that requires the minimum number of such assignments and the results of its application are given below:

The Negation Classes as initially derived

(*In* LISP *format each element on the left-hand side is followed by a class in brackets*)

  ((THIS (STUFF NOTSTUFF THIS NOTTHIS THING SIGN FOLK NOTHING
    NOTSIGN NOTFOLK))
  (THING (STUFF NOTSTUFF KIND NOTKIND THING NOTHING THIS NOTTHIS
    SIGN NOTSIGN GRAIN NOTGRAIN MAN NOTMAN))
  (DO (DO NOTDO BE NOTBE))
  (BE (BE NOTBE DO NOTDO PAIR NOTPAIR CHANGE NOTCHANGE
    CAUSE NOTCAUSE HAVE NOTHAVE BE NOTBE))
  (SIGN (KIND NOTKIND SIGN NOTSIGN THING NOTTHING THIS NOTTHIS
    FOLK NOTFOLK MAN NOTMAN GRAIN NOTGRAIN))
  (FOLK (FOLK NOTFOLK SIGN NOTSIGN THIS NOTTHIS MAN NOTMAN))
  (PAIR (PAIR NOTPAIR BE NOTBE))
  (GRAIN (GRAIN NOTGRAIN THING NOTTHING SIGN NOTSIGN))
  (CHANGE (CHANGE NOTCHANGE BE NOTBE))
  (CAUSE (CAUSE NOTCAUSE BE NOTBE))
  (MAN (KIND NOTKIND MAN NOTMAN THING NOTTHING SIGN NOTSIGN
    FOLK
  (HAVE (HAVE NOTHAVE BE NOTBE))
  (PART (PART NOTPART WHOLE NOTWHOLE))
  (WHOLE (WHOLE NOTWHOLE PART NOTPART))
  (ASK (ASK NOTASK))
  (BEAST (BEAST NOTBEAST))
  (CAN (CAN NOTCAN))
  (COUNT (COUNT NOTCOUNT))
  (DONE (DONE NOTDONE))
  (FEEL (FEEL NOTFEEL))
  (FOR (FOR NOTFOR))
  (FORCE (FORCE NOTFORCE))

(FROM (FROM NOTFROM))
(HOW (KIND NOTKIND HOW NOTHOW))
(IN (IN NOTIN))
(KIND (THING MAN STUFF SIGN NOTMAN NOTTHING NOTSTUFF
 NOTSIGN HOW NOTHOW KIND NOTKIND))
(LET (LET NOTLET))
(LIFE (LIFE NOTLIFE))
(LIKE (LIKE NOTLIKE))
(LINE (LINE NOTLINE))
(MAY (MAY NOTMAY))
(MORE (MORE NOTMORE))
(MUST (MUST NOTMUST))
(ONE (ONE NOTONE))
(MUCH (MUCH NOTMUCH))
(PLANT (PLANT NOTPLANT))
(PLEASE (PLEASE NOTPLEASE))
(POINT (POINT NOTPOINT))
(SAME (SAME NOTSAME))
(SELF (SELF NOTSELF))
(SENSE (SENSE NOTSENSE))
(SPREAD (SPREAD NOTSPREAD))
(STUFF (STUFF NOTSTUFF KIND NOTKIND THING NOTTHING THIS
 NOTTHIS)
(THINK (THINK NOTTHINK))
(TO (TO NOTTO))
(UP (UP NOTUP))
(WHEN (WHEN NOTWHEN))
(WHERE (WHERE NOTWHERE))
(WORLD (WORLD NOTWORLD)) (WRAP (WRAP NOTWRAP))) NEGL))

4.3 The second template matching cycle

Matching full templates on to fragments

The full templates are the items with which the system really operates,
and they are derived from bare templates by looking at the *remaining*
formulae in the frame, i.e. more than the three in the bare template
output above. A full template is not a triple of formulae but a
sextuple; it is the three formulae associated with the bare template
plus the formulae which precede those bare template formulae in the

frame. Any of these latter three may be absent and will then be represented by LISP NILS.

I want to distinguish between what I have called internal and external rejection procedures: roughly speaking, internal procedures are those which case out bare templates that have been matched with fragments by means of criteria which apply *only within* the fragment in question. They do not 'look outside' the fragment.

In terms of the system above this means taking the output from TEMPO (i.e. all the bare templates that can be matched on to a fragment), and rejecting the templates that do not satisfy the Rules 13–15 of Chapter 3 above. For each fragment, it will be remembered, TEMPO returns a list consisting of the fragment name and a (second) list of objects like the following:

((HEAD1 HEAD2 HEAD3)(SENSE-PAIR1 SENSE-PAIR2 SENSE-PAIR3))

I shall call these 'I objects'.

The top-level LISP function that performs the internal rejections for a fragment is PICKUP, which takes an actual fragment-name as its argument. What it does is (*a*) to examine the semantic formula for the sense of each word to which TEMPO has attached a template head; and (*b*) to examine the coded formulae immediately preceding (left-right order) that formula in the frames for the fragment. (These left-ward formulae have been tagged to words which possibly *qualify* the 'head word.') On the basis of closeness relations between the head formula and its predecessors, and the preference scale given in Rules 12–14 above, PICKUP makes a decision in the case of each template whether or not to reject it from further consideration. Those templates that survive are then considered further by the *external* rejection procedures. The survivors from PICKUP represent a stage of ambiguity resolution beyond that given by TEMPO. If, for example, PICKUP examines a template that has been matched on to a fragment containing the words 'round box', where a template head had been attached to a formula for 'box', then, hopefully, PICKUP keeps *at least* the template in which 'round' is coded by its 'spatial property sense' and 'box' is coded by its 'container' sense.

PICKUP is internally identical to TEMPO except that, for each search function TEMPO contains, PICKUP has returned to it not simply a list of 'I objects' but the value of REFINE of that list.

The *value* of REFINE is a list of 5 lists; these are lists of full templates in a preference order, the first list contains those templates which are 'formally close' internally in 4 ways . . . and so on down to the fifth list of templates with *no* internal 'formal closenesses'. The objects on these lists are not 'I objects' (bare templates), but 'II objects' (full templates) which have the following form:

((HEAD1 HEAD2 HEAD3)(SENSE-PAIR1 SENSE-PAIR2 SENSE-PAIR3 SENSE-PAIR4 SENSE-PAIR5 SENSE-PAIR6)),

where SENSE-PAIR4 is the pair preceding SENSE-PAIR1 in the frame it matches, and so on down to SENSE-PAIR6 which precedes SENSE-PAIR3. The way in which REFINE keeps a 'closeness score' within the function PICKUP can be seen by looking again at the way the bare templates that matched with the fragment 'The old transport system' are examined and expanded into full templates.

PICKUP looks first at FOLK+DO+GRAIN, which are the heads of formulas for 'old', 'transport' and 'system' respectively. In no case is there any qualifier formula in the frame that is not already in the bare template, except one for the vacuous 'The'. In the frame for the first GRAIN+BE+KIND form there is the qualifier formula for 'transport' whose head is KIND, but no other qualifier not already in the bare template. I say *qualifier*, because that sense of 'transport' has head KIND and precedes a noun-like formula (for those who like to think in conventional grammatical terms) whose head is GRAIN. This is a *form-closeness* and PICKUP keeps a score of these as it turns each bare template into a full one. It also counts verb-like formulae preceded by adverb-like ones, adjective-like formulae preceded by adverb-like ones and so on. It also scores one for the form N+BE+KIND where N is a noun-like head, as GRAIN is. So then, PICKUP can score from 0 to 4 for any template; up to 3 for the predecessors of the heads and one for the N+BE+KIND form. In this case it will score 0 for FOLK+DO+GRAIN; 2 for the first GRAIN+BE+KIND; and only 1 for the second GRAIN+BE+KIND, since the KIND sense of 'old' is not a proper qualifier for the KIND sense of 'transport' (i.e. adjectives do not qualify adjectives in English).

As well as keeping this score PICKUP builds up a full template form by adding, on to the bare template, those formulae that are qualifiers in the required sense. The full templates for the first and third of the above bare ones will be just the same as the corresponding bare ones except for three NILS, inserted to mark the absence of any of the three possible preceding qualifiers. In the case of the second bare template, PICKUP will build up the item

((GRAIN BE KIND)
 (((WHOLE GRAIN) (SYSTEM AS AN ORGANIZATION))
 ((BE BE) (DUMMY))
 (((MUCH WHEN) KIND) (OLD AS HAVING BEEN THROUGH MUCH TIME))
 (((THING FOR) ((WHERE CHANGE) KIND)) (TRANSPORT AS PERTAINING
    TO MOVING THINGS ABOUT)) NIL NIL))

The fourth formula is the proper qualifier for the first, and, if such had been found for the second and third, they would have appeared in place of the NILs in the fifth and sixth places respectively.

The closeness functions within REFINE differ in only two respects from Rules 13:

(1) One of the formulae for the word 'TO' is acceptable as a qualifier for a verb-type formula. This seems in accord with common sense, since its presence before a verb is a safe indicator of an infinitive verb-sense.

(2) The preceding formula is given in each case by PREC, though in certain cases it yields the preceding formula but one. For example, where the true predecessor is the character 'FO' (thus giving the 'predecessor' from within a qualifying phrase bounded by 'FO') or where the true predecessor is 'AND' or 'OR', the next predecessor will be not a true qualifier but a noun in apposition whose content would otherwise be lost, or spread over too many templates. Thus in (President and Congress are separately elected) one sense of 'President' is admitted as a qualifier of 'Congress'.

Inside PICKUP the same preference choices are made that were made by TEMPO earlier. Of those templates so chosen the value of the first non-empty sublist of REFINE is taken (i.e. those *most* form-close) and the value of function CLOS of that list is returned as the value of PICKUP. CLOS inspects these 'II objects' that are the most 'form-close' and implements Rule 16 to take only those of them that are also 'content-close', if there are any.

There are other facilities within REFINE that express the general rule 'pack the sense-frames as tightly as possible'. For example, the function DUPLICATES prefers templates in which the same sense-pair has not been picked up twice, as both qualifier *and* provider of a template head. Clearly if there are templates *without* this duplication they will pick up more information from the fragment than one with duplicates. Thus, if the following two templates are produced internally for a fragment, the first will be preferred.

((SIGN BE GRAIN)
(((COUNT SIGN) (ONE AS THE FIRST INTEGER))
((IN BE) (IN AS INSIDE))
(((DO HOW) GRAIN) (FASHION AS MANNER IN WHICH))
NIL NIL ((SELF FOR) KIND) (OWN AS SIGNIFYING POSSESSION))))
((GRAIN BE KIND)
((((DO HOW) GRAIN) (FASHION AS MANNER IN WHICH))
((BE BE) (DUMMY))
(((SELF FOR) KIND) (OWN AS SIGNIFYING POSSESSION))
(((SELF FOR) KIND) (OWN AS SIGNIFYING POSSESSION)) NIL NIL))[9]

Nothing corresponding to a 'syntax-semantics' distinction is enshrined in the distinction between the form and content functions. For example, the form functions examine formulae for appropriate 'agents' for other verb-type formulae, and most true believers in a 'semantic-syntax distinction' would say that *that* was a *semantic* activity.

The effect of the PICKUP functions, applied to the initial bare template matchings provided by the function TEMPO, is to reduce the number of templates attaching to each fragment of text. As the bare templates are expanded by PICKUP, some are rejected by means of the procedures I described so that output from PICKUP consists of fragments tied to a list of full templates which must necessarily be either the same length or shorter than the list output from TEMPO shown in Section 4.2 above.

In the case of some fragments, the PICKUP cycle is sufficient to reduce the list of full templates to one member. That is, only one full template attaches to a fragment, and there is no ambiguity left to be resolved by what I called external procedures. That is the case with the two fragments whose bare template output (see 4.2 above) contained five and two templates respectively. The output from PICKUP for these fragments is as follows.

((BRITAINS TRANSPORT SYSTEM ARE CHANGING)
((GRAIN BE KIND)
(((WHOLE GRAIN) (SYSTEM AS AN ORGANIZATION))
((BE BE) (ARE AS HAVE THE PROPERTY))
((CHANGE KIND) (CHANGING AS ALTERING))
(((THING FOR) ((WHERE CHANGE) KIND))
(TRANSPORT AS PERTAINING TO MOVING THINGS ABOUT)) NIL NIL)))
((WITH IT THE TRAVELLING PUBLICS HABITS)

((GRAIN BE KIND)
 (((MUCH (((MAN FOR) (MUCH DO)) GRAIN))
  (HABITS AS REPEATED ACTIVITIES))
 ((BE BE) (DUMMY))
 (((WHOLE FOLK) KIND)
  (PUBLICS AS CONNECTED WITH THE WHOLE PEOPLE))
 (((WHOLE FOLK) KIND)
  (PUBLICS AS CONNECTED WITH THE WHOLE PEOPLE))
 NIL (((WHERE CHANGE) HOW)
  (TRAVELLING AS MOVING FROM PLACE TO PLACE)))))

Each full template in LISP format is as easy to interpret as the bare templates, provided it is remembered there are six formulae instead of three, where NILS count vacuously as (missing) formulae.

However, in the case of most fragments more than one full template still attaches to them after the PICKUP cycle, and the resolution of that ambiguity is tackled by the 'semantic parser' that resolves external ambiguities.

4.4 The 'semantic parser'—resolving a paragraph

The procedures considered so far have rejected possible interpretations for fragments in two ways: first, by matching preferred classes of bare templates on to coded fragments; second, by preferring interpretations that can be expanded to fill the coding frame as fully as possible, and with as much content connexion as possible. All these I call *internal* rejection procedures, in that they operate over the span of single text-fragments, and may still leave a fragment tied to more than one full template.

The remaining, *external*, rejection procedure spans texts consisting of a number of fragments. It seeks for closeness relations between the markers of full templates matching on to different fragments. These closeness relations are somewhat weaker than the content closeness defined within a full template, in that they also make use of the weaker *negation-class inclusion* between markers, discussed above (p. 113. Moreover, these relations do not simply establish preferences, as with the full template matching; they are used to provide a criterion of closeness between a pair of full templates, which any actual pair may or may not satisfy.

In this subsection I describe how the top-level function PARSPARA takes fragments of a paragraph, produces those full templates for the fragments that survive the internal resolution routines described in the last section, and returns the fragments nested, or parsed. More importantly, for the overall purposes of this work, the function PARSPARA also has access to the full templates that give rise to each nested form, and so it can return a word-sense resolution for the paragraph (since a full template is simply a selection from among the possible word-senses of a fragment).

The function PICKPARA returns a paragraph as a list of items, each item being a fragment name and a list of possible full templates for that fragment. The full templates at this point are simply sextuplets of sense-pairs (formulae and sense explanations), rather than a sextuplet of sense-pairs *and* the head triple (or bare template) that I described in the last section (as II forms). The reason for this contraction is that the II forms, described above and reproduced in figure form, were essentially for display, in that the actual form of the template triple is available for inspection. However, it is not necessary for further computation by the system, to have a copy of the head triple (or bare template), since the triple can be reconstructed at any time from the first three sense-pairs of the (full template) sextuplet.

Thus the output from PICKUP is in fact an item like the following:

```
(
(fragment name)
    ((SENSE-PAIR1 . . . . . . . .      SENSE-PAIR6)
    (    . . .              . . .           )
    (    . . .                            )))
```

I shall refer to the simple sextuples as the 'III forms' of full templates. PICKPARA returns a list of 'III-form' items as the value of a paragraph, and it can be seen that the form of this value of a paragraph is the same as that of the *word*-dictionary described at the outset. That is to say, the form is 'one natural language item tagged to a list of possible representations of it'. So what we now have is a 'dictionary' for the fragments of a paragraph in terms of the full templates which can represent the fragments.

Thus, just as the computational purpose of the whole system is to choose, for each word occurrence in a text one from among the sense-pairs in the dictionary entry for the word, so we see that this choice can be reduced, as it were, to the selection of one full template from among those in the 'dictionary entry' for the fragment in this 'fragment dictionary' produced by PICKPARA.

For the exposition of PARSPARA, some mention of the FIT and JAM functions must be made. These express the Rule 18 of Chapter 3 above; that is to say they test for 'semantic closeness' between two full templates and, if found, the two full templates are replaced by a single item with the form of a full template. Or, to put it in terms of the two function names: if the full templates FIT they are then JAMmed.

FIT takes an ordered pair of full templates as its arguments. If the three main formulae (those contained by the first three sense-pairs of the sextuple) of the first full template are connected to the three main formulae of the second full template by *any two* of the ten connexions illustrated schematically below, then the two full templates FIT.

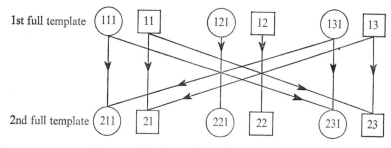

The 'round items' in the above figure indicate the qualifier formulae of the 'square item' formulae. That is to say, the verb-type formula (second formula in left-right order) may only be connected to its counterpart, but the substantive-type formulae may be connected to either of their counterparts. 'Connected' is expressed by the rules in terms of the 'semantic closeness' that was also used above to select proper qualifiers. A connectivity *holds* in the above diagram if the head of the lower (square) formula is in the negation class of the head of upper (square) formula and the two (square or round) formulae are 'semantically close' in the sense defined. The replacement 'full template', for pairs of them which FIT, is constructed using the following simple algorithm (which expresses Rule 18 of Chapter 3 above):

(i)   If two sense-pairs fit, put them in the corresponding positions in the replacement frame, *unless* they are both in the same left-right positions in their templates, in which case insert only the upper (first) sense-pair of that position in the replacement frame.

(ii) If this procedure leaves any of the six positions in the replacement frame empty, fill it with the sense-pair from that position in the upper (first) template.

This may sound complex, but is expressed very easily in LISP; FIT simply builds up a list of triples, one for each formula pair for which OK returns the value T (true). Each triple so constructed consists of the sense-pairs considered by the function OK (in their own left-right positions in the triple), unless both are in the same left-right position, in which case only the first is written. Blanks left are filled by the null list. If the final list of triples has two or more members (number of connectivities) then the JAM triple of sense-pairs is returned. JAM takes as its arguments the two full triples and the list of triples built up by FIT in the way described.

PARSPARA takes as its argument the name of a paragraph, and immediately constructs the PICKPARA value for it. From this it constructs FRAMEFRAG for the paragraph. FRAMEFRAG builds up all possible strings of *message-pairs*.

Def. 22: A *message-pair* is a two-item list: one item is a list of the first three sense-pairs of some full template, the other item is a list containing the name of some fragment with which the full template matches.

Thus a message-pair is to a fragment what a sense-pair is to a word, in that it contains both *the* name and *one possible* semantic representation.

PARSPARA next examines the frames of message-pairs. Each frame is in fact *a semantic representation* of the paragraph and also a *possible resolution* for the whole paragraph. It is recursively rewritten to see if it can be expressed as *two* message-pairs (see Rule 17 above: $P \rightarrow T_r + T_s$). Each frame is scanned by the rewriter, and if it can find a left-right pair of message-pairs whose full templates satisfy FIT, then it deletes the first message-pair and replaces the second by a message-pair consisting of (1) the JAM value of the two 'fitting' full templates, and (2) *a list of the names of the fitting templates*.

PARSPARA constructs a new frame for each pair rewritten, and when it has finished (i.e. has rewritten all possible left-right pairs in the frame), it attempts to rewrite each of the new (rewritten) frames. This rewriting continues recursively until either a frame with two members is reached or all paths are blocked. If it reaches a two-member frame, that is to say it succeeds '*in reaching the paragraph point P*', then it examines no more rewrites of that particular frame since they all correspond to the same original frame— that is to say, to the same word-sense resolution of the paragraph.

However, it is possible that other frames from FRAMEFRAG may give rise to (possibly different) resolutions for the whole paragraph. Hence, whether it succeeds or fails with a particular frame, PARSPARA always goes on to the other frames. It keeps a list of successful frames together with their *parsing pattern*.

What is meant here by 'parsing pattern' can be seen by going back for a moment to the operation of the string rewriter in PARSPARA. It forms new strings of message-pairs in each of which two 'fitting' message-pairs are replaced by a single message-pair. The replacement pair contains (as left-hand member) a list of the contents of the name-lists of the two fitting pairs, and (as a right-hand member) the JAM value of the full templates, one from each of the fitting pairs.

Thus, in the frame for the first paragraph containing the two message-pairs:

((BRITAINS TRANSPORT SYSTEM ARE CHANGING)
(((WHOLE GRAIN) (SYSTEM AS AN ORGANIZATION))
 ((BE BE) (ARE AS HAVE THE PROPERTY))
 ((CHANGE KIND) (CHANGING AS ALTERING))
 (((THING FOR) ((WHERE CHANGE) KIND))
  (TRANSPORT AS PERTAINING TO MOVING THINGS ABOUT)) NIL NIL))
and
((AND WITH IT THE TRAVELLING PUBLICS HABITS)
(((MUCH(((MAN FOR)(MUCH DO))GRAIN))
  (HABITS AS REPEATED ACTIVITIES))
 ((BE BE) (DUMMY))
 (((WHOLE FOLK)KIND)
 (PUBLICS AS CONNECTED WITH THE WHOLE PEOPLE))
 NIL (((WHERE CHANGE)HOW)
 (TRAVELLING AS MOVING FROM PLACE TO PLACE)))))

Then since the two full templates in those message-pairs are a fitting pair, we shall expect them to be replaced in the string by the form:

(((BRITAINS TRANSPORT SYSTEM ARE CHANGING)
  (WITH IT THE TRAVELLING PUBLICS HABITS))
 ((((WHOLE GRAIN) (SYSTEM AS AN ORGANIZATION))
  ((BE BE) (ARE AS HAVE THE PROPERTY))
  ((CHANGE KIND) (CHANGING AS ALTERING))
  (((THING FOR) ((WHERE CHANGE) KIND))
   (TRANSPORT AS PERTAINING TO MOVING THINGS ABOUT))
  NIL (((WHERE CHANGE) HOW)
   (TRAVELLING AS MOVING FROM PLACE TO PLACE)))))

The first item in the replacement form is a list of the two fragment names, and *is* thus the parsing pattern of those two items.

The function PARSFRAME (within PARSPARA) scans a frame of message-pairs and tests for 'fits': when successful it replaces the right-most message-pair by a 'jam' in the fashion just described. As this procedure is applied recursively to frames then the left-member of the jam pair (which is always a *list* of the left-members of the fitting pairs) becomes an expression of the parsing pattern of the jamming done so far, for it can always be expressed as a tree structure for the fragments it 'contains'. PARSFRAME stops when it encounters a frame of only two message-pairs, for this means that the 'top' of the paragraph has been reached.

In fact PARSFRAME makes two passes at every paragraph frame: during the first it seeks to fit only contiguous message-pairs (see Rule 19 above); and it rewrites noncontiguous pairs only if it finds no contiguous ones. If PARSFRAME reaches the top of the paragraph it returns the topmost parsing pattern (the left-hand member of the last message-pair formed), but if all paths for that frame are blocked it returns only the null list. PARSPARA stores on a list that last (non-null) parsing pattern, along with the original frame itself which now constitutes one ambiguity resolution for the paragraph.

When a frame for the paragraph has been found that can be fully parsed, output is handled by the function SCOOP. SCOOP returns (in print) a list of the fragments of the paragraph, and with each fragment it returns (1) a list of the sense-expressions for all the words of the fragment that are resolved or which have only a single sense entry in the dictionary initially, (2) a list of words (if any) preceded by the rubric (WORDS NOT RESOLVED).

After listing the fragments and the resolution (or non-resolution) of their constituent words, PARSPARA prints out the 'successful' parsing pattern for the paragraph so that an operator of the system can see which 'semantic compatibilities' between fragments have given rise to any particular resolution. If it can find no resolutions at all, for any frame, PARSPARA prints at the typewriter (NO RESOLU-TION ALL PATHS BLOCKED).

Below is a sample output from the overall resolution of the first paragraph, printed out at the teletypewriter.

Sample output from the semantic parser
(first seven fragments of the first paragraph)
(((BRITAINS TRANSPORT SYSTEM ARE CHANGING)
  ((WORDS RESOLVED IN FRAGMENT)
   ((TRANSPORT AS PERTAINING TO MOVING THINGS ABOUT)
    (BRITAINS AS HAVING THE CHARACTERISTIC OF A PARTICULAR PART OF THE WORLD)
    (SYSTEM AS AN ORGANIZATION)
    (ARE AS HAVE THE PROPERTY) (CHANGING AS ALTERING)))
  ((WORDS NOT RESOLVED IN FRAGMENT) NIL))
 ((WITH IT THE TRAVELLING PUBLICS HABITS)
  ((WORDS RESOLVED IN FRAGMENT)
   ((TRAVELLING AS MOVING FROM PLACE TO PLACE)
    (IT AS INANIMATE PRONOUN)
    (PUBLICS AS CONNECTED WITH THE WHOLE PEOPLE)
    (HABITS AS REPEATED ACTIVITES)))
  ((WORDS NOT RESOLVED IN FRAGMENT) NIL))
 ((IT IS THE OLD PERMANENT WAY)
  ((WORDS RESOLVED IN FRAGMENT)
   ((IT AS INANIMATE PRONOUN)
    (IS AS HAS THE PROPERTY)
    (OLD AS HAVING BEEN THROUGH A LOT OF TIME)
    (PERMANENT AS UNCHANGING) (WAY AS PATH OR ROUTE)))
  ((WORDS NOT RESOLVED IN FRAGMENT) NIL))
 ((WHICH ONCEMORE IS EMERGING)
  ((WORDS RESOLVED IN FRAGMENT)
   ((ONCEMORE AS ONE MORE TIME)
    (IS AS HAS THE PROPERTY)
    (EMERGING AS MOVING OUT OF SOMETHING)))
  ((WORDS NOT RESOLVED IN FRAGMENT) NIL))
 ((AS THE PACEMAKER)
  ((WORDS RESOLVED IN FRAGMENT)
   ((AS AS CORRESPONDING TO)

(PACEMAKER AS ANYTHING THAT MOVES FAST)))
((WORDS NOT RESOLVED IN FRAGMENT) NIL))
((AIRLINES LATELY HAVE BEEN LOSING TRAFFIC)
  ((WORDS RESOLVED IN FRAGMENT)
  ((AIRLINES AS PUBLIC TRANSPORT ORGANIZATIONS)
  (LATELY AS NEAR THE PRESENT IN TIME)
  (HAVE AS POSSESSES)
  (BEEN AS HAVING EXISTED)
  (LOSING AS NO LONGER POSSESSING SOMETHING)
  (TRAFFIC AS VEHICLES))) ((WORDS NOT RESOLVED IN FRAGMENT)
  NIL))
((TO MODERNIZED RAILWAYS)
  ((WORDS RESOLVED IN FRAGMENT)
  ((TO AS TOWARDS OR CORRESPONDING TO)
  (MODERNIZED AS BROUGHT UP TO DATE)
  (RAILWAYS AS TRANSPORTERS BY RAIL)))
  ((WORDS NOT RESOLVED IN FRAGMENT) NIL))

What follows is a diagrammatic representation of the parsing of the first data paragraph. The parsing pattern is given on the right of the page in an intuitively obvious tree fashion; the continuous lines on the paragraph itself indicates the connexions between word-sense codings upon which the parsing was based. These are rather like the kind of 'anaphoric' connexions across words in paragraphs given in Olney and Londe [209]. All the paragraphs except two philosophical ones were resolved in this way (see below on what was done with the two recalcitrant ones).

(Lines drawn on the left-hand side of the page between words indicate connexions between word-senses that gave rise to a parsing. Lines on the right-hand side of the page indicate the parsing itself in the usual tree structure manner; dotted lines indicate the parsing of non-contiguous items. If the page is turned on its left edge then above the words is a conventional tree diagram of the kind discussed in connexion with phrase structure grammars in Chapter 2 above.)

There is an important possible case, discussed in Chapter 3, though not actually instantiated by any of these ten paragraphs. That is the case in which *each* of the fragments of the paragraph is revolved internally—i.e. only one template for each fragment is supplied to the semantic parser. As I indicated above, in this case PARSPARA would return (RESOLVED INTERNALLY NO PARSING SOUGHT)

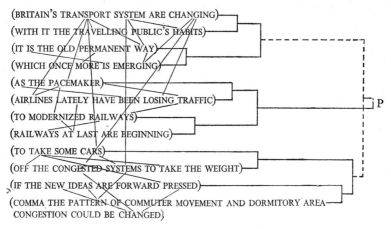

(BRITAIN'S TRANSPORT SYSTEM ARE CHANGING)
(WITH IT THE TRAVELLING PUBLIC'S HABITS)
(IT IS THE OLD PERMANENT WAY)
(WHICH ONCE MORE IS EMERGING)
(AS THE PACEMAKER)
(AIRLINES LATELY HAVE BEEN LOSING TRAFFIC)
(TO MODERNIZED RAILWAYS)
(RAILWAYS AT LAST ARE BEGINNING)
(TO TAKE SOME CARS)
(OFF THE CONGESTED SYSTEMS TO TAKE THE WEIGHT)
(IF THE NEW IDEAS ARE FORWARD PRESSED)
(COMMA THE PATTERN OF COMMUTER MOVEMENT AND DORMITORY AREA CONGESTION COULD BE CHANGED)

P

together with the corresponding sense resolution.

It would do this (as a matter of programming efficiency) even though the sequence of fragments might be coherent, i.e., it might be possible to parse their representations 'up to the paragraph symbol P'. However, *for the purpose of ambiguity resolution* there is clearly no need to do this, and no further theoretical questions arise here since none of the ten paragraphs examined was of this type.

4.5 The sense constructor (or Expand algorithm)

The problem that remains is what to do when the 'semantic parser' of paragraphs returns the diagnostic (NO RESOLUTION ALL PATHS BLOCKED). I am now assuming the discussion of Chapter 3 above, and specifically that it would be worth identifying the 'recalcitrant' word, if any, with another word in the paragraph, then running the system again to see if it unblocks, and so resolves the paragraph after all. If it does so, it seems reasonable to claim that the identification is an extension of sense as described in Chapter 3.

There are, then, two distinct problems involved in doing this:

(i)   How to identify the 'recalcitrant word', or point of breakdown of the semantic parser;

(ii)   With *which* other word's sense in the paragraph to identify the recalcitrant word, once it has been found.

Two further assumptions, then, are required and the following seemed, and have been proved, reasonable first tries:

(i)   Look for the template which has been *rewritten least* at the level of rewriting at which the parsing function, PARSPARA, breaks down. This seems a reasonable algorithmic expression of the fact that the template that has been least rewritten is the one that it is least easy for PARASPARA to make 'cohere' with the rest of the paragraph, and hence the one most appropriate to have one of its word-senses extended so as to fit the semantic compatibility rules.

(ii)   Given the least-rewritten template(s), then it follows it will be of level 1 (i.e. not rewritten at all) or it will be of some other level, in which case it will be a rewrite of more than one template. If the latter, let us assume that one can have access to the rewritten templates in text-order, and that one can apply the following procedure to them in order. Any such template will be of one of two forms; 'an entity is of a certain kind' or 'some entity is or affects another entity'. If the second case, the rule is 'identify the first entity with that sense of the second entity'. If that fails, or if the case is the first case, the rule is 'identify the first entity with the *closest* sense for any word occurring in the paragraph'. Here 'closest'[10] is used in a way slightly wider than it was defined earlier for formulae, with the proviso that if more than one sense is *close* to the same degree, then the *closest* is the first one found and so on. This whole constitutes the metarule, or Expand algorithm, of Chapter 3 above.

Thus, if the paragraph explicitly asserts the identity of a concept with some other concept already in play then, hopefully, this procedure will find it. If there is no such explicit assertion, then it seems reasonable to try replacing, as it were, the recalcitrant sense with one already closest to it. Doing this has the effect, crudely speaking, of making the paragraph more analytic,[11] and is the principled move most likely to allow the resolution procedure to continue.

These suggestions are effected within the system as follows:

Each time PARSPARA fails to resolve one frame from FRAMEFRAG it examines the value of a free variable BESTPARS to see if it contains a blocked parsing containing a template at a 'lower level' of rewriting than the one then under examination. If it does it passes on, but if not it resets the value of BESTPARS to the new 'lowest-level' parsing. Thus, if PARSPARA finds that *all* the frames block, then BESTPARS will at that time contain the lowest-level rewrite of all. Since the functions to be described also require access to a frame of templates, the actual value of BESTPARS is not just a parsing but a pair consisting of a (blocked) parsing and the appropriate frame of full templates for the paragraph.

M

If a blocked situation arises in that no resolution results from any frame, then PARSPARA prints (NO RESOLUTION ALL PATHS BLOCKED) as described above, and *also evaluates a function of no variables called* CONSTRUCTOR. This immediately prints 'CONSTRUCTOR MODE' and controls all subsequent operations via READ and PRINT functions under on-line teletype control. The importance of the teletype control here is that an operator can, as it were, veto any suggestions for sense extension which he considers absurd, even though they might, if substituted and rerun, produce a resolution of the paragraph.

Dialogues of the following kind are then possible (machine responses are preceded by a '$' sign):

$ RECALCITRANT TEMPLATE IS FOR (FRAGMENT NAME) CONTINUE
    YES OR NO
    YES

$ SUGGEST (X AS Y) SHALL I TRY IT YES OR NO
    YES

$ STILL BLOCKED AT TEMPLATE FOR (FRAGMENT NAME) (1)

$ SUGGEST (X′ AS Y′) SHALL I TRY IT YES OR NO
    NO

$ THEN SUGGEST (X′ AS E′) SHALL I TRY IT YES OR NO
    YES (2)

This procedure will continue from point (2) until either the whole range of possibilities mentioned has been exhausted, in which case CONSTRUCTOR returns (CANNOT RESOLVE PARAGRAPH BY CONSTRUCTION), and, since this is returned and not merely printed, it has the effect of taking the system back to the standard EVALQUOTE (or operating) mode, *or* it gets a non-blocked response from a rerun PARSPARA, in which case, too, CONSTRUCTOR MODE is left and the PARSPARA output printed. Point (1) in the dialogue above represents simply a diagnostic, in that the suggestion that follows it is not a suggestion for unblocking *that* template but *another* suggestion for unblocking at the original point. So, in the transition from point (1) to the next line CONSTRUCTOR resets the sense value, i.e. it cancels the addition to the sense-dictionary it had earlier suggested, but which had failed to produce any desirable result.

As I described in the last section above, there was no need to call upon the present procedures in the case of the data paragraphs (numbers 1–5), nor in the cases of three of the experimental paragraphs. Successful, and somewhat surprising, constructions were made in the cases of the two 'odd' ones, which were the passages from Spinoza and Wittgenstein respectively.

In the case of the paragraph from Spinoza's writings the following dialogue occurred after the system went into CONSTRUCTOR MODE:

(CONSTRUCTOR MODE)
((NO RESOLUTION ALL PATHS BLOCKED)
  (BEST PARSING CONTAINS)
  (((((KIND SIGN) (ATTRIBUTE AS A PARTICULAR KIND OF PROPERTY))
    ((BE BE) (DUMMY))
    ((SAME KIND) (SAME AS IDENTICAL))
    ((WHOLE (MUST (KIND SIGN)))
     (NATURE AS ESSENCE OR ESSENTIAL PROPERTIES))
     NIL NIL)))
  (RECALCITRANT TEMPLATE IS FOR)
  (THE SAME NATURE OR ATTRIBUTE)
  (CONTINUE YES OR NO)
YES
  (SUGGEST ATTRIBUTE AS NATURE) (SHALL I TRY IT YES OR NO)
YES
  (((IF THERE WERE TWO OR MORE DISTINCT SUBSTANCES)
   ((WORDS RESOLVED IN FRAGMENT)
   ((THERE AS AT A POINT)
   (WERE AS EXISTED)
   (OR AS DISJUNCTION)
   (MORE AS IN AN INCREASED MANNER)
   (DISTINCT AS DIFFERENT) (SUBSTANCES AS SORTS OF THING)))
   ((WORDS NOT RESOLVED IN FRAGMENT)
   (TWO(((COUNT SIGN) (TWO AS A NUMBER))
   ((COUNT KIND) (TWO AS HAVING THE PROPERTY OF TWOITY)))))

Dialogue in CONSTRUCTOR MODE *together with first part of subsequent resolution.**

As can be seen the sense construction in this case (for the word 'attribute') was successful in that it enabled a resolution to take place. In the case of the paragraph from Wittgenstein's writings, the system at first suggested a construction that proved to be of no use, in that it did not enable a resolution to take place. After that, however, it suggested an extension of the sense of the word 'propositions' that did allow a resolution to take place. Here is the Wittgenstein

* From the demonstration of prop. iv, in Part I of Spinoza's *Ethics*.

paragraph in the same format as the editorial from *The Times* above: the full lines now show the connexions up to the breakdown point, and the broken lines on the left show the connexions found by the system *after* construction, which enabled PARSPARA to resolve the whole paragraph:

(The diagram adopts the same conventions as the earlier one, based on a straightforward semantic parsing, except that on the left-hand side of the page dotted lines indicate those connexions that were only possible after CONSTRUCTOR had suggested an extension of sense for 'propositions'. The words parsed are [303, §§2.02– 2.023]).

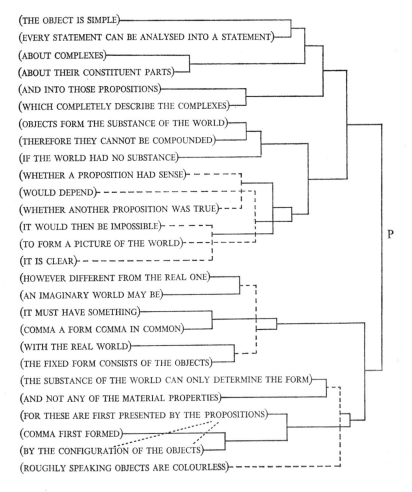

(THE OBJECT IS SIMPLE)
(EVERY STATEMENT CAN BE ANALYSED INTO A STATEMENT)
(ABOUT COMPLEXES)
(ABOUT THEIR CONSTITUENT PARTS)
(AND INTO THOSE PROPOSITIONS)
(WHICH COMPLETELY DESCRIBE THE COMPLEXES)
(OBJECTS FORM THE SUBSTANCE OF THE WORLD)
(THEREFORE THEY CANNOT BE COMPOUNDED)
(IF THE WORLD HAD NO SUBSTANCE)
(WHETHER A PROPOSITION HAD SENSE)
(WOULD DEPEND)
(WHETHER ANOTHER PROPOSITION WAS TRUE)
(IT WOULD THEN BE IMPOSSIBLE)
(TO FORM A PICTURE OF THE WORLD)
(IT IS CLEAR)
(HOWEVER DIFFERENT FROM THE REAL ONE)
(AN IMAGINARY WORLD MAY BE)
(IT MUST HAVE SOMETHING)
(COMMA A FORM COMMA IN COMMON)
(WITH THE REAL WORLD)
(THE FIXED FORM CONSISTS OF THE OBJECTS)
(THE SUBSTANCE OF THE WORLD CAN ONLY DETERMINE THE FORM)
(AND NOT ANY OF THE MATERIAL PROPERTIES)
(FOR THESE ARE FIRST PRESENTED BY THE PROPOSITIONS)
(COMMA FIRST FORMED)
(BY THE CONFIGURATION OF THE OBJECTS)
(ROUGHLY SPEAKING OBJECTS ARE COLOURLESS)

P

I have discussed the CSD system only from a linguistic point of view: as a system designed to do a fairly pedestrian, though difficult, job. The system is still in a rudimentary state, and needs a great deal of improvement if it is to deal with less common forms of expression. It also needs to be tested over a much wider range of sorts of text.

The five philosophical, or more correctly metaphysical, texts served the purpose of contrasting in tone and content with the more straightforward editorial texts. Their analysis by the CSD system also had a number of more speculative interests: not only the role of the suggested word-sense constructions in the analysis of the arguments contained by the metaphysical paragraphs; but also the possibility of distinguishing metaphysical texts from others by the particular pattern of word-sense changes they display. I have discussed these matters elsewhere [298].

In another way, too, the analysis of metaphysical texts brings the argument of this book to a point of rest. In Chapter 1 I described Carnap's theory of logical syntax, the purpose of which was to separate off the meaningful from the meaningless by means of a system of rules. It is quite clear from considering Carnap's work as a whole that one of the main motivations of his theory was to be able to analyse metaphysical texts and dismiss them as meaningless [see 44]. In that chapter I argued against logical syntax that it was never applied in any systematic way, but was always discussed with reference to illustrative examples. That criticism applies equally well to Carnap's handling of metaphysical examples (though I would not for one moment want to defend the sentences from Heidegger's works that Carnap analyses in detail in [44]).

In the same chapter I argued for a more sophisticated notion of meaningfulness, one put in terms of sense resolvability and possible sense constructions. In the terms of that criterion, applied systematically in the way I have described, the five metaphysical texts analysed survived rather better than Carnap might have led us to believe.

The linguistic results at this early stage of development promise well, and if the system were successful on a larger scale it might have other, equally improbable, applications in different fields. One such speculative interest of the system might be its application to the speech patterns of schizophrenics. Schizophrenic discourse seems [see Laing, 157] to be meaningful within the boundaries of units of the order of length of the clause or phrase. The trouble is that these units don't seem to fit together in a coherent way in the schizophrenic's speech pattern. A system of the present sort, which tries to make such items cohere, might conceivably provide a measure of 'semantic disorder' in such cases.

Notes

1 *Meaning and machines*

1 These notions all refer to the ability of suitably designed systems to return themselves to a condition of stability, and they are usually illustrated by describing Watt's self-regulating governor for steam engines. However, with more complicated systems it is not always a simple matter to decide whether a particular system contains a reflexive element or not. If ELIZA gets confusing replies from a human being it can ask such questions as are likely to get it back into an appropriate part of its 'script'. However, it is not capable of modifying its script in novel circumstances and *in that sense* ELIZA might be said not to be a paradigm of AI. This case illustrates the general difficulty of drawing a hard and fast line between AI and CL. That distinction was made only to illustrate a very general difference of approach.

2 One short way with any such proposal, of course, is to say that either these two notions are the same, in which case the whole business is trivial, or they are different, in which case it is circular. This is the form of the Paradox of Analysis, whose application to these situations Miss Boden has called the Paradox of Explanation [34]. I shall assume that its unhelpfulness has been thoroughly explored.

3 There might seem to be a useful distinction between 'being meaningful, yet ambiguous because of *two* possible interpretations' and 'being meaningless because of many (more than two) interpretations'. This possibility is clear in the case of poetry, much of which is rightly considered meaningful when it has two (though not usually *many*) interpretations. The same goes for jokes, allegories, and other special cases.

4 Failure to observe this fact has been a prolific fallacy in this century. For example, Russell's 'Given the syntax of a language, the meaning of a sentence is determinate as soon as the meaning of the component words is known' [255, p. 8]. That is either a dubious definition of syntax, or is almost certainly false of syntax in the normal sense.

5 One cannot even infer that the smallest items in a meaningful utterance are words. Consider ' "Frulligo" he shouted as the drug began to take effect'.

6 And in terms of the same characterization there can be no real survey of meaningful utterances either (other than with respect to particular dictionaries or contexts), as any paradigm of meaningfulness might be ambiguous (and so meaningless) with respect to some possible dictionary: for example, one with an arbitrary word-sense added to it. The normally unambiguous 'I must take these letters to the post' would be ambiguous with respect to a conventional dictionary *plus* the entry 'post as franking machine'. The fact that that entry does not describe a sense of 'post' in contemporary English is neither here nor there.

7 Cf. Wittgenstein's 'If someone were to draw a sharp boundary I could not acknowledge it as the one I too had always wanted to draw,

or had drawn in my mind. For I did not want to draw one at all.' [305, §76.]

8 The actual application of the linguistic system described to philosophical texts is set out in [298].

2   *The contemporary background*

1 See also Y. Bar-Hillel [15] for the debt of Carnap to Husserl. I say 'resurrection' of Universal Grammar because it might well be held that Dalgarno's, Wilkins's and Leibniz's essays on a 'Universal Characteristic' also required the construction of a Universal Grammar.

2 I take it that Gardiner's insertions into larger contexts *were* 'procedures' in the required sense.

3 Bar-Hillel [15] argued for an extension of Carnap's techniques to linguistics; and later championed Chomsky's work as being such an extension. On the other hand Cohen [65] has argued that Chomsky's work is not a proper extension of Carnap's.

4 These formulae are normally referred to as 'sentences' even without logic since Tarski [276, p. 30].

5 This is made quite clear in Garvin [99].

6 The distinction here rests not on the existence of an appeal to intuitions, but on the way the appeal is made. It is, of course, true that there are appeals in logic to 'actual inference', and one might say that the possibility of such an appeal serves to separate logic within, or from, mathematics proper.

7 Cf. 'Under many circumstances it is quite *appropriate* to use deviant utterances.' [54, p. 28.]

8 This means no more than that the word produced at any instant depends only on some or all of the words that have already been produced.

9 It is important to see that this dispute is about the *generation* or *production of sentences* not their analysis. Chomsky and Miller have not really concerned themselves with models for *hearers*. When Mandelbrot [178] writes as follows he is talking about hearers, '. . . we cannot follow Galanter and Miller in the opposition they establish between stochastic *models* and grammatical *explanations*. It is clear from their comment that they exhibit some impatience with the philosophy which has underlain American psychology in this century, that one should study what people do and not what they plan to do.'

10 Cf. 'Comprehensiveness of coverage does not seem . . . to be a serious or significant goal in the present state of linguistic science.' [54, p. 53.]

11 Though this would not allow us to 'know' in that it would allow us to choose between equivalent sets of such rules. Nor would we know that there was not some other equivalent set of rules that it made equally good sense to say was the one 'being used by' the human being under examination. To adapt an example of Professor Sutherland's: examination of the output of a computer does not, in general, allow us to decide

whether it is a digital or analogue machine. And we know that it is one of those two kinds only because we know how machines are put together, and that those are the only two kinds of computers that there are. In the case of human beings we lack both sorts of information.

12 [52, p. 28] '. . . the fact that a certain noise was produced, even intentionally, by an English speaker, does not guarantee that it is a well-formed specimen of his language.'

13 I am not saying that there are not perfectly proper intuitions about language. What I am claiming, and will argue for in detail later, is that intuitions about grammatical structure are not among them. One can see how easily Chomsky falls into confusion between intuition and what one might call 'mere introspection' in the following passage: '. . . the late view of Wittgenstein that there is no necessity to suppose the whole "calculus of language" to be present to the mind as a permanent background for each act of language use.' Chomsky is attacking this 'view' of Wittgenstein's. There is no real need to defend Wittgenstein from this charge, for, not only was he discussing the entirely different question of 'mentalistic terms' (i.e. what is or is not 'present to the mind') in the passage referred to by Chomsky, but he too stressed that to understand a piece of language it is necessary to 'lay on the whole calculus of language' [see 308, §§15 and 43–46]. What is astonishing here is that Chomsky really does seem to think that a linguistic theory that accounts adequately for features of language behaviour must also be present to the mind of the language user when he is performing!

14 The point at issue between Chomsky and Skinner does not concern the existence or non-existence of 'mechanisms in humans' for they are both concerned to produce explanatory mechanisms of the kind introduced into modern psychology by Craik. The point at issue is about the *relative simplicity* of such a mechanism, as I think the following quotation makes clear:

> It is important to see just what it is in Skinner's program and claims that makes them appear so bold and remarkable. It is not primarily the fact that he has set functional analysis as his problem, or that he limits himself to the study of observables i.e. input-output relations. What is so surprising is the particular limitations he has imposed on the way in which the observables of behavior are to be studied, and, above all, the particularly simple nature of the function which he claims, describes the causation of behavior. [Chomsky, 49.]

15 Substantially the same as Quine's '—', as defined in [230]. Some, like Curry, maintain that rewrite rules are best stated in terms of unordered sets, but the present one is the orthodox exposition. [See 72.]

16 Particularly in respect of the way in which (1) discontinuous substituent rules can handle constructions like 'either . . . or', and (2) in which context-sensitive grammars can permute the elements of a sentence-string. [See Kugel, 155.] Both these facilities have been claimed

by Chomsky on behalf of transformational grammars. Yngve, in his paper [310] has shown how discontinuous substituents can be handled formally within a PSG (I shall use the abbreviations PSG and TG for phrase structure and transformational grammars respectively, from now on). A good recent exposition of the PSG case is Harman's [116]. In it the author constructs a PSG which generates a set of sentences that includes the set generated by one of Chomsky's transformational grammars. However, Harman admits that 'not all the sentences constructed in accordance with this grammar are well-formed' (p. 611). It should also be noticed that the PSGs described by Harman do not consist of an unordered set of rewrite rules, but of rules whose constituents have subscripts which limit their order of application. This is an extension to PSGs not discussed here, for reasons of simplicity in exposition.

17 Having its origin, in this century, in Russell's attempt to locate different 'logical forms' under the same 'grammatical form'.

18 See Section 2.22 below.

19 I.e. [48, p. 39] A reader may wonder what is the distinguishing feature of TGs, beyond the fact that they need not conform to the restrictions on PSGs. There is no answer to that question, since TGs have never, to my knowledge, been strictly defined by Chomsky. A number of attempts have been made by others, such as Ginsberg and Partee [100.].

20 Chomsky concludes discussion of this example with: '[A PSG] must necessarily impose further structure in quite an arbitrary way.' That is, he accepts the notion of an infinite sentence, but he rejects that of an infinite number of rules. But why, since in this case the rules required would be as susceptible of recursive definition as the sentence in question?

21 L. J. Cohen has pointed out that since one would never get to the full stop, then for that reason alone we could not call an *infinite* word-string a sentence. The notion of the 'infinite sentence' seems curiously important to Chomsky, yet he is unclear about it. In a more recent book Chomsky [56, p. 198] takes Dixon to task for writing, 'We are clearly unable to say that there is any definite number, N, such that no sentence contains more than N clauses', while on the same page objecting to Chomsky's assertion that 'there are [sic] an infinite number of sentences in a language'. This, Chomsky says, is either a blatant self-contradiction, or Dixon has some new sense of the word 'infinite' in mind. But it is not a self-contradiction, and Chomsky is simply confusing 'infinite' with 'unbounded'. That one *could* 'go on' does not commit one to doing so, nor does it ever give one a completed infinity: it simply defines unboundedness.

22 He does mention PSGs with discontinuous constituents [48, p. 41n] but only to say that they do not affect his case. On the face of it they do, and he nowhere shows that they do not.

23 [48, p. 15] There is a further confusion of Chomsky's about the notion of sentence. He sometimes speaks of explicating simply 'sen-

tence in L' [48, p. 55] in which case (2) above *isn't* a sentence for him.

24 Transformations, too, were defined at this stage in Chomsky's work in such a way that 'meaning' was not mentioned. It was contingent that 'active-passive' transformations 'preserved meaning' while 'negativizing' ones did not.

25 Cf. '. . . words have those meanings which we give them; and we give them meanings by explanations'. [Wittgenstein, 307, p. 26.]

26 Putnam refers to the Chomsky rule 'If S1 and S2 are grammatical sentences, and S1 differs from S2 only in that X appears in S1 where Y appears in S2, and X and Y are constituents of the same type in S1 and S2, respectively, then S3 in a sentence where S3 is the result of replacing X by X+and+Y in S1'. It is unfortunate that Putnam should have picked that example, since putting S1 ='John is a unique human being' and S2='Mary is a unique human being' is quite enough to show that this 'rule' will not do.

27 Cohen has made out a case that assessments of grammaticalness are 'resistant to statistical support' because the 'grammaticalness of a string is to be judged only in the light of its supposed method of generation' [64, p. 39].

28 See also Chomsky's recent invocation of the old notion of 'innate ideas' to try and back up this view [54, pp. 27 *seq.* and 56].

29 L. J. Cohen for example, in [65].

30 [52, p. 7]: 'Normal mastery of a language involves not only the ability to understand immediately an indefinite number of new sentences, but also the ability to identify deviant sentences, and, on occasion, to impose an interpretation on them.'

31 It is a phrase structure grammar because Chomsky is concerned here with what he calls a 'base'. This has much the same function as did the 'kernels' (and the PSG that produced them) in earlier expositions of his system.

32 'Dashed' boxes are mine to include lattices (see below). It is worth noting that Chomsky's often repeated claim, that he is taking syntax back to the path of *traditional* grammar, is not borne out by his analysis of this sentence which shows no connexion at all between the verb and what one naturally calls *its* auxiliary.

33 [54, p. 159] 'A decision as to the boundary between syntax and semantics (*if there is one*) is not a prerequisite for theoretical and descriptive study of syntactic and semantic rules.' [My italics.]

34 [54, pp. 79 and 82–96] Chomsky is only pointing out the well-known truth about classification that one cannot classify a random sample of objects *per genus et differentiam* unless one also makes arbitrary decisions about the order of the categories.

35 I am not suggesting that it can, since I argued earlier that 'meaningfulness', or 'intelligibility', would not allow of such a simple demarcation.

36 See, for example, [Cohen 65], [Weinreich 290], [Sgall 265].

37 See, for example, [Sparck-Jones 272], [Dixon 77].

38 Katz and Fodor, 'The structure of semantic theory' [145] (to be referred to as KF) and Katz and Postal, *An Integrated Theory of Linguistic Descriptions* [146] (to be referred to as KP).

39 That is, I think, because they share the 'logistic' view that the meaning of an utterance is simply some sum of the meanings of its words plus the syntax. Chomsky holds the view [54, pp. 161–2], and a particularly clear statement of it occurs in Weinreich [290, p. 36]: 'The goal of a semantic theory is to explicate the way in which the meaning of a specified sentence is derivable from the fully specified meanings of its parts.'

40 Ambiguity of reference of this sort also occurs in text, where it is some-times called 'anaphora'. A clear case of it is prior reference of pronouns. I shall consider this a special case, and not deal with it further. [See Robinson, 251.]

41 See further below on the complex and vexed notion of reference. Their work is certainly non-referential by contrast with Chomsky's view that 'ambiguity is referential ambiguity' [48, p. 86].

42 Chomsky does, of course, take account of parts of speech in his lexicon.

43 [146, p. 22] KP are writing in the 'generative mode', that is of generating a reading, or structure, for a piece of language. But it will be clear that if they do this successfully then they will *ipso facto* have 'resolved the ambiguity' of the constituent words, since for each word there will be only one sense representation in the structure generated.

44 See Weinreich [290] who points out that KF cannot fall back on an appeal to the sufficiency of the senses plus the *grammatical* structure when challenged about this.

45 *Sophistical Refutations* 165a, for example. It also goes back, possibly further, to the story in Genesis of Adam naming the things of the world. Cassirer has argued that evidence fails to reveal a period when humans had a simple object language, and that belief in it is a nineteenth-century myth.

46 [261, p. 295] '. . . the idea or phonic substance that a sign contains is of less importance than the other signs that surround it. Proof of this is that the value of a term may be modified without either its meaning or its sound being affected, solely because a neighbouring term has been modified.'

47 It can already be seen how the polysemy of 'semantics' is like that of 'meaning', which I have outlined above. The old sense of the word going back to Bréal (and traced in Ullman [281]) concerns the con-nexions between the senses of words, and corresponds roughly to the notion of internal sense or meaning *which is not a referential concept at all.* In its modern use in 'formal semantics' it covers much the same spread of notions as does 'referential meaning'. It has been most developed by Tarski and Carnap, on the basis of distinctions drawn by Pierce [218, Vol. II, p. 136 seq.] and Morris [197, pp. 77–137], although it was Chwistek who first used 'semantics' in this sense in 1922 [see Carnap, 42, pp. v–vii]. Tarski and Carnap's theories had

differences of emphasis; Tarski's was on 'satisfaction' and Carnap's on 'singular denotation'. Since then, however, *intensional* theories of semantics have been put forward by Church [59], Carnap [43] and R. M. Martin [179]. These are also *referential* theories; Martin pins down the difference between the two kinds by showing that in a denotational theory a word refers to a class of members, whereas in an intensional theory it refers to a class of classes i.e. of defining properties.

48 [305, §§28–30] 'An ostensive definition can be variously interpreted in every case'... 'the ostensive definition explains the use—the meaning—of the word when the overall role of the word in the language is clear'. Cf. Quine's '. . . the specific objective reference of foreign terms is inscrutable. . . . ' [235, p. 80].

49 Cf. Cohen, [65, pp. 81–3] 'Logical grammar suggests that the conceptual study of meanings is concerned with the timeless'.

50 I am indebted to Mr D. S. Linney for this point.

3 Computable semantic derivations

1 A survey of current work on computational semantics, in the sense of 'semantics' I have now settled for, would be difficult for the same reason as a survey of work in artificial intelligence would be difficult, namely, that there is no overall agreed theory in use. All one can do is describe and try to compare the different enterprises. There are no generally agreed terms, or standards of judgment. Work that would have to be surveyed would include [Bobrow, 33], [Raphael, 241], [Simmons, 266], [Quillian, 228], [Su and Harper, 275] and [Shank and Tessler, 262].

2 This is so although the output from the analysis described in this section is a list of word-senses. For the structured form from which the appropriate senses are read off remains available as possible output for some purpose other than ambiguity resolution pure and simple.

3 I am not suggesting for a moment that Wittgenstein or Bambrough *discovered* what classifiers call 'polythetic' or overlapping classifications. Dr Needham has pointed out that these have been known since the eighteenth century at least.

4 One consequence for linguistic classification of this 'relativist' view of classification is that it is not just a contingent matter that word occurrences can be classified into sense classes. That fact is important for the suggested explication of meaningfulness of Chapter I. For, if all uses of words are always 'in the same sense' (as Antal claims), or even if it is merely contingent that words have a number of senses, in that it might be otherwise, then the explication of meaningfulness in terms of resolving ambiguity would be vacuous. If there was no ambiguity in the first place then anything defined in terms of its resolution would be pointless.

5 The assumption that the entries in dictionaries for natural languages can be interpreted as 'substitution licences' also has the effect of limiting the method to a single language in a non-extensible way. For the entries in a French-English dictionary could not be substituted for each other in any sentence at all.

6 It is most important that the work of Sparck-Jones attempts to construct a reasonable notion of word-sense. There is a familiar demonstration in books on mathematical linguistics that the set of word-senses in a vocabulary is infinite, even non-denumerably infinite. But that rests on an absurd initial definition of word-sense, namely *any* occurrence of a word symbol in *any* symbol string, of *any* length, which is to say that every occurrence of a word is a new sense of it!

7 Public lecture, Cambridge, 1965.

8 Needham's point that we cannot *know* in advance that such a system will cope with everything that can be said, is of course correct. But it cannot be contrasted with syntax in this respect, for we do not have any more secure *knowledge* in the case of syntax: all we have is the facility to *reject* anything that does not fit.

9 In that sense a system using message-forms may be said to incorporate some of the information about the real world that is again being said to be necessary to any system of computational linguistics [Hays, 120]. The dispute about how much such knowledge is necessary to any linguistic system is one that crops up at regular intervals.

10 This notion owes a considerable debt to the general discussions of Guberina and Masterman concerning an overall coherence in text between pairs of items longer than individual words and, generally, shorter than sentences. [See 108, 184.]

11 I make no attempt here to invent a 'metatheory' in which to place the CSD system. That notion has been gaining some publicity lately, for example [Schwarz, 264], and its use in linguistics of this sort is wholly unnecessary and misleading. The term is borrowed from the work of Tarski, where it refers to description of formal items of a theory. In that sense of 'metatheory' the present section is, vacuously, metatheory. However, when used by linguists, like the one I referred to, it seems to mean 'psycholinguistic assumptions' or what is sometimes called 'motivation'. But formal analysis of language has no need of psychological assumptions, for the analysis either works, or it doesn't. Talk of 'metatheory' is only a way of imposing a wordy screen that obscures what should be the subject under discussion, namely language.

12 See, for example Hockett in [129] and Ullmann and Jakobson in the same volume. There is also the literature on Universal Languages back to Leibniz, Lully, Dalgarno and Wilkins. (There is a large bibliography in Sparck-Jones, *op cit*.).

12 Quine. [235, p. 83], 'In effect, therefore, we must credit the child with some sort of pre-linguistic quality space.'

14 At Systems Development Corporation, Santa Monica, California, John Olney has available the whole of Webster's dictionary in computer-readable form. He has listed, in order, the words used most frequently

by the dictionary makers in the definitions that constitute the dictionary. The fifty most frequent words show a remarkable overlap with the fifty-three defining elements listed overleaf: an extraordinary correspondence between the inductive and the *a priori*.

15 I use upper-case letters for the elements. That should not lead to any confusion with the names (in Chapter 4) of functions in the LISP language, which are also in upper-case letters.

16 Thus the element 'NOTTHING' would mean that what it applied to was not a thing, and so on.

17 Some linguists claim that the feature method is also reducible to a substitution criterion, but, if it is, it is so in quite a different sense from the Sparck-Jones criterion.

18 The present notion of template owes a great deal to Margaret Masterman's notion of a 'semantic shell'; see [186].

19 Halliday has also suggested the thematic organization of text clauses in terms of a notion of 'message', see [113].

20 A more felicitous name might be Wittgenstein's 'Logical Space' [304]. The notion is also closely related to notions of opposition made use of by Jakobson, and in another field by Lévi-Strauss.

21 By 'fragment ambiguity' I mean only that the previous procedures have attached a number of possible meaning structures to each fragment, and so the fragment is ambiguous until some subsequent decision is made between the structures so attached.

22 The form of these rules is simply a convenient abbreviation of a more conventional form. Thus:

R5 iv. (N1→SIGN) + . . . + N2→PART, STUFF,

is simply an abbreviated expression of the two context-dependent phrase structure rules.

SIGN + . . . + N2→SIGN + . . . + PART
SIGN + . . . + N2→SIGN + . . . + STUFF

23 The choice of rules is clearly such as to produce intuitively acceptable templates: to get the system to do something that one feels humans do (i.e. rule out impossible message-forms in that way). But there is, I repeat, no inference here (or *attempted* inference, for it would be a first-order howler) from *what* humans do to *how* they do it.

24 Rules 11 i–iv can be thought of as 'transformation rules':
i.e. (i) can be put in the form:

N1+KIND→KIND + . . . + N1

But it is not necessary, or formally homogeneous, to do so.

25 The term 'template' will now be taken to refer to 'full template' unless confusion would result from doing so.

26 It will be seen that this general form of expression, taken with Def. 21, is a summary form of ninety rules (the number of ways of producing templates with two of ten possible different connexions).

27 Sentence (1) is really a *definition* of the second sense, and (2) is a real example.

4 Practical semantic experiments

1 I shall use upper-case letters for function and file names (a list of the major functions constructed is given in Appendix x of [298]).

2 One coding for each preposition, that is, *not* a single coding for all prepositions.

3 Since the formulae for, say, 'Congress' and 'elected' would then correspond to different fragments.

4 These lists are largely derived from Earl [85].

5 I have not taken space to set out the conditions for fragmenting text in detail, though they are set out in [298 Appendix x]. These procedures are, as it were, theoretically dispensable, and their task might be accomplished in many different ways.

6 In fact, the phrase would be passed on as 'A of rules fo book'. The (empty) character 'fo' is inserted in the fragmented texts to delimit such shifted phrases.

7 CDR is a basic LISP function which returns a list of all members of a list *except the first*. Thus, after searching for all possible bare templates containing the head of the first formula SEARCHER repeats this with the CDR of the frame, and so on until the frame is empty.

8 This is part of the output value from the LISP function TEMPO. TEMPO ties each fragment name to a list of items each of which had the form

  ((HEAD1   HEAD2   HEAD3)
   (SENSEPAIR1   SENSEPAIR2   SENSEPAIR3)).

So in the output, (BRITAINS TRANSPORT SYSTEM ARE CHANGING) (the apparent grammatical howler comes from the form of the fragmentation, and is unimportant for semantic purposes) is tied to five such items, of which the second is the intuitively correct one. The string of three heads is the bare template, and it has matched on to the three formulae contained in the three following sense-pairs, in order. So, for example, HEAD1 is the head of the formula in SENSEPAIR1, and so on. Each matched bare template has picked up three formulae from a frame for a fragment.

9 A LISP NIL is inserted if there was no qualifying formula to be found at that point in the frame examined.

10 The function CLOSEST uses the functions described earlier to determine closeness between formulae, together with one that seeks for pairs of atoms related by membership of the same negation class. CLOSEST ranks closeness by different tests in a 'poker-hand' of preferred kinds of closeness, and finally produces a list of word-senses ordered with the closest at the top of the list.

11 In the sense of *diminishing its semantic representation*, since after a sense construction there will be fewer word-senses distributed over the set of text-words than was possible before the construction.

Bibliography

Note: A considerable number of the papers referred to occur in one of three collections of papers, and I shall use abbreviations as follows to refer to those collections:

Teddington *Proceedings of the First International Conference on Machine Translation, Teddington, Middlesex, 1961* (HMSO, London, 1961).
XII Vol. XII of the *Symposia in Applied Mathematics*, American Mathematical Society.
COLING *Proceedings of the International Conference on Computational Linguistics, Stockholm, Sweden, 1969.*

1 Adjukiewicz, K., 'Die syntaktische Konnexität', *Studia Philosophica*, 1935: tr. Geach, in *Review of Metaphysics*, 1967.
2 Alt, F., and Rhodes, I., 'Recognition of clauses and phrases in machine translation of languages', in *XII*.
3 Ambrose, A., 'Proof and the theorem proved', *Mind*, 1959.
4 Anderson, J. F., 'Some basic propositions concerning metaphysical analogy', *Review of Metaphysics*, 1952.
5 Anderson, J. F., 'Mathematics and the Language Game', *Review of Metaphysics*, 1958.
6 Anderson, J. F., and Belnap, N., 'A modification of Ackermann's rigorous entailment', *Journal of Symbolic Logic*, 1958.
7 Antal, L., *Questions of Meaning*, The Hague, 1963.
8 Ashby, R., 'Entailment and modality', *Proc. Arist. Soc.*, 1962–3.
9 Austin, J. L., *Philosophical Papers*, Oxford, 1961.
10 Austin, J. L., *How to do Things with Words*, Oxford, 1962.
11 Ayer, A. J., *Language, Truth and Logic* (2nd edn.), London, 1946.

N

12 Bambrough, J. R., 'Universals and family resemblances', *Proc. Arist. Soc.*, 1960–1.
13 Bar-Hillel, Y., 'A quasi-arithmetic notation for syntactic description', *Language* 29, 1953.
14 Bar-Hillel, Y., 'Logical syntax and semantics', *Language* 30, 1954.
15 Bar-Hillel, Y., 'Husserl's conception of a purely logical grammar', *Philosophical and Phenomenological Research*, 1957.
16 Bar-Hillel, Y., review of Martin, R. M., *Truth and Denotation*, *Language* 35, 1959.
17 Bar-Hillel, Y., 'On a misapprehension of the status of theories in linguistics', *Foundations of Language*, 1966.
18 Bar-Hillel, Y., 'Measures of syntactic complexity', in Booth (ed.), *Advances in Machine Translation*, N. Holland, 1967.
19 Bar-Hillel, Y., 'Dictionaries and meaning rules', *Foundations of Language*, 1967.
20 Bar-Hillel, Y., and Carnap, R., *An Outline of a Theory of Semantic Information*, Research Laboratory of Electronics, Massachusetts Institute of Technology: Tech. Report 247, 1952.
21 Bar-Hillel, Y., Perles, M., and Shamir, E., 'On the formal properties of simple phrase structure systems', *Phonetik Sprach. Kommunikationsforsch.*, 1961.
22 Belnap, N., 'Entailment and relevance', *Journal of Symbolic Logic*, 1960.
23 Belnap, N., *A Formal Analysis of Entailment*, Sociology Dept., Yale Univ., 1961.
24 Bennett, J. F., *Rationality*, Studies in Philos. Psychology, London, 1964.
25 Bennett, J. F., 'Meaning and implication', *Mind.*, 1954.
26 Bennett, J. F., 'On being forced to a conclusion', *Arist. Soc. Supp. Vol.*, 1961.
27 Bennett, J. F., 'Analytic-synthetic', *Proc. Arist. Soc.*, 1958–9.
28 Birkhoff, G., *Lattice Theory*, American Mathematical Association, Symposia in Pure Mathematics, 1949.
29 Black, M., 'Vagueness', in *Language and Philosophy*, Ithaca, N.Y., 1949.
30 Black, M., 'Metaphor', *Proc. Arist. Soc.*, 1954–5.
31 Bloomfield, L., *Language*, New York, 1933.
32 Bobrow, D., 'Syntactic analysis by computer—a survey', *Proc. Fall Joint Computer Conf.*, 1963.
33 Bobrow, D., 'Natural language input for a computer problem-solving system', Ph.D. Thesis, Massachusetts Institute of Technology, 1964.
34 Boden, M., 'The paradox of explanation', *Proc. Arist. Soc.*, 1961–2.
35 Bolinger, D., 'The atomization of meaning', *Language* 41, 1965.
36 Booth, A. D., Cleave, J. P., and Brandwood, L., *Mechanical Resolution of Linguistic Problems*, London, 1958.
37 Borko, H. (ed.), *Automated Language Processing*, Wiley, New York, 1967.

38 Bosanquet, R., 'Remarks on Spinoza's ethics', *Mind*, 1945.
39 Cambridge Language Research Unit, 'Essays on and in Machine Translation', mimeo, 1960.
40 Carnap, R., *Philosophy and Logical Syntax*, London, 1935.
41 Carnap, R., *The Logical Syntax of Language*, London, 1937.
42 Carnap, R., *Introduction to Semantics*, Cambridge, Mass., 1942.
43 Carnap, R., *Meaning and Necessity*, Chicago, 1947.
44 Carnap, R., 'The elimination of metaphysics', reprinted in Ayer (ed.), *Logical Positivism*, New York, 1959.
45 Charney, E. K., 'On the semantic interpretation of entities that function structurally', in *Teddington*.
46 Chomsky, N., 'Systems of syntactic analysis', *Journal of Symbolic Logic*, 1953.
47 Chomsky, N., 'Three models for the description of language', *IRE Transactions on Information Theory*, Vol. IT 2, No. 3, 1956.
48 Chomsky, N., *Syntactic Structures*, Janua Linguarum, 1957.
49 Chomsky, N., review of Skinner, B. F., *Verbal Behaviour*, *Language* 32, 1956.
50 Chomsky, N., 'On the notion of "Rule of grammar" ', in *XII*.
51 Chomsky, N., 'Logical basis of linguistic theory' (unpublished).
52 Chomsky, N., *Current Issues in Linguistic Theory*, Janua Linguarum, 1964.
53 Chomsky, N., 'On degree of grammaticality', in Katz and Fodor (eds.), *Readings in the Philosophy of Language*, Englewood Cliffs, N.J., 1965.
54 Chomsky, N., *Aspects of the Theory of Syntax*, Cambridge, Mass., 1965.
55 Chomsky, N., 'Topics in the theory of generative grammar', in Sebeok (ed.), *Current Trends in Linguistics*, Vol. 3, The Hague, 1966.
56 Chomsky, N., *Language and Mind*, Cambridge, Mass., 1969.
57 Chomsky, N., and Schützenberger, P., 'An algebraic theory of context-free languages', in Braffort and Hirshberg (eds.), *Computer Programming and Formal Systems*, Amsterdam, 1963.
58 Church, A., 'The need for abstract entities in semantic analysis', *Proc. Amer. Acad. of Arts and Sciences*, 1951.
59 Church, A., 'A formulation of the logic of sense and denotation', in Henle (ed.), *Structure, Method and Meaning*, New York, 1951.
60 Church, A., *Introduction to Mathematical Logic*, Vol. I, Princeton, N.J., 1956.
61 Chwistek, L., *The Limits of Science*, tr. Brodie and Coleman, London, 1948.
62 Cohen, L. J., 'On the project of a Universal Character', *Mind* 1954.
63 Cohen, L. J., 'On a concept of degree of grammaticalness', *Logique et Analyse*, 1959.
64 Cohen, L. J., 'A logic for evidential support', *Brit. Jl Phil. of Sci.*, 1966.
65 Cohen, L. J., *The Diversity of Meaning* (2nd edn.), London, 1966.
66 Collingwood, R. G., *An Essay on Philosophical Method*, Oxford, 1933.

67 Collingwood, R. G., *An Autobiography*, London, 1939.
68 Corbe, M., and Tabory, J., 'Introduction to an automatic English syntax', in *Teddington*.
69 Cowan, J., 'The uses of argument—an apology for logic', *Mind*, 1964.
70 Curry, H. B., *Foundations of Mathematical Logic*, New York, 1963.
71 Curry, H. B., 'Remarks on inferential deduction', in Tymieniecka and Parsons (eds), *Contributions to Logic and Methodology in Honour of I. M. Bochenski*, Amsterdam, 1965.
72 Curry, H. B., 'Logical aspects of syntactic structure', in *XII*.
73 Darlington, J., *Translating Ordinary Language into Symbolic Logic*, Memorandum MAC–M–149, Project MAC, Massachusetts Institute of Technology, 1964.
74 Davis, M., *Computability and Unsolvability*, New York, 1958.
75 Davis, M., 'Eliminating the irrelevant from mechanical proofs', *Proc. Sympos. App. Maths.*, Vol. XV, Amer. Math. Soc., 1963.
76 Delavenay, E., *An Introduction to Machine Translation*, London, 1960.
77 Dixon, R. W., 'A trend in semantics', *Linguistics*, 1963.
78 Dixon, R. W., *Linguistic Science and Logic*, The Hague, 1963.
79 Dixon, R. W., *What is Language?*, London, 1965.
80 Dolby, J., and Resnikoff, H., 'The algorithmic determination of the possible parts of speech of written English words', *Mechanical Translation*, 1965.
81 Drange, T., *Type Crossings*, The Hague, 1966.
82 Dreyfus, H., *Alchemy and Artificial Intelligence*, RAND Mem P–3244, Santa Monica, 1965.
83 Dummett, M., 'The philosophical significance of Gödel's theorem', *Ratio*, 1963–4.
84 Dummett, M., 'Wittgenstein's philosophy of mathematics', *Philosophical Rev.*, 1957.
85 Earl, L., *An Algorithm for Automatic Clause Delimitation in English Sentences*, Lockheed Missiles and Space Co., Tech. Report, 5.13.64.5, 1964.
86 Feigenbaum, E. A., 'Artificial intelligence: themes in the second decade', *Proceedings of the International Conference on Information Processing*, New York, 1969.
87 Findlay, J., 'The teaching of meaning', *Logique et Analyse*, 1962.
88 Fodor, J., review of Antal, L., *Questions of Meaning*, *Language* 39, 1963.
89 Fodor, J., 'Projection and paraphrase in semantic analysis', *Analysis*, 1961.
90 Fodor, J., and Katz, J., *The Structure of Language—Readings in the Philosophy of Language*, Englewood Cliffs, N.J., 1965.
91 Forman, B., *An Experiment in Semantic Classification*, Univ. of Texas, Linguistic Research Center, 1965.
92 Fowler, R., 'Sentence and clause in English', *Linguistics*, 1965.
93 Frege, G., *Foundations of Arithmetic*, tr. Austin, Oxford, 1950.
94 Frege, G., *Translations*, tr. Geach and Black, Oxford, 1960.

95 Gaifman, H., *Dependency Systems and Phrase Structure Systems*, RAND Mem. P–2315, Santa Monica, 1961.
96 Galanter, P., and Miller, G., 'Some comments on stochastic models and psychological theories', *Mathematical Models in the Social Sciences*, 1960.
97 Gardiner, A., 'A grammarian's thoughts on a recent philosophical work', *Transactions of the Philological Society*, 1951.
98 Garvin, P. (ed.), *Natural Language and the Computer*, New York, 1963.
99 Garvin, P., review of *XII, Language* 39, 1963.
100 Ginsberg, S., and Partee, B., *A Mathematical Model of Transformational Grammars*, Systems Development Corp., Santa Monica, TM–7380–4800, 1968.
101 Givòn, T., *Transformation of Ellipsis, Sense Development and Rules of Lexical Derivation*, Systems Development Corp., Santa Monica, SP–2896, 1967.
102 Gödel, K., *On Formally Undecidable Propositions of PM and Related Systems*, tr. Meltzer, Edinburgh, 1961.
103 Gorn, S., 'Ambiguity and paradox in mechanical languages', *Proc. Sympos. Pure Maths.*, Vol. V, Amer. Math. Soc., 1952.
104 Goodman, N., 'On likeness of meaning', *Analysis*, 1949.
105 Goodstein, R., 'Significance of the incompleteness theorems', *Brit. Jl Phil. of Sci.*, 1953–4.
106 Green, C., *et al.*, 'Baseball—an automatic question-answer', *Proc. Winter Joint Computer Conf.*, New York, 1961.
107 Greenberg, J. H. (ed.), *Universals of Language*, Cambridge, Mass., 1963.
108 Guberina, P., *La Logique de la logique et la logique de la language*, Zagreb, Yugoslavia, 1957.
109 Guiraud, P., 'Diacritical and statistical models for language in relation to the computer', in Hymes (ed.), *The Use of Computers in Anthropology*, The Hague, 1965.
110 Hacking, I., *Logic of Statistical Inference*, Cambridge, 1965.
111 Halliday, M., 'Categories of the theory of grammar', *Word*, 1961.
112 Halliday, M., 'Some notes on deep grammar', *Journal of Linguistics*, 1966.
113 Halliday, M., *Some Aspects of the Thematic Organization of the Clause*, RAND Mem. P–5224, 1957
114 Hampshire, S, 'The progress of philosophy', *Polemic*, 1946.
115 Hardwick, S., *et al.*, *Fact Correlation Experiment*, Radio Corp. of America, Maryland, 1964.
116 Harman, G., 'Generative grammar without transformation rules', *Language* 39, 1963.
117 Harris, Z. S., *Methods in Structural Linguistics*, Chicago, 1951.
118 Harris, Z. S., 'Co-occurrence and transformation in linguistic structure', in Fodor and Katz (eds), *Readings in the Philosophy of Language* (*q.v.*).
119 Hays, D., 'Dependency theory, a formalism and some observations', *Language* 40, 1964.

120 Hays, D., 'Applied computational linguistics', *Proceedings of the Second International Congress on Applied Linguistics*, Cambridge, 1969.
121 Hermes, H., *Enumerability, Decidability, Computability*, Berlin, 1965.
122 Hesse, M. B., 'On defining analogy', *Proc. Arist. Soc.*, 1959–60.
123 Hesse, M., 'The explanatory function of metaphor', *Proc. Internat. Cong. Logic, Methodology and Phil. of Sci.*, N. Holland, 1964.
124 Hiz, H., 'Intuitions of grammatical categories', *Series on Transformational Analysis*, No. 29, Univ. of Pennsylvania, 1961.
125 Hiz, H., 'Types and environments', *Phil. of Sci.*, 1957.
126 Hiz, H., 'Questions and answers', *Journal of Philosophy*, 1962.
127 Hockett, C. F., *A Course in Modern Linguistics*, New York, 1958.
128 Hockett, C. F., 'Chinese versus English; an exploration of the Whorfian thesis', in *Language and Culture*, Univ. of Chicago, 1960.
129 Hockett, C. F., 'The problem of universals in language', in Greenberg (ed.), *Universals of Language*, Cambridge, Mass., 1963.
130 Hockett, C. F., *The State of the Art*, The Hague, 1968.
131 Holloway, J., *Language and Intelligence*, London, 1951.
132 Householder, F., review of Chomsky, N., *Current Issues in Linguistic Theory*, *Journal of Linguistics*, 1966.
133 Husserl, E., *Logische Untersuchungen*, Leipzig, 1900.
134 I.B.M. *Final Report on Computer Set AN/GSQ–16(XW–1)*, I.B.M. Research, Yorktown Heights, New York, 1959.
135 Jacobsen, S. N., 'A modifiable system for relating connected sentences in English text', in Garvin and Spolsky (eds), *Computational Linguistics*, Bloomington, Ind., 1966.
136 Jakobson, R., 'Linguistics and communication', in *XII*.
137 Janotis, A., and Josselson, H., 'Multiple meaning in machine translation', in *XII*.
138 Johnson, S., *A Dictionary of the English Language*, London, 1755.
139 Jordan, Z., *Polish Science and Learning*, London, 1944.
140 Katz, J., 'The semantic component of a linguistic description', *Proc. Conf. on Structural Linguistics*, Magdeburg, 1964.
141 Katz, J., 'Semantic theory and the meaning of "grammatical" ', *Journal of Philosophy*, 1964.
142 Katz, J., *The Philosophy of Language*, New York, 1966.
143 Katz, J., 'Recent issues in semantic theory', *Foundations of Language* 1967.
144 Katz, J., and Fodor, J., 'What's wrong with the philosophy of language?', *Inquiry*, 1962.
145 Katz, J., and Fodor, J., 'The structure of semantic theory', *Language* 39, 1963.
146 Katz, J., and Postal, P., *An Integrated Theory of Linguistic Description*, Cambridge, Mass., 1964.
147 Kleene, S., 'Lambda-definability and recursiveness', *Duke Math. Jl*, 1963.
148 Kleene, S., 'Computability and lambda-definability', *Journal of Symbolic Logic*, 1937.

149 Klein, S., 'Control of style with a generative grammar', *Language* 41, 1965.
150 Klein, S., 'Automatic paraphrasing in essay format', *Machine Translation*, 1965.
151 Klein, S., *Disseminer*, Carnegie Institute of Technology, 1967.
152 Klein, S., and Simmons, R., 'Syntactic dependence and the computer generation of coherent discourse', *Machine Translation*, 1963.
153 Kneale, W., 'Universality and necessity', *Brit. Jl Phil. of Sci.*, 1961.
154 Kneale, W., and M., *The Development of Logic*, Oxford, 1962.
155 Kugel, P., 'Sets of grammars between context-free and context-sensitive', *Proc. Conf. of Assn. for Mach. Trans. and Comp. Ling.*, New York, 1965.
156 Kuhn, T. S., *The Structure of Scientific Revolutions*, Chicago, 1963.
157 Laing, R. D., *The Divided Self*, London, 1960.
158 Lakoff, G., 'Towards generative semantics', Internal memorandum, Mech. Trans. Group, Massachusetts Institute of Technology, 1963.
159 Lambek, J., 'The mathematics of sentence structure', *Amer. Math. Monthly*, 1958.
160 Lambek, J., 'On the calculus of syntactic types', in *XII*.
161 *Language and Machines: Computers in translation and linguistics*, available from the Printing and Publishing Office, 2101, Constitution Ave., Washington D.C.
162 Lepschy, G., 'Problems of semantics', *Linguistics*, 1965.
163 Lesniewski, S., *Principles of the General Theory of Sets*, Moscow, 1916.
164 Lesniewski, S., 'Grundzüge eines neuen Systems der Grundlagen der Mathematik,' *Fund. Math.*, 1929.
165 Levien, R., and Maron, M., 'A computer system for inference execution and data retrieval', *Communications of Assn for Computing Machinery*, 1965.
166 Lewis, C. I., and Langford, C. H., *Symbolic Logic*, New York, 1932.
167 Lewy, C., 'Entailment and proposition identity', *Proc. Arist. Soc.*, 1963-4.
168 Lieberman, D., *et al.*, *Specification and Utilization of a Transformational Grammar*, I.B.M. project 4641, 1966.
169 Lindsay, R., 'Inferential memory as the basis of machines which understand natural language', in Feigenbaum and Feldman (eds), *Computers and Thought*, New York, 1963.
170 Linsky, L. (ed.), *Semantics and the Philosophy of Language*, Urbana, 1952.
171 Locke, W. N., and Booth, A. D., *Machine Translation of Languages*, Cambridge, Mass., 1955.
172 Longacre, J., 'Prolegomena to lexical structure', *Linguistics*, 1965.
173 Lukasiewicz, J., *Aristotle's Syllogistic*, Oxford, 1951.
174 Lyons, J., 'A Structural Theory of Semantics and its Application to some Lexical Sub-Systems in the Vocabulary of Plato', Ph.D. Thesis, University of Cambridge, 1961: published as *Structural Semantics*, No. 20 of the Publications of the Philological Society, Oxford, 1964.
175 Lyons, J., and Wales, R., *Psycholinguistic Papers*, Edinburgh, 1966.

176 Mace, C., 'Logic of elucidation', in *Essays in Memory of L. S. Stebbing*, London, 1948.
177 Malcolm, N., 'The nature of entailment', *Mind*, 1940.
178 Mandelbrot, B., 'Word frequencies and Markovian models of discourse', in *XII*.
179 Martin, R. M., *Truth and Denotation—a Study in Semantical Theory*, London, 1958.
180 Masterman, M., 'Words', *Proc. Arist. Soc.*, 1953–4.
181 Masterman, M., *Potentialities of a Mechanical Thesaurus* (Appendix by A. F. Parker-Rhodes), *Mechanical Translation*, 1956.
182 Masterman, M., 'The thesaurus in syntax and semantics', *Mechanical Translation*, 1956.
183 Masterman, M., 'Translation', *Arist. Soc. Supplementary Volume*, 1961.
184 Masterman, M., 'Commentary on the Guberina hypothesis', *Methodos*, 57–58, 1963.
185 Masterman, M., 'Semantic algorithms', *Proc. Conf. on Computer-related Semantics*, Wayne State Univ., 1965.
186 Masterman, M., 'Semantic message detection for machine translation using an interlingua', in *Teddington*.
187 Masterman, M., and Kay, M., 'Mechanical Pidgin translation', in Booth (ed.), *Advances in Mechanical Translation*, 1967.
188 Masterman, M., Needham, R. M., and Sparck-Jones, K., 'The analogy between machine translation and library retrieval', *Proc. Internat. Conf. on Scientific Information*, Washington, 1959.
189 Matthews, G., 'Analysis by synthesis of natural language', in *Teddington*.
190 Mays, W., 'Carnap on logic and language', *Proc. Arist. Soc.*, 1961–2.
191 McCarthy, J., 'Computer programs for checking mathematical proofs', *Proc. Sympos. on Recursive Function Theory*, Amer. Math. Soc., 1961.
192 McCarthy, J., 'A basis for a mathematical theory of computation', in Braffort and Hirschberg (eds), *Computer Programming and Formal Systems*, Amsterdam, 1963.
193 McCarthy, J., *et al.*, LISP *1.5 Programmer's Manual*, Cambridge, Mass., 1962.
194 Minsky, M. (ed.), *Semantic Information Processing*, Cambridge, Mass., 1968.
195 Moore, G. E., *Philosophical Studies*, London, 1922.
196 Moravscik, J., 'Linguistic theory and the philosophy of language', *Foundations of Language*, 1967.
197 Morris, C. W., *Foundations of the Theory of Signs*, Internat. Encyclopedia of Unified Science, 1.ii, Chicago, 1938.
198 Myhill, J., 'Problems arising in the formalisation of intensional logic', *Logique et Analyse*, 1958.
199 Naess, A., *Communication and Argument*, Oslo, 1966.
200 Needham, R. M., 'Semantics for mechanical translation', *Proc. Internat. Conf. on Information Processing*, New York, 1965.

201 Needham, R. M., and Parker-Rhodes, A. F., *The Theory of Clumps*, Cambridge Language Research Unit, mimeo, 1960.
202 Needham, R. M., and Sparck-Jones, K., 'Keywords and clumps', *Journal of Documentation*, 1964.
203 Nelson, E. J., 'Intensional relations', *Mind*, 1930.
204 Newell, H., *et al.*, 'Empirical explorations with the logic theory machine' in Feigenbaum and Feldman (eds), *Computers and Thought*, New York, 1963.
205 Nidditch, P., *The Development of Mathematical Logic*, London, 1962.
206 Oettinger, A. D., *Automatic Language Translation*, Cambridge, Mass., 1960.
207 Ogden, C., and Richards, I., *The Meaning of Meaning*, London, 1936.
208 Olney, J., 'Some patterns observed in contextual specialisation of word senses', *Information Storage and Retrieval*, 1964.
209 Olney, J., and Londe, D., *An Analysis of English Discourse Structure, with particular attention to Anaphoric Relationships*, Systems Development Corp., Santa Monica, SP–2769, 1967.
210 *The Oxford English Dictionary* (Corrected re-issue with Introduction, Supplement and Bibliography of a New English Dictionary on Historical Principles, edited by Murray, Bradley, Craigie, and Onions), Oxford, 1933 (abbreviated as O.E.D.).
211 Panov, D. Y., *Automatic Translation*, London, 1960.
212 Pap, A., 'Logic and the concept of entailment', *Journal of Phil.*, 1950.
213 Pap, A., *Semantics and Necessary Truth*, New Haven, 1958.
214 Pap, A., 'Types and meaninglessness', *Mind*, 1960.
215 Parker-Rhodes, A. F., 'Some recent work on thesauric and inter-lingual methods in machine translation', *Internat. Conf. on a Common Language for Machine Literature Searching and Translation*, Cleveland, Ohio, 1959.
216 Parker-Rhodes, A. F., 'A new model of syntactic description', in *Teddington*.
217 Passmore, J., *Philosophical Reasoning*, London, 1961.
218 Pierce, C. S., *Collected Papers*, New York, 1925.
219 Popper, K., 'Logic without assumptions', *Proc. Arist. Soc.,* 1947–8.
220 Popper, K., 'On the theory of deduction', *Proc. Roy. Neth. Acad. of Sci.*, 1948.
221 Popper, K., *The Logic of Scientific Discovery*, London, 1959.
222 Popper, K., *Conjectures and Refutations*, London, 1963.
223 Post, E., 'Finite combinatory processes', *Journal of Symbolic Logic*, 1936.
224 Post, E., 'Recursively enumerable sets of positive integers and their decision problems', *Bull. American Math. Society*, 1944.
225 *Proceedings of the National Symposium on Machine Translation*, Los Angeles, 1960 (ed. Edmundson), London, 1961.
226 *Proceedings of the 1961 International Conference on Machine Translation of Languages and Applied Language Analysis*, National Physical Laboratory, 1961, London, 1962.
227 Putnam, H., 'Some issues in the theory of grammar', in *XII*.

228 Quillian, R., 'The teachable language comprehender', *Communications of the Assn for Computing Machinery*, 1969.
229 Quine, W. V. O., 'Notes on existence and necessity', *Journal of Philosophy*, 1943.
230 Quine, W. V. O., 'Concatenation', *Journal of Symbolic Logic*, 1946.
231 Quine, W. V. O., *Mathematical Logic*, Cambridge, Mass., 1947.
232 Quine, W. V. O., *From a Logical Point of View*, Cambridge, Mass., 1953.
233 Quine, W. V. O., 'Meaning and translation', in Brower (ed.), *On Translation*, Cambridge, Mass., 1959.
234 Quine, W. V. O., 'Carnap and logical truth', *Synthese*, 1960.
235 Quine, W. V. O., *Word and Object*, Cambridge, Mass., 1960.
236 Quine, W. V. O., 'Logic as a source of syntactic insight', in *XII*.
237 Quine, W. V. O., 'Two dogmas of empiricism', in *From a Logical Point of View* (q.v.).
238 Quirk, R., and Svartik, J., *Investigating Linguistic Acceptability*, The Hague, 1966.
239 Ramsey, F., *Foundations of Mathematics*, London, 1931.
240 Raphael, B., 'SIR—A computer program for semantic information retrieval', Ph.D. Thesis, Massachusetts Institute of Technology, 1965.
241 Raphael, B., 'A computer program which "understands"', *Proc. Fall Joint Computer Conf.*, New York, 1964.
242 Reichenbach, H., *Elements of Symbolic Logic*, New York, 1947.
243 Rescher, N., *Hypothetical Reasoning*, Amsterdam, 1964.
244 Rescher, N., *The Logic of Commands*, London, 1966.
245 Richards, I. A., *The Philosophy of Rhetoric*, Oxford, 1936.
246 Richards, I. A., 'Why generative grammar doesn't help', *English Language Teaching*, 1968.
247 Richens, R. H., 'Interlingual machine translation', *Computer Journal*, 1958.
248 Robison, H., co-author, *Research in Automatic Informative and Extracting*, Lockheed Missiles and Space Co., LSMC–894736, 1966.
249 Robinson, J., 'Theorem proving by computer', *Journal Assn for Computing Machinery*, 1963.
250 Robinson, J., 'A review of automatic theorem proving', *Sympos. in App. Math.*, Amer. Math. Soc., 1967.
251 Robinson, R., 'Ambiguity', *Mind*, 1948.
252 Rosenbloom, P., *The Elements of Mathematical Logic*, New York, 1950.
253 Russell, B., 'On vagueness', *Australasian Journal of Psych. and Phil.*, 1923.
254 Russell, B., *A Critical Exposition of the Philosophy of Leibniz*, 2nd edn, London, 1937.
255 Russell, B., Introduction to Wittgenstein's *Tractatus Logico-Philosophicus*, London, 1922.
256 Ryle, G., 'Formal and informal logic', in *Dilemmas*, Cambridge, 1954.
257 Ryle, G., 'Categories', in Flew (ed.), *Logic and Language*, Vol. I, Oxford, 1951.

258 Ryle, G., review of Carnap, R., *Meaning and Necessity, Philosophy*, 1949.
259 Ryle, G., 'Systematically misleading expressions', in Flew (ed.), *Logic and Language*, Vol. I, Oxford, 1951.
260 Salton, G., and Thorpe, R. W., 'An approach to the segmentation problem in speech analysis and language translation', in *Teddington*.
261 Saussure, F. de, *Cours de linguistique générale*, Paris, 1916.
262 Schank, R., and Tessler, L., 'A conceptual dependency parser for natural language', in *COLING*.
263 Schlick, M., 'Meaning and verification', *Phil. Rev.*, 1934.
264 Schwarz, R. M., 'Towards a computational formalization of natural language semantics', in *COLING*.
265 Sgall, P., 'Generation, production and translation', *Proc. Conf. of Assn. for Mach. Trans. and Comp. Linguistics*, New York, 1965.
266 Simmons, R. F., Burger, J. F., and Long, R. E., 'An approach toward answering English questions from text', *Proc. Fall Joint Computer Conference*, San Francisco, 1966.
267 Simmons, R. F., 'Automated language processing', in Cuadra (ed.), *Annual Review of Information Science and Technology*, Vol. I, New York, 1966.
268 Slagle, J., 'Experiments with a deductive question-answering program', *Comm. of the Assn for Computing Machinery*, 1965.
269 Sloman, A., 'Rules of inference or suppressed premises', *Mind*, 1964.
270 Sparck-Jones, K., *Synonymy and Semantic Classification*, Ph.D. Thesis, Cambridge, 1964.
271 Sparck-Jones, K., *Notes on Semantic Discourse Structure*, Systems Development Corp., Santa Monica, SP–2714, 1967.
272 Sparck-Jones, K., 'Semantic Markers', Cambridge Language Research Unit, mimeo.
273 Sparck-Jones, K., 'Experiments in semantic classification', *Mechanical Translation*, 1965.
274 Sparck-Jones, K., 'Semantic classes and semantic message forms', *Proc. Conf. on Computer-related Semantic Analysis*, Wayne State Univ., 1965.
275 Su, S. Y. W., and Harper, K. E., 'A directed random paragraph generator', in *COLING*.
276 Tarski, A., *Logic, Semantics and Metamathematics*, Oxford, 1965.
277 Toulmin, S., *The Uses of Argument*, Cambridge, 1958.
278 Turbayne, C., 'The myth of metaphor', *Brit. Jl Phil. of Sci.*, 1964.
279 Turing, A., 'Computability and lambda-definability', *Journal of Symbolic Logic*, 1937.
280 Turing, A., 'Computing machinery and intelligence', *Mind*, 1950.
281 Ullman, S., *The Principles of Semantics*, 2nd edn, Oxford, 1959.
282 Ullmann, S., *Semantics: An Introduction to the Science of Meaning*, Oxford, 1962.
283 Waismann, F., 'How I see philosophy', in *Contemp. Brit. Phil.* (3rd series), London, 1956.
284 Waismann, F., *Principles of Linguistic Philosophy*, London, 1965.

285 Waismann, F., 'Verifiability', in Flew (ed.), *Logic and Language*, Vol. I, Oxford, 1951.
286 Wales, R., and Marshall, J., 'The organization of linguistic performance', in Lyons and Wales (eds), *Psycholinguistic Papers (q.v.)*.
287 Walker, R., *et al.*, 'Recent developments in the MITRE syntactic analysis procedure', *Proc. Conf. of Assn. for Mach. Trans. and Comp. Linguistics*, New York, 1966.
288 Wang, H., 'Mechanical methods and inferential analysis', in Breffort and Hirschberg (eds), *Computer Programming and Formal Systems*, Amsterdam, 1963.
289 Wang, H., 'Proving theorems by pattern recognition', *Comm. of the Assn for Computing Machinery*, 1960.
290 Weinreich, U., 'Exploration in semantic theory', in Sebeok (ed.), *Current Trends in Linguistics*, Vol. 3, The Hague, 1966.
291 Weiss, P., 'Relativity in logic', *Monist*, 1928.
292 Weissman, C., LISP *1.5 for the Q–32*, Systems Development Corp., Santa Monica, TM–2337, 1965.
293 Weizenbaum, J., 'ELIZA—A computer program for the study of natural language communication between man and machine', *Comm. of the Assn for Computing Machinery*, 1966.
294 Wells, R., 'Immediate constituents', *Language* 23, 1947.
295 Whorf, B., *Language, Thought and Reality*, Cambridge, Mass., 1956.
296 Wilks, Y. A,. *Semantic Consistency in Text—an Experiment and some Suggestions*, Systems Development Corp., Santa Monica, SP–2758, 1967.
297 Wilks, Y. A., *Transformational Grammars Again*, Systems Development Corp., Santa Monica, SP–2936, 1967.
298 Wilks, Y. A., *Computable Semantic Derivations*, Systems Development Corp., Santa Monica, SP–3017, 1968.
299 Wilks, Y. A., review of Chomsky, N., *Current Issues in Linguistic Theory*, *Linguistics*, 1967.
300 Wilks, Y. A., 'On-line semantic analysis of English texts', *Mechanical Translation*, 1968.
301 Wilks, Y. A., 'Decidability and natural language', *Mind*, 1971.
302 Wimburne, J. N., 'Sentence sequence in discourse', *Proc. 9th Congress of Linguists*, The Hague, 1964.
303 Wittgenstein, L., *Tractatus Logico-Philosophicus*, London, 1922.
304 Wittgenstein, L., 'On logical form', *Proc. Arist. Soc.*, 1929.
305 Wittgenstein, L., *Philosophical Investigations*, Oxford, 1953.
306 Wittgenstein, L., *Remarks on the Foundations of Mathematics*, Oxford, 1956.
307 Wittgenstein, L., *The Blue and Brown Books*, Oxford, 1957.
308 Wittgenstein, L., *Philosophische Bemerkungen*, Oxford, 1965.
309 Wooley, G., 'Syntax analysis beyond the sentence', *Proc. Assn. for Mach. Trans. and Comp. Linguistics*, New York, 1966.
310 Yngve, V., 'A model and hypothesis for language structure', *Proc. Amer. Philosophical Soc.*, 1961.
311 Zipf, G., *The Psycho-biology of Language*, Cambridge, Mass., 1935.

312 Ziff, P., *Semantic Analysis*, Ithaca, N.Y., 1961.
313 Ziff, P., 'About ungrammaticalness', *Mind*, 1964.
314 Ziff, P., 'About what an adequate grammar couldn't do', *Foundations of Language*, 1967.

Index of Names

Date Due

Demco 38-297